Changing Patterns
of Management Development

Andrew Thomson, Christopher Mabey, John Storey,
Colin Gray and Paul Iles

BLACKWELL
Business

First published 2001

2 4 6 8 10 9 7 5 3 1

Blackwell Publishers Ltd
108 Cowley Road
Oxford OX4 1JF
UK

Blackwell Publishers Inc.
350 Main Street
Malden, Massachusetts 02148
USA

British Library Cataloguing in Publication Data

A CIP catalogue record for this book is available from the British Library.

Library of Congress Cataloging-in-Publication Data

Changing patterns of management development / Andrew Thomson . . . [et al.].
     p.   cm. — (Management, organizations, and business series)
   ISBN 0–631–20998–0 (acid-free) — ISBN 0–631–20999–9 (pbk. : acid-free)
   1. Executives—Training of—Great Britain. 2. Management—Study and teaching—Great Britain. I. Thomson, A. W. J. II. Series.
   HD30.42.G7 C48 2001
   658.4'07124—dc21

                                                        00–010409

Typeset in 10 on 12pt Book Antiqua
by Graphicraft Limited, Hong Kong
Printed in Great Britain by TJ International, Padstow, Cornwall

This book is printed on acid-free paper.

for Rosie
1940–1998
Wife, Colleague, Friend and Team Member
with all our love

Contents

Acknowledgements

We are grateful to a number of colleagues for their help in the preparation of this book. In particular, we would like to thank Nick Rubashow, whose firm Makrotest carried out the surveys, not only for the efficiency with which this was done, but also for his contribution to the creation and piloting of the questionnaires. Colin Taylor gave invaluable help with the design and carrying out of the regression analysis of the surveys. Eion Farmer was an early team member who carried out some of the interviews. Rosie Thomson was a team member and author until she tragically died just as the writing of the book began. We are also very grateful to those people and organizations who made the surveys possible. We received funding from the Department for Education and Employment through the Management Charter Initiative, from the Small Business Research Trust, from the Association of MBAs, and from the Open University Business School. Roger Young as Director-General of the Institute of Management was helpful in contacting companies for our interview panel, and Karen Charlesworth in co-ordinating this. Roger McCormick as Director-General of the Association of MBAs suggested the MBA survey, and his successor, Mike Jones, was happy to carry it on. Several people assisted by reading various drafts: Tricia Bradley, Brian O'Neill, Penny Tamkin, John Wilson, Karen Charlesworth. There are also a large number of unsung heroes, namely those managers who were interviewed or who filled in questionnaires and returned them, often at some inconvenience to themselves. In almost every instance, there was great interest in and complete co-operation with the surveys; without these the results would not have been as robust as they are. We think that the development of its managers is an important issue for Britain; they clearly thought so too. Finally, we are especially grateful to the project secretaries who have produced several successive drafts of the book, Liz Micallef and the overall team secretary, Jackie Connell.

Figures

Tables

About the Authors

Colin W. J. A. Gray is a senior lecturer and, until recently, the Director of External Affairs at the Open University Business School. He is also Deputy Director-General of the Small Business Research Trust (a leading UK non-profit SME research institute) and a board member of the Institute for Small Business Affairs (SME academics and support practitioners). His publications include *Management Development in the Republic of Ireland: Patterns and Trends* (2000; with Robert Graham, Kieran Donoghue and Christopher Mabey); *Enterprise and Culture* (1998); *The Barclays Guide to Growing the Small Business* (1990); and *A Portrait of Management Development* (1997; with Andrew Thomson, John Storey, Christopher Mabey, Eion Farmer and Rosemary Thomson). His most recent articles are published in the *Journal of Small Business and Enterprise Development* and *Higher Education in Europe* (1999).

Paul Iles is a Professor of Human Resource Development and Head of the Liverpool Centre for Human Resource Development at Liverpool Business School, John Moores University. A chartered psychologist, Associate Fellow of the British Psychological Society and Fellow of the Institute for Personnel and Development, he is also a visiting professor at the University of Paris II, Panthéon-Assas. His books include *Managing Staff Selection and Assessment, Managing Learning* and *Assessing Managerial Skills,* and he has published widely in national and international scholarly and professional journals. He is currently working with a variety of local authorities and health authorities, as well as companies such as Rover, Ford, Littlewoods and Urenco. He also works in the Middle East and Asia.

Christopher Mabey is Head of the Centre for Human Resource and Change Management at the Open University Business School, where he lectures and leads action research projects examining how companies successfully orchestrate change, especially HR strategies. He has a doctorate in industrial management from Brunel University and has written and edited seven books, including a major text, now in its second edition, entitled *Human Resource Management: A Strategic Introduction* (1998). As a chartered occupational psychologist he has been involved with a number of organizations of varying size and sector as a change consultant, working with individuals on their personal development, carrying out team-building events and contributing to culture-change programmes. Initially this was done as an internal adviser at British Telecom and at Rank Xerox, where he was responsible for management development for UK operations, but more recently he has worked in a freelance capacity.

John Storey is Professor of Human Resource Management at the Open University Business School. His previous books include *Managers in the Making: Careers, Development and Control in Corporate Britain and Japan* (1997; with Paul Edwards and Keith Sisson); *The Realities of Human Resource Management* (2000; with Keith Sisson); and *Human Resource Management: A Critical Text* (2000). He is editor of the *Human Resource Management Journal*.

Andrew Thomson is Professor at the Open University Business School, and has also taught at Glasgow University, where he was Professor of Business Policy, and, as visiting professor, at the Chicago Graduate School of Business. He was chairman of Council of University Management Schools from 1985 to 1987, of the Joint SERC–ESRC Committee from 1985 to 1988, and of the British Academy of Management from 1990 to 1993. His main interest is in the area of management development in organizations. His publications include *A Portrait of Management Development* (1997; with John Storey, Christopher Mabey, Colin Gray, Eion Farmer and Rosemary Thomson); *Management Development: The Views of the Membership of the Association of MBAs* (1998; with John Storey, Christopher Mabey, Rosemary Thomson, Colin Gray and Eion Farmer); and *Achieving Management Excellence* and *A Comparison of IM Members with Other Managers* (2000; both with Christopher Mabey).

chapter 1

Introduction

INTRODUCTION: THE ROLE OF MANAGEMENT DEVELOPMENT

Over the last two decades, and more particularly since the publication of two seminal reports, the Handy Report *The Making of Managers* and the Constable–McCormick Report *The Making of British Managers*, which were jointly published on the same day in 1987, management development has been seen as a key dimension of economic success in Britain. This has now reached a high point with the setting up early in 2000 of a Council for Excellence in Management and Leadership, which we will discuss further in chapter 4. Without adequate development of the management cadre, it has been accepted by policy-makers, companies, and perhaps most important of all, managers themselves, that a modern industrial economy cannot maintain its competitiveness, that organizations cannot be sufficiently flexible to respond to the rapidly changing circumstances of the late twentieth and early twenty-first centuries, and that managers cannot adjust to career patterns considerably removed from the expectations of their predecessors. But this appreciation of management's importance was not always so, as chapter 3 relates. Indeed Britain has only recently recognized what many of its competitors recognized long ago.

In the last decade or so, the modern theory of the firm has moved away from a market focus, in which competitive positioning in relation to rivals was the key, to a resource-based view of the firm, in which management is one of the most important resources. Perhaps the focus on the role of management is best explained in Chandler's magisterial book, *The Visible Hand* (1977: 1):

> The theme propounded here is that modern business enterprise took the place of market mechanisms in coordinating the activities of the economy and allocating its resources. In many sectors of the economy the visible hand of management replaced what Adam Smith referred to as the invisible hand of market forces. The market remained the generator of demand for goods and services, but modern business enterprise took over the functions of coordinating flows of goods through existing processes of production and distribution, and of allocating funds and personnel for future production and distribution. As modern business enterprise required functions hitherto carried out by the market, it became the most powerful institution in the American economy and its managers the most influential group of economic decision makers.

The modern theory of the firm has incorporated resources and especially 'core competencies' as the central focus for competitive advantage. How these competencies, whether skills, knowledge, technology, brands, or operational systems, are exploited and integrated is the role of the managers, who are the active component in strategy. But to define, create, and exploit the organization's resources in this way requires the managers to possess a portfolio of suitable personal competencies of their own. Creating this portfolio is what management development is all about; we would argue that effective management is a *sine qua non* of a resource-based approach. Thus the next step of focusing on management development as a means of achieving effective management becomes a logical and indeed necessary one. We accept that this is a somewhat idealistic position. It is far from easy to disaggregate strategic competencies into personal competencies, and indeed, very few organizations have made a serious attempt. Even the principle of management development is only at the point of being recognized as being a key requirement at the organizational level in some organizations. But in spite of the problems of cause and effect and of measurement, the evidence of this book is that more and more companies have moved to accept the general argument. Indeed, recent trends in management theory are pushing further down this road as managing knowledge, which largely means the knowledge held by managers, becomes central to resource-based theory (Scarbrough et al. 1999).

▶ The Main Arguments of the Book

The intention of this book is to discuss where management development in Britain now stands on the cusp of a new century. We are primarily interested in the way organizations develop their managers, and in how the managers themselves view this development. The main arguments in the book are based on empirical data. Our primary source is the surveys which we carried out in the late 1990s and which are described in more detail below and in appendix 1, but we are also interested in other research and sources of information. There are important focal points of development other than the organization, such as business schools, professional institutes, and consultants, but we only relate to these as part of the total scheme of development as seen from the organization and not in their own context, important as that may be. Similarly we are interested in national policy in education, training, and the labour market, but only as it affects management development, and in changing career and labour market patterns for the same reason. We are primarily interested in the British situation, but seek to place this in the wider setting of other national systems.

Within this context we make a number of propositions, which serve as the central arguments of the book. These are:

- There has been a very considerable change in the amount and significance of management development since the mid-1980s. This trend reflects recognition of the importance of management development by both organizations and individual managers.
- Organizations operate their management development system along a spectrum from a 'strong' policy framework to a 'weak' one. This positioning is largely determined by the way the organization chooses to prioritize and manage its provision rather than being determined primarily by structural factors.
- This differentiation between strong and weak systems is reinforced by findings from all of our surveys, both company and individual, and consistently associates with the quality of the management development process.

- There is broad agreement between the surveys about 'objective' issues such as the amount of training, but there are differences in perception, especially between the organizational view and that of the individual manager, where more 'subjective' issues are concerned.

We need, however, to unpack and qualify these statements to some extent. Although the first proposition is true as a general statement when compared to the mid-1980s, the picture is nevertheless distinctly patchy. Some organizations report a great deal of training, others very little or none at all; some use a range of formal methods, others leave development to informal methods. Some report that management development has a very high priority, others that it has a very low one; some leave the responsibility for the process to the individual manager, while others assume that it is entirely a company responsibility. A majority of organizations still do not have any written document which states their policy on the subject. Some report that management development has a great deal of impact on the organization, others that it has very little; some report that their management development objectives are fully achieved, others that this has not happened at all. It follows that there are relatively few cases of completely 'strong' or 'weak' organizations; most sit in other positions along the spectrum.

But if the story is far from completely upbeat, and only a limited proportion have 'strong' policy frameworks, it also needs to be said that at the other end of the spectrum, the existence of a 'weak' policy framework does not imply that such organizations do not engage in management development. That management development occurs in almost all organizations is a major step forward, since Britain started the last two decades of the twentieth century from a much weaker base in management development than its main economic competitors. Why there was a weaker base and what has caused the willingness to change is part of our story.

Therefore the story as we tell it is very mixed, with significant weaknesses identified in perception and operation. So how to report this mixture of situations? There is undoubtedly a spectrum, and in analysing the results of our surveys we have defined 'strong' and 'weak' policy frameworks for management development as the key determinants of the overall situation. This in turn of course raises the question of what we mean by 'strong' and 'weak'. In general, the change over the last decade towards a greater significance and amount of management development is associated with a move from a 'weak' policy framework towards a 'strong' one. 'Strong', in other words, is associated with positive aspects of management development, 'weak' with negative ones. But of course this is taking an external and national perspective. It may well be that some companies over the last decade have deliberately moved from the 'strong' end of the spectrum towards the 'weak'. Thus some of the relatively few companies which in the mid-1980s had a very sophisticated policy framework may have chosen to dismantle it in part and leave development more for the individual manager to take the initiative. Nevertheless, our reporting of positive change is connected with an overall move from weak to strong. But this still leaves the question of how we have chosen to define which are 'weak' and which are 'strong'. We have utilized three dimensions of organizational policy as a cluster for regression analysis and found them to achieve high levels of significance. But there is an element of arbitrary demarcation in choosing these three, and we would not want to argue that they are the only factors influencing the situation. In addition, the factors we have chosen are by no means entirely independent variables; as with any policy variables other factors underlie them. And they by no means always coexist to the same extent. So for a number of reasons we do not want to overemphasize a limited number of variables. But we do think the spectrum exists and is a useful way of describing the overall situation, and that strong and weak policy frameworks, however defined, are a key to understanding it. Moreover it is not just the policy framework itself to which we need to draw attention, because the policy framework is associated with a range of other variables comprising the process, the output and the outcome of the management development system in each organization, and it is this chain of connections within the model of this system which forms a major part of the book.

Thus as well as the idea of a strong–weak spectrum, we also put forward a model as part of an attempt to develop a more robust theoretical framework within which to discuss management development. In our earlier work we set out to provide a 'portrait' of the state of management development in the mid-1990s to compare with that in the mid-1980s, and this term was used in our initial publication (Thomson et al. 1997). But the question then arose of how to explain the findings in causal terms, and this led to a series of regression analyses on three of the surveys, and the postulation of a working model to underpin this work. The model thus became part of our framework of analysis and is presented in its most simple form in figure 1.1, but then elaborated in the next chapter. We hasten to add that there is still a great deal to be done in this area before there can be real confidence in the emerging model. It is better to think of it as a 'working' model than a proven one in terms of the conclusions we derive from it. In particular, we feel that it will be necessary to obtain longitudinal data sets and be able to compare change over time

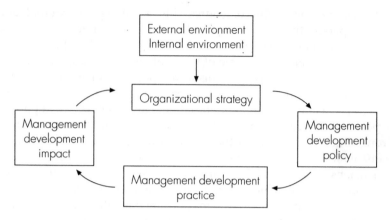

Figure 1.1 A model of management development

and in the light of different economic circumstances. Nevertheless, we do feel that we have empirical support for the propositions above.

The model essentially reflects a circular flowchart in the form of a clock consisting of the various dimensions of management development, which also provide a convenient map of the central part of the book, since the empirically based chapters take up these dimensions in turn:

- The **context** of management development, which for regression purposes becomes some of the main **inputs**. These include the external and internal structural and cultural environment and various aspects of wider organizational strategy outside management development.
- The **policy and responsibilities** by which management development operates within the organization. This is the subject area of chapter 6.
- The **practice** of management development, which can be split into two parts. First there is the internal **process**, usually in the form of a development cycle, which is the subject area for chapter 7. In addition there are **outputs** in the form of the methods and amounts of development, which are covered in chapter 8.
- The **impact** of management development, which also represents its **outcomes**. This is covered in chapter 9 and also includes the **evaluation** of management development.

We did not initially set up the model in order to test it; the original intention was to provide a portrait of management development. The model is thus an attempt to explain the findings rather than provide a hypothesis for testing, although further research would desirably start from the latter position. In an analytic sense the model can be used in two ways. One is diagrammatic in order to visualize variables involved in the overall system of management development. The other way is to identify causality and to permit statistical analysis, albeit taking account of a rather smaller range of variables than shown in the diagrammatic form. The conclusions from our findings are primarily derived from the regression analysis we carried out using independent and dependent variables and clusters of variables to obtain the differentiation between 'strong' and 'weak' management development policies which we argue are a matter of choice rather than circumstance.

▶ The Empirical Evidence

We have carried out a number of surveys of the state of management development in the late 1990s. They are intended to build on the work done for the Constable–McCormick Report of 1987, which was itself based on four separate surveys carried out in 1986. One of these, the Thomson Working Party Report (Thomson 1987), assessed employers' views on management education and training, and this is the main reference point for our surveys, although one which has been extended in its scope and perspective. There are three separate approaches in our surveys:

1. Surveys of employers, carried out in 1986. In each case the person in charge of management development was the intended respondent. The organizations covered were:

   (a) A panel of 18 large employers which had participated in the 1986 survey and which were visited by members of the research team.
   (b) A telephone survey of 501 organizations with more than 100 employees each.
   (c) A postal questionnaire of 389 small businesses.

2. A survey of MBA graduates drawn from the membership of the Association of MBAs. A structured sample of 500 was drawn from a questionnaire sent to the whole membership in May 1997. A sub-sample of 50 self-employed MBAs was taken from this, leaving a main sample of 450.

3. A survey of 215 managers from 55 companies which had already participated in surveys 1(b) and 1(c) above and had volunteered to help with follow-up research. The purpose of this survey was

to match the views of managers with those of their company's response. It was carried out in September 1997, and the data from the 1(*b*) and 1(*c*) company managers are available as separate databases.

In addition to the surveys themselves, which primarily provide cross-tabulation data, we have carried out regression analyses on three of the surveys: 1(*b*), the 501 telephone interviews; 1(*c*), the 389 small company questionnaires; and 2, the MBA graduates. More information on the sample structures and base data from these surveys is provided in appendix 1, while information on the regression analyses, including the variables used to identify the strong–weak spectrum, is supplied in appendix 2. Discussion of these variables is also provided in chapter 6.

There is also a need to reflect on the strengths and weaknesses of the surveys themselves. We can say that their contribution, both separately and collectively, provides both breadth and depth of coverage in the field to an extent not found in previous work, in the following ways:

- There are over 900 responses with an organizational perspective and over 700 from individual managers reflecting the views of the 'consumer' of management development.
- There is coverage of both formal and informal management development, and of the neglected area of the internal processes of management development.
- The surveys also provide a triangulation of perspectives from Human Resource Development managers, MBA graduates, and managers in the organizations, and these perspectives are mutually reinforcing.
- There is an additional perspective across size barriers, with five categories, from 100–299 employees to over 5,000, and with a separate survey devoted to small businesses with 6–100 employees.
- There are some longitudinal links in the surveys with the mid-1980s, and a longer-term historical framework in which to set the wider story.
- Using data from the surveys, we have examined the determinants of effective management development, with essentially the same results in each case. As with the triangulated perspectives, this compatibility of results gives great confidence in the overall picture being presented.
- We have also included other literature and survey material about management development, in order to provide as comprehensive a review of the state of management development as possible.

In spite of these very considerable advantages, we also need to accept that surveys of our type may have weaknesses. One issue is that very few data are kept about management development, even in large organizations. Even if there might be information about individuals, this is rarely, if ever, accumulated across the organization to provide a reliable picture. Thus those speaking on behalf of the organization are giving their own perception of the situation rather than a completely objective report. For managers trying to report the situation in their organization the position may be even more difficult in that they have much less of an overview of the wider picture of management development than the organizational spokesman. It may also be argued that those providing such a perception may, even if unconsciously, give a gloss on the situation. Secondly, there are potential difficulties of sampling procedure; as noted above, fuller details of sample sizes and structures are given in appendix 1. We would argue that the telephone interviews were based on a reliable sampling procedure, with an enthusiastic commitment in the interviews themselves and relatively few refusals to co-operate. We are therefore reasonably satisfied that this survey is representative. The others, however, are rather more problematic. The small business survey was taken from an existing panel, but we accept that the respondents are perhaps unusual amongst small businesses in being willing to answer this and other surveys as part of the panel. Nevertheless, the panel itself is probably the best available in Britain. The members of the Association of MBAs are hardly representative of managers as a whole, and we have no means of checking how representative the respondents are of its membership. Nevertheless they represent an important viewpoint as major consumers of management development and being likely to be knowledgeable about the subject. The final group of managers in co-operating companies also presents a problem. We had no control over their selection, and only a small proportion of companies were willing to co-operate. They did, however, add a valuable perspective on consistency in that their answers could be compared with those of the companies and with each other.

We also want to acknowledge a different sort of problem. The type of surveys we have carried out deal much more easily with the formal, the tangible, and the quantifiable than they do with the informal, intangible and unquantifiable aspects of learning. We fully accept that informal learning is critical, that management is essentially an experientially based occupation, and that the really influential aspects of knowledge are tacit rather than explicit. We shall shortly come to table 1.1 which puts formal development in its place as a contribution to what makes a good manager. We have tried to examine the relevance of informal methods of development, and used scales which permit subjective attitudes to be expressed. But at the end of the day our mode of approach is still biased to the more formal.

These issues should be borne in mind when reading the book. Nevertheless, we think that the benefits greatly outweigh the disadvantages. As Mumford (1997) has noted, 'articles and books about management development more often appear to be works of advocacy than analysis'. We believe that this book comes closer than most to a work of analysis. Moreover, these weaknesses become less apparent if they are reinforced by other views from a different perspective, and this is one of the main reasons for carrying out several surveys. Even so, cross-sectional analysis can never be totally trustworthy, and we recognize that only when results have been confirmed by a number of corroborating findings over a period of time will they be definitive.

▶ The Scope of Management Development

Another role of this introductory chapter is to define the scope of what we mean by management development. We have used the term in a comprehensive sense to encompass the different ways in which managers improve their capabilities. It includes management education, which is often taken to refer to formal, structured learning in an institutional context, and management training, which is often used to mean acquiring knowledge and skills related to work requirements, also by formal means. But our use of the term 'development' goes beyond the sum of these to mean a wider process than the formal learning of knowledge and skills, which includes informal and experiential modes of human capital formation. Management development is thus a multi-faceted process, in which some aspects are easier to identify and measure than others.

One way of putting these different dimensions into perspective is by trying to compare their relative contribution to the outcome of a good manager. Indeed, views as to what factors create a good manager naturally underlie views about the role and potential value of management development. We will see in chapter 3 that there has been an ongoing debate about the nature of management: whether managers are born, not made, and whether management is an art or a science. It would clearly be wrong to jump from the historical perception that managers are born not made and that management development is therefore irrelevant to the opposite pole that management development is the sole requirement for making a good manager.

There is no absolute way of measuring what constitutes or creates a good manager; indeed, the term 'good manager' itself begs various questions. But the views of managers themselves and changes in these

Table 1.1 What makes a good manager (mean and rank on 1–5 scale)

Factors influencing management ability	1986	1996	1997 (MBAs)	1998 ('Large' managers)	1998 ('Small' managers)
Inherent ability/personality	4.61 – 1	4.19 – 1	4.01 – 1	4.41 – 1	4.49 – 1
Job experience	4.11 – 2	3.85 – 2	3.55 – 2	4.06 – 2	4.11 – 2
Initial vocational education	3.17 – 3	2.83 – 5	2.48 – 5	3.00 – 5	3.15 – 5
In-company training	2.93 – 4	3.67 – 3	2.81 – 4	3.63 – 3	3.95 – 3
Initial non-vocational education	2.49 – 5	2.67 – 6	2.35 – 6	2.72 – 6	2.80 – 6
External education after joining	2.34 – 6	3.12 – 4	2.96 – 3	3.26 – 4	3.21 – 4

over time provide perhaps the most reasonable starting-point. A question on this issue was incorporated as part of the survey of industry for the Constable–McCormick Report (Thomson 1987), and we have repeated it in our later surveys. The question in table 1.1 has now been asked of five separate groups of people, organizational respondents in the 1986 and 1996 surveys, and customers of management development in the other three: MBAs in the 1997 survey and 'ordinary' managers in both small and larger companies in the 1998 surveys.

The results show a very high level of consistency in ranking. Differences are examined below, but the outstanding feature is that the main factors by far in each of the surveys are inherent ability and job experience, with the various dimensions of education and training trailing far behind. What is more, Handy et al. (1988) note of the 1986 survey (Thomson 1987) that in this they were in agreement with employers in the other four countries in the comparative survey. They must therefore be seen as having a substantial level of credibility.

Looking at the results in a little more detail it will be seen that in each survey inherent ability scores considerably higher than any other factor, even job experience. The conclusion from this might seem to be a continuation of the historical belief that managers are born, not made. We would not want to deny the importance of such inherent traits, but in spite of their continued high ranking, there has been a change since 1986, and in the light of the gradual recognition and expansion of management development in the post-Second World War period we can be reasonably sure that there was considerable change in the years leading up to 1986. The spread of scores in 1986 was such that inherent ability scored almost twice the level of external education after joining, then the lowest-ranked factor. But in all the surveys since then the gap has closed, with inherent ability being scored somewhat lower and the various aspects of education/training somewhat higher. A second point is that since 1986 the relative rankings have changed to favour in-company training and external education after joining at the expense of initial education. Also of interest is that small company managers' views were very similar to their counterparts in medium-sized and large companies; there is a widespread view that small companies have a less positive attitude towards training and development than bigger companies which is not borne out by these findings. The final point of note is that the MBAs favour external education after joining over in-company training, whereas the other four surveys reverse this. But this is only to be expected of MBAs, the vast majority of whom did their MBA after starting work. In fact perhaps the surprising thing is that these individuals, for whom the MBA is a major feature of their career, still rank it far below inherent ability and job experience.

We do not want to make too much of the detailed differences given the different make-up of the groups, but their unanimity on the basic rankings is important. The conclusion to be drawn from these surveys is that certain personality attributes are necessary in a competent manager, that experience is still a key dimension, but that development of various types makes a significant if not overriding contribution to management competence. On the art–science divide, the pendulum has moved towards science, but by no means all the way. We accept these views as our own starting-point.

Conclusion

As a final point in this introduction to the concept of management development, we accept that there is still uncertainty about the value of training, which has always reinforced the scepticism and prejudices of those who believed solely in the 'character' theory of management. Even very recently, the Skills Audit, the most comprehensive governmental attempt to benchmark skills, has admitted 'Yet while there is much research into UK management, none has established to what extent good training contributes to good management, and good management to good company performance' (DfEE 1996: 43). One of the tasks of this book is to make a contribution to this ongoing debate, and chapter 9 looks at this issue in more detail.

2

Models of Management Development

INTRODUCTION AND BACKGROUND THEORIES

The purpose of this chapter is to examine the theoretical context of management development, initially by reviewing the main social science theories on which management development is based, then by reflecting on various issues that lead to the creation of a management development policy, and finally by looking at previous attempts to create a theory of management development. We then move to our own working model; this will become the theoretical touchstone for chapters 6 to 9, each of which explores and tests key elements of this model. Chapters 10 and 11 also utilize the model from rather different perspectives.

It should be noted that the state of theory in management development leaves something to be desired; this is partly because the main building-blocks themselves leave many important questions unanswered, and partly because the area of management development has yet to benefit from a coherent theoretical approach, being stronger on prescription than analysis to date. Management development theory is part of a wider family of theories each contributing building-blocks which help to explain key dimensions of the way managers are typically developed in organizations. Ultimately these relate to the basic social science disciplines of economics, psychology and sociology. In the economic domain human capital theory provides a rationale for development while labour market theory focuses on the way in which managers as employees provide a resource for organizations. In terms of psychology, learning theory draws attention to the cognitive and processual sides of skill formation, while sociology informs organization theory and human resource strategy in dealing with the role of development in an organizational context. Table 2.1 provides a framework of these background contributions to management development.

▶ Human Capital and Labour Market Theory

Human capital theory is built on the recognition of the role of human skills in economic activity. It assumes that the processes of human and physical capital accumulation are similar, and that human capital acquisition should be seen as an investment in the same way as investing in plant or equipment. Although this formulation is associated with Becker (1964), the general assumption of neo-classical economics has always been that earnings relate to productivity in an occupation and that such productivity might be increased by education or on-the-job training (Mincer 1970). The issue is how to create the optimum portfolio of skills required in the labour market, both now and for the future, and it is a key issue for each of the major parties, namely the state, the organization, and the individual. For the purposes of this discussion we are regarding the manager as the consumer of management development. The key questions are: who gains from development, who has responsibility for organizing it, and, most important, who should pay for it?

The state has traditionally seen education as its responsibility in terms of organization and funding, but increasingly the funding of higher education is being pushed towards the individual (or the employer), especially in areas such as postgraduate management which have a high payback to the individual. The state in Britain traditionally took a laissez-faire attitude towards post-school training, but since the 1960s has been rather more proactive, and currently has a wide range of active labour market policies. We shall return to these in so far as they affect management in chapter 4. We should note, however, that there are those who have taken a sceptical view of the role of the state in this area, arguing that the market failure case for intervention

Table 2.1 Theoretical contributions to our understanding of management development

Theory	Dominant discipline(s)	Primary unit of analysis	Concerns re management development	Favoured methodology
Human capital and labour market	Macro-economics political science	State	– National competitive performance – Constraints of government policy	Broad surveys
Organizational: contingency	Micro-economics	Sector	– 'Fit' between management development and corporate strategy – Constraints structure, culture, technology	Quantitative analysis
Organizational processual	Sociology	Organization	– External, internal, historical context of management development – Constraints of organizational politics, plural interests and personalities	In-depth (longitudinal)
Management learning	Psychology	Individual	– Constraints of unstructured development opportunities and individual learning styles – Process of natural learning in the workplace	Interviews, work diaries, observation

is not made, and that policies are often generated by the need to be seen to be doing something about unemployment (Shackleton 1992). Individuals have traditionally expected either the state or the employer to pay for skill development, although in practice they have often paid for development outside the aegis of the organization, especially at higher occupational levels. The organization has various choices to make in terms of whether to develop, who to develop, how to develop and for what; it also has to make a decision about the timescale over which the development should take place (whether to train for immediate job needs or for future career roles). In practice, many organizations cope perfectly well by obtaining the necessary skills from the labour market, and not infrequently by deliberately poaching staff from other employers, thus both saving themselves the training costs and ensuring that organizations that do train have reason to fear that their investment will be appropriated by others. A further reason for not training has typically been the uncertainty of the outcome; this causes difficulties in terms of accurately defining the costs of training and even more in measuring the rate of return. But if there are logical reasons for not training, there is a compelling case for doing so, as in the benefits of a well-formulated management development policy in providing key skills to the organization.

However, it is arguable that a firm's management development policy and processes can only be understood in the context of the labour markets in which it operates. For instance, one firm may have a policy to operate an internal labour market, in which there are recognized 'ports of entry' such as traineeships and thereafter an assumed career ladder in which internal promotion is the expected mode of upward progress. Such a stance is in stark contrast to an organization with an orientation towards using the external labour market, whereby all vacancies at whatever level are open to outside recruitment, so that any appointment is for the job and not for a career. Naturally, the implications for training and development policy in each case are quite different. In an internal labour market, the employer will be seeking to train individuals for long-term as well as short-term development, and to do so in ways which provide skills specific to the firm rather than transferable ones. These skills may be to do with procedures, culture, the creation of teams, both explicit and tacit knowledge about the firm and its operations, or other firm-specific issues. Training may also be used to induce loyalty in the individual, and to help reduce turnover and its attendant costs. As Doeringer and Piore (1971) have pointed out, training for specific skills tends to increase the proportion of training costs borne by the employer as opposed to the employee, and also to increase the absolute level of those costs. If a firm operates in the external labour market, it may wish to avoid the training costs of widely available skills, seek new types of skill not available internally, and prevent inbreeding and complacency. It may also be able to avoid the overhead costs of manpower and succession planning and of being a training organization. It will take a short-term view of recruiting for the job, and not encourage expectations of a career in the firm. Some of these issues are taken up in chapter 10 in discussing managerial careers.

Sonnenfeld, Peiperl and Kotter (1988) have provided a framework based on the US context in which different industries have different labour market dynamics, and propose that this interacts both with career patterns and development systems. Thus *academies* are firms with internal labour markets, and reward systems based on individual contribution. They are characterized by stability and low turnover. These companies hire from outside only at entry levels, and expect a large proportion of their employees to stay until retirement. The key human resource function is development. These firms obtain needed talent, and create barriers to the exit of labour, by developing firm-specific skills and, in many cases, a deep-seated loyalty in their employees. Industries which follow the 'academy' model include consumer products, pharmaceuticals, and electronics manufacturers. *Clubs* also employ internal labour markets, but group factors are more important than individual contribution, and they are more concerned with seniority and status than innovation and profitability. The critical human resource function is the retention of membership. Such industries include utilities, government, insurance, and the military. *Baseball teams* are open to external labour markets at all levels, and seek out those individuals who make the largest individual contribution. The major human resource function is recruitment, to keep the firm fully staffed and performing. In many of these firms there is little training; employees either come fully skilled or develop skills very quickly on the job. People in baseball teams tend to identify more with their profession than any firm, and the industries they work in include accounting, consulting, medicine, advertising, investment banking, and entertainment. Finally, *fortresses* are firms preoccupied with survival which cannot afford to focus on individual members, so that group factors predominate in a context of retrenchment. Such industries include publishing, textiles, natural resources, and retailing. This type of categorization is useful in classifying the way in which different types of labour market operate and whether the key contribution is made by the individual or the organization. Each of the categories has a different implication for management development: clearly the commitment to it will be greater in the internal as opposed to the external labour market, and there will also be a difference where the skills required are purely individual or part of a group.

Explorations by Pettigrew et al. (1988) into vocational and management training systems in the late 1980s also took explicit account of internal and external labour markets. In their analysis of 20 companies, they identified a number of important factors that stimulated human resource development (HRD) initiatives: (i) the recognition of the need for a business strategy which enabled the organization to manage increased complexity; (ii) a positive internal labour market where there was an open skill and career structure and training and development opportunities were seen as an aid to recruitment; and (iii) an organizational context where the 'internal actors and systems' favoured an integrated approach to recruitment, learning and career development. Inhibiting factors included a preoccupation with immediate tasks, where there was a lack of a qualifications culture and where training was perceived as a low status activity.

In our modelling of management development we acknowledge the importance of labour markets, both as a competitive, strategic trigger for human resource activity and as a shaper of recruitment and training choices as mediated by the external and internal labour markets within which an organization is located. But such a perspective neglects the processes and activities that facilitate learning. This takes us to a very different field of theory.

▶ Learning Theory

Learning theory shifts the focus to the methods by which individuals and organizations acquire new knowledge, skills and ways of doing things: the basic argument is that effective development activities can be designed only when the purposes, conditions and methods of learning have been established. Various attempts have been made to identify the qualities, or mix of qualities, being sought in management learning. An early and enduring typology is that proposed by Burgoyne and Stuart (1976) who use three overlapping categories: basic data and information representing those facts which pertain to the specific work environment and relevant professional knowledge; situation-specific skills and response tendencies including analytical, problem-solving, judgement/decision-making skills; social skills and abilities; emotional resilience and proactivity – the inclination to respond purposefully to events; and qualities for self-development including creativity, mental agility, balanced learning habits and self-knowledge. The authors point out that when designing learning and development activities it is essential to know which of these qualities – or mix of qualities – are being sought in order to choose the appropriate learning methods and approaches. Closely related to this issue is that of different approaches to competency definition, which is taken up in chapter 7.

Also important is an understanding of the degree of learner autonomy: that is, the freedom of choice exercised by managers over the content of what they want to learn and the process by which they wish to learn it. This is a subject which has been a major area for researchers (e.g. Revans 1980; Simpson 1980; Schon 1983; Knowles 1984). The value of understanding the conditions conducive to individual learning is that it again helps to identify appropriate management development approaches for any given subject-matter (Burgoyne 1977). For instance, the notion of learner autonomy has been used to assess the most appropriate computer-based courseware for training management accountants (Mabey, Kaye and Topham 1998).

While this kind of analysis yields valuable insights into the goals and methods of learning, it tends to assume that managers' development needs can be – and typically are – addressed by the organization setting up some kind of training programme or learning activity for the individuals concerned. Such a view needs to be counterbalanced by two other perspectives. First, the fact that a great deal of on-the-job coaching and unstructured personal development takes place on a daily basis in all organizations. For instance, in their report on how well 144 directors from 41 UK organizations were equipped for their responsibilities Mumford et al. (1987) concluded that 'most directors have learned through a mixture of relatively accidental and unstructured experiences. Systems of management development have not been widely influential.' From this study Mumford (1993) puts forward a so-called 'integrated managerial' type of management development (a self-conscious use of everyday work experience for developmental purposes), which combines the virtues of *ad hoc* and more formal development while eliminating their deficiencies. In a more theoretical analysis which argues the case for a resource-based view of strategic human resource management (SHRM), Kamoche (1996) also notes the value of skill formation arising from tacit knowledge, action-centred learning, learning from mistakes, learning by doing and as a by-product of other activities; it is the very embeddedness of these activities in daily work routines (as compared with isolated, formalized training programmes) which makes them 'resource mobility barriers' because competitors will find them difficult to imitate. In a similar vein, Mueller notes:

> HR policies such as employee training and management development are unlikely to be the basis of the creation of SAs [strategic assets], unless they tie into subsequent or contemporaneous skill formation activities, including ongoing operational routines. Ongoing skill formation activities result in a 'reservoir' of skills, a certain part of which will not explicitly be recognised as such by management, i.e. is a 'hidden reservoir'. However, HRM policies can play a role as part of a process aimed at preventing obsolescence of skills by re-activating (part of) the reservoir. (Mueller 1996: 773)

Indeed it might be argued that the boundary between knowledge creation and management development is becoming increasingly blurred.

For example, in an influential book on the way organizations build their competitive capability, Nonaka and Takeuchi (1995) characterize Western managers as relying upon quantifiable data, codified procedures and explicit information-processing; in contrast, they maintain the success of Japanese corporations is based on the fact that managers are encouraged to derive knowledge from intuition, internalize their discoveries and then find ways of migrating this tacit knowledge into the wider organization so that constant renewal can occur. Such a mindset would seem to favour on-the-job learning and informal development as against the programmatic management training so typical in the West (Storey et al. 1997).

The second problem with much writing on management development is that it assumes individual learning takes place to exclusively serve the current purposes of the organization, which by definition remains in control of the learning processes that have been 'constructed'. This is at odds with other conclusions derived from the adult learning literature. For instance, it is known that truly innovative learning is more likely to occur in situations which lack certainty and controllability (e.g. Kotter 1995; Sitkin et al. 1994). The work of Kolb (1984) has shown that individuals have different learning preferences, which will predispose them towards certain developmental opportunities and to be indifferent or resistant to others. Mumford's application of these ideas to management development predicts a very mixed response to 'one-for-all' training programmes (Mumford 1993). And in the same way that individuals tend to have preferred learning styles, it has been suggested that organizations have preferred learning orientations; these comprise the values and attitudes that determine where learning is likely to take place and the nature of what is learned (Dibella et al. 1996).

Finally, irrespective of wider questions and choices arising from different theories of learning, Rogers (1986) identifies certain general characteristics of adult learning. Thus any management development programme needs to engage with: the learner's processes of maturation, self-fulfilment and self-determination; the learner's knowledge and emotional investment in the learning they are embarking on; the learner's past experience of learning and their expectations about both the way in which learning occurs and their own capabilities to learn.

Applying learning theory research to management development significantly enriches our view of how learning takes place in organizations and helpfully questions many of the assumed benefits of management development programmes. In particular, it serves to underline the importance of understanding both individual and organizational goals/expectations as they embark on management development, the variety of methods that can be called upon to 'deliver' management development, the range of factors that can 'interfere' with the learning process and the potent place of informal approaches in the development of managers. To these issues must be added an understanding of the role that development can play in the creation of a good manager, and by what means. Table 1.1 has already noted that managers of all kinds, whether they are providers or customers, whether they have had a great deal of external education, such as our MBA cohort, or whether they are 'average' managers, such as the client manager groups, have very similar views and rankings as to what makes a good manager and the role of development in it. Our research model attempts to take into account these various features of management development. We also try to take account of the different forms of development and the satisfaction which the actors express for them in chapter 8. In particular, we are conscious of the need to analyse the balance between formal and informal methods. The third theoretical perspective which we review restores management development very firmly to a more strategic setting.

▶ Organization and Human Resource (HR) Theory

Organizational structure is a key factor in determining requirements for managerial skills of different kinds. The idea of management as a profession has been greatly enhanced by the growth of large divisionalized and diversified corporations (Chandler 1977). A second feature of this trend is the increasingly specialist nature of many managerial tasks while at the same time managers are required to be aware of the wider objectives of the organization. A third dimension of the same development is the need for many managers to be able to make the transition from functional specialisms to more general management skills as they take on more senior management and/or project roles. There are also requirements for other sorts of management skills, both specialized and general awareness. These are the types of skills which need to be provided to managers earlier in their careers. Indeed, there is a strong tendency for management skills to migrate down the occupational hierarchy as job definitions and responsibilities are broadened.

The possibility of HR strategies having the effect of delivering appropriate management skills, enhancing quality, cutting costs and improving creativity and ultimately profitability – in short, maximizing shareholder value – is highly attractive. For many years evidence to support such a connection between HR investment and business performance has remained elusive. However, in recent years there has been growing interest in the elevation of human resource issues into the strategic performance equation and the use of quantifiable data to measure it (e.g. Ulrich 1997).

Evidence for the impact of a combination of human resource policies and practices is growing, the argument being that it is the very synergy between different HR activities that makes them potentially strategic and powerful in their enhancement of organizational performance. Dyer and Reeves (1995) note that the packages or bundles of typical strategic HR elements are defined somewhat differently by different authors: 'The superior packages are variously labelled "Innovative", "Commitment" and "Flexible (or Lean) Production". All incorporate a dimension of employee involvement, and a majority also involve careful selection, extensive training and contingent compensation' (1995: 668). Purcell's list of strategic HR elements that apparently have consequences for corporate performance slightly expands this: 'careful recruitment and selection (with emphasis on competencies); extensive use of systems of communication; teamworking with flexible job design; emphasis on training and learning; involvement in decision-making with responsibility; and performance appraisal with links to pay' (Purcell 1996: 4). This issue of impact on performance is further reviewed in chapter 9.

While training, and in some cases management development, features centrally in most accounts of so-called high-performance or high-commitment management, pursuing a best-practice model of human resource strategies can lead to some apparent contradictions in practice. For instance: how is it possible for a firm to pursue individualized HR policies (such as development centres, personal development plans, fast tracking) at the same time as initiatives to improve teamwork and cross-functional learning (such as quality circles, functional flexibility)? How does an organization reconcile long-term strategies to improve quality by a steady enhancement of managerial capabilities over time with simultaneous requirements to attain cost savings via functional flexibility which may imply deskilling and or delayering? How can a firm achieve a 'strong' culture of shared values and corporate commitment at the same time as cultivating a flexible and adaptable workforce of managers with portfolio careers?

Two schools of thought prevail as to how this alignment of HR strategies and organizational strategies is actually accomplished. Some propose a universal set of HR policies and practices that, if pursued by a given firm, will lead to superior performance. Guest's (1992) model of human resource management falls into this category. His view is that competitive advantage will accrue only when four HR policy goals of integration, commitment, flexibility and quality are present. Guest's approach is useful because, in his words, it offers a set of testable propositions which can be used as an interpretative framework to make sense of the reality of human resource management within different contexts. This contrasts with a contingent approach which emphasizes the need for a package or bundle of HR measures to be appropriate to the particular circumstances and strategies of the organization concerned, without prescribing what these should be. Different authors have chosen different contingencies in this regard. For Schein (1985) the life-cycle stage – embryonic, growth, maturity or decline – will predefine the cultural and strategic profile of the organization concerned, which in turn will imply distinctive approaches to strategic human resource development. Schuler and Jackson (1987) itemize specific HRM policies predicated upon the required employee role behaviour, which arises from whether the prevailing company strategy is innovation, quality enhancement or cost reduction. This echoes the central idea of labour market theory reviewed above. Harrison (1997) goes the further step of describing the learning strategies that match different business needs. So, for example, coaching, mentoring, continuous learning and self-development all help to ensure an ongoing 'fit' between business needs and human performance, whereas training in organization development processes might come to prominence at a time when the organization is responding to emergent challenges and needs.

Finally, attention needs to be given to the pluralist/stakeholder versus organizational/unitarist assumptions of organizational theory. They are important not only in their own right, but also because our methodology depends on being able to compare and contrast the views of different actors. Much of the theory reviewed so far has taken an organizational or managerial stance towards the development of managers. Clearly, however, there are other parties that have vested interests in how training and development is conceived, implemented and how its effects are measured in a given organization. This pluralist perspective is typically underestimated by human capital and labour market theorists. Figure 2.1 shows the application of stakeholder theory to management development.

Different authors have sought to theorize this pluralism in different ways. For instance, Van der Krogt and Warmerdam (1997) propose a network approach, which takes account of labour markets, dominant actors and the interplay between labour and training networks. This, they argue, overcomes the deficiencies of seeking to explain management development from a functionalist, a systems, or an actor perspective alone. Burgoyne and Jackson (1997) describe the learning domain as an arena 'within which the conflicting purposes and values

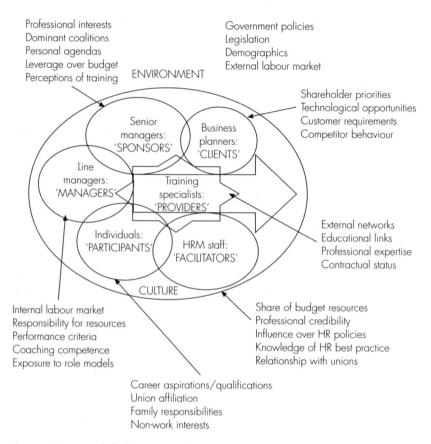

Professional interests
Dominant coalitions
Personal agendas
Leverage over budget
Perceptions of training   ENVIRONMENT

Government policies
Legislation
Demographics
External labour market

Shareholder priorities
Technological opportunities
Customer requirements
Competitor behaviour

Senior managers: 'SPONSORS'

Business planners: 'CLIENTS'

Line managers: 'MANAGERS'

Training specialists: 'PROVIDERS'

Individuals: 'PARTICIPANTS'

HRM staff: 'FACILITATORS'

External networks
Educational links
Professional expertise
Contractual status

CULTURE

Internal labour market
Responsibility for resources
Performance criteria
Coaching competence
Exposure to role models

Share of budget resources
Professional credibility
Influence over HR policies
Knowledge of HR best practice
Relationship with unions

Career aspirations/qualifications
Union affiliation
Family responsibilities
Non-work interests

Figure 2.1 A stakeholder approach to management development
Source: Mabey and Salaman 1995: 174.

within an organization meet to be reinforced, reconciled or proliferated' (1997: 61). They maintain that, provided important differences are aired and the opportunities for compromise and synergy between different interest groups are not lost, the arena can be managed despite its pluralist and contested nature. Others are more sceptical, suggesting that investing in management development often becomes little more than collusive game-playing between those investing in, designing and participating in such activities (e.g. Clarke 1999). The value of analysing policies and processes from a pluralist perspective is that it legitimizes a full range of stakeholder groups, each with their own predispositions, priorities and degrees of proactivity in a given arena of organizational life, and this is something our methodology seeks to do.

Figure 2.1 is intentionally fluid, and while there is an underlying sense of business direction (represented by the arrows), agreement with or commitment to this is by no means taken as given. Different stakeholders might helpfully be seen as organizational sub-systems, each with a different interest in, influence over and ownership of training and development strategies and outcomes. The intersection of boundaries in the figure signifies that such sectional agendas will in some cases overlap and align. But, broadly speaking, the nature of training and development can be seen as central, negotiated territory with the power of the providers of such activities ebbing and flowing between the client, sponsor, manager, participant and facilitator groupings within the organization, each influenced in turn by a host of factors – many of them beyond the boundary of the organization itself.

This interplay of competing and contested views, together with the influence of external environmental forces, will shape the pathway of training strategies and implementation in a given organization. So, taking this pluralist perspective, it is not surprising that investment in management training does not automatically translate into improved performance. There are a myriad reasons why this may be the case: a poor matching of training provision to managers' requirements; a failure to understand the situational factors that shape behaviour; mixed motives on the part of senior management for investing in management development; collusion between what the organization thinks it wants in the way of management development and what external/ internal providers actually deliver (a case of the 'performance' becoming more important than the 'plot', see Clark and Salaman 1996); the incipient resistance of existing authority structures; and the difficulty of developing appropriate levels of trust, mutual support and collaboration essential for effective learning to take place.

It can be seen, then, that a stakeholder approach to management development is predicated in part upon systems thinking. Management training and development is characterized as an open system interpreting and acting upon changes in the environment (organizational objectives, internal labour markets), receiving resources (in the form of managers, information, budget, etc.), transforming them (with knowledge, skills, growth and development) and exporting them back into the environment. At the same time the management training function is made up of a number of sub-systems controlling and co-ordinating its internal activities (Garavan et al. 1995). There are a number of benefits from taking such a systemic view of management development. It makes more visible some of the interference factors mentioned above, which create barriers and constraints to development; it draws attention to everyday organizational learning not normally considered to be part of the management development process; it helps to question some of the fundamental assumptions upon which existing conceptions of management development are premised; and it elevates the importance of wider organizational influences when planning and implementing management development (Doyle 1996). Because of its dynamic and contested conception of management development, we draw heavily upon this pluralist approach when developing our own model of management development.

However, we must also recognize that a stakeholder perspective is not universally accepted or utilized, whatever the rhetoric that most organizations use. The alternative approach is a shareholder perspective in which labour, whether managerial or from other parts of the workforce, is merely treated as a factor of production whose contribution and productivity are maximized in the interests of the owners. Since in modern capitalism the owners are remote from direct involvement in the organization and usually consist of financial institutions or individual investors whose only objective is to maximize their returns, the interests of other stakeholders are hardly considered. Although these other stakeholders may be involved in management development to an extent to which the owners are not, they ultimately have little power if their interests clash with those of the shareholders. Management, and especially the chief executive, tend to be judged by the extent to which they create shareholder value, almost to the exclusion of other issues. Such a viewpoint might require the human resource function generally, including management development, to justify itself only in terms of the bottom line and have little sense of responsibility towards those involved. This perspective is often, but by no means exclusively, associated with American approaches (Ulrich et al. 1997) and would argue that wherever possible the individual manager should be responsible for their own management development, except possibly for narrowly job-related skills.

To return to the general topic, the contribution of organization theory, and the strategic human resource management approach in particular, is that it re-frames management development in at least three new ways. First, it underscores the importance of seeing management development as internally integrated with, rather than in isolation from, other HR policies. Second, it suggests that, when seen as part of a thoughtfully devised business strategy, management development has the potential to make a strategic difference to the organization. Third, it would appear that the realization of this potential depends, at least in part, on a number of internal and external contingencies which should guide the detailed design of management development policies. Finally, we register the need to avoid unitarist assumptions when exploring the enactment of management development policy.

In summarizing the contribution of the background theories, we can see how each approach contributes to our understanding of developing managers in organizations. Human capital theory legitimately addresses the accumulation of appropriate skills in a particular nation, sector, organization or individual; this helps us to understand the debate over paying for development and why there has been a tendency for qualifications to be seen as a benchmark and key criterion for occupational selection and promotion, at least as part of a sifting process within recruitment. Labour market theory also regards external conditions as the catalyst for decisions about the acquisition and development of management capability, elaborating a number of choices organizations can make contingent on their market circumstances. Learning theory privileges the role of learning and the conditions – for organizations at a collective level and managers at an individual level – conducive to the effective acquisition of new knowledge, skills, and attitudes. For its part, organization theory generally, and the SHRM approach in particular, counsels against divorcing management development activities from other HR policies and procedures on the one hand, and from wider organizational strategies on the other.

▶ Previous Models of Management Development

So far, we have been considering what different background theories and policy considerations have to offer an investigation of management development in British organizations. Helpful though the above observations are, the sources we have drawn upon have been largely theoretical; writers extrapolating from their favoured fields of knowledge and coming up with their own versions of what best practice management development might look like. It is now time to put some of these ideas to the test. If we are to move forward our understanding of management development and its strategic role in today's organizations, we need to work towards some kind of model and tentative hypotheses which can be examined empirically, refined and built upon by successive research.

We are by no means the first to recognize this need. For instance, in an article attempting to set the HRM agenda for the 1990s, Hendry and Pettigrew drew attention to the gaps, with particular reference to training issues:

> Research into the factors which facilitate, inhibit, and stabilise HRM change, among firms of different size, in different sectors, age, and even

localities, would be of direct interest to policy makers. Our VET [vocational education and training] findings and the model derived from the case study research (Pettigrew et al. 1988: 92ff) would benefit from multivariate, quantitative application to more precisely defined settings of change. (1990: 37)

Yet, having conducted their own review of the institutional and practical evidence of training and development in the UK five years later, Ashton and Felstead were led to conclude that: 'Dedicated research data on the role of training and development in the management of human resources is most pressing and ripe for future enquiry' (1995: 241). Furthermore, this is not simply a case of academic commentators lamenting the paucity of data. Practitioners have also highlighted the dire consequences of management development continuing to be poorly researched and ill informed:

> Unless the gap between social science research and training practice is bridged more effectively, the phenomenon of genre management training will persist. In so doing, a training version of Gresham's law will apply: the presence and momentum of too much mediocre and inappropriate training will prevent more effective training from flourishing. (Mole 1996: 24)

It is not difficult to find prescriptions for the ideal model of management development and the steps necessary to achieve it. In chapter 1 we referred to the Constable–McCormick and Handy reports of 1987. There have been other sets of recommendations, perhaps most notably Geoffrey Holland's 'national manifesto' for management development in Britain, incorporating ten objectives for the decade to come (Holland 1986). Based on research over many years at the Centre for the Study of Management Learning at Lancaster University, Burgoyne proposed a six-step model describing organizations in ascending order of maturity with regard to their management development (Burgoyne 1988). This ranged from a total reliance upon natural, laissez-faire, uncontrived processes of MD at one extreme to a situation where MD not only fed corporate policy-making, but actually enhanced the processes by which such strategies are arrived at. This typology was echoed by the Ashridge 4F model (Wille 1990), which described organizational approaches to management development as fragmented (training seen as a cost and/or luxury, formally delivered with low learning transfer), formalized (more links to organizational systems and involvement from line management), focused (more emphasis on the mutual benefit to the individual and the organization) and fully integrated (learning is interwoven with everyday work). These observations, like the linking of management development with the so-called hard systems of HRM on the one hand and collaborative career planning on the other, the potential contribution of management development to strategy formation and the notion of seamless learning, anticipated many of the key themes that were to dominate management development thinking in the 1990s.

Nickie Fonda was an early proponent of the need to link management development to business performance. She cited several organizations where management capability was proving to be a decisive factor in sustaining competitive advantage (Fonda 1989) and attempted to demonstrate the contribution of managerial competence, commitment and capability for change to the strategic aims of the organization (Fonda 1988). In his enumeration of 10 success factors of management development, Margerison also puts a strong emphasis upon quantifiable results (Margerison 1990). Among his action-based rules for management development are five off-the-job training days for all managers each year, concentrating on managers with 'potential' (giving them at least one secondment and one job with profit and loss accountability before the age of 35) and involving all managers in a structured process of management development diagnosis and planning in the context of business plans. McLagan (1989) maintains that individual, group and organizational effectiveness will only be achieved when there is an integrated use of training and development, organization development and career development. This leads her to prescribe carefully the multiple roles, competencies and ethical requirements of HRD practitioners. Thomson and Mabey (1995) develop McLagan's ideas by identifying the central part played by human resource development in the effective management of change: their model depicts the synergistic links with all the other aspects of a firm's human resource management, showing how such collective activities are both informed by, yet also help to fulfil, the mission of the organization concerned. However, as they admit, this depiction, like others referred to above, is not really a model. They do little more than represent the way management development might operate in an ideal world, and as such, explain little. Furthermore they tend to make sweeping assumptions about the rationality of decision-making and policy implementation in organizations.

In spite of these early attempts to theorize management development it has to be said that the field of management development remains theoretically immature. Still lacking is a careful delineation of the important variables influencing the uptake, design and implementation of management training and development activities, and any analysis of the mutual interaction between such variables as well as their single or combined impact upon organizational performance. It is to this challenge that we now pass.

▶ Towards a New Model of Management Development

In this section we put forward a working model of management development, which is based on an elaboration of the circular flowchart presented in figure 1.1. Building on current knowledge, reviewed above, we start from the assumption that any model of management development needs to be contingent. We also recognize the need to contextualize organizational strategies and policies within the national system of management development. We focus on the organization, but the basic principles can also be applied at the individual and state level.

Figure 2.2 is intended to provide a working model within which the issues relating to management development at the level of the organization can be discussed. It will be seen that there is a cycle of four stages, leading from organizational strategy which provides the context for management development. From this comes some attempt to formulate policies governing training, which, in turn, lead to the management development practice unique to each organization. These activities comprising management development practice will create an impact of some kind which feeds back into aspects of organizational performance, which in turn affect subsequent organizational strategy and the relationship with its environment. By acknowledging the importance of national, sectoral and firm context, identifying organizational and HR strategy, this contingent model is informed by the literatures reviewed above. Our intention has been to explore the strength and direction of implied relationships, and successive chapters of the present volume will report the findings relating to different stages of the model. In the questionnaires we used for each of the surveys (see appendix 1) there is a range of questions which relate to each of the stages and provide variables for analysis, whether through cross-tabulation or statistical regression.

We will now explain more fully each of the stages in the model, although the precise way in which the range of variables within them is analysed in our study is given in appendix 2. Drawing upon systems thinking, the four stages can be seen as providing inputs, processes, outputs, and outcomes and thus also potentially acting as independent and dependent variables for statistical analysis. This is the same terminology which Tamkin and Hillage (1998) have used in creating a framework for management development performance indicators. The terms are complementary to the more static descriptions used in figure 2.2. Although there are arrows between the different stages to indicate that the direction of causation is clockwise, none of

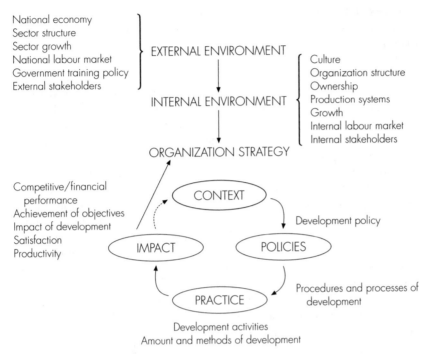

National economy
Sector structure
Sector growth
National labour market
Government training policy
External stakeholders

EXTERNAL ENVIRONMENT

Culture
Organization structure
Ownership
Production systems
Growth
Internal labour market
Internal stakeholders

INTERNAL ENVIRONMENT

ORGANIZATION STRATEGY

Competitive/financial
    performance
Achievement of objectives
Impact of development
Satisfaction
Productivity

CONTEXT

Development policy

IMPACT

POLICIES

PRACTICE

Procedures and processes of
development

Development activities
Amount and methods of development

Figure 2.2   A model of organizational management development

the linkages are necessarily either direct or complete. Indeed it is one of our central propositions that although policy is understandably a crucial explanatory variable there is a spectrum of strong and weak management development policies which are themselves a matter of choice rather than being driven solely by the context and circumstance of the first stage. And the same is true between the links to the other stages. In particular, the outcomes or impact from a policy framework and a set of development activities that are sought by the organization and are the rationale of the whole management development system are very difficult to measure in terms of improved performance. While we recognize that our model is far from comprehensive, we believe that it does provide a framework within which the system can be explored, both conceptually and statistically. Furthermore, acknowledging the legitimate criticism of systemic analysis that it neglects the plural nature of organizations, as reviewed above (Van der Krogt and Warmerdam 1997; Burgoyne and Jackson 1997), our model deliberately solicits the views of several stakeholders in the training process: human resource development designers, line managers, developers and participants in management development activities (see appendix 1).

Context (inputs). The aspects of the external and internal environment influencing organization strategy are many and varied; the main ones are included in figure 2.2, but they are themselves difficult to capture without further disaggregation. It would, for instance, be very difficult to capture organizational strategy in a holistic sense and we have no such measure. For our statistical analysis we have identified three 'clusters' of independent variables, with just three indices for each cluster. Thus the external environment is measured by organization size, sector and nationality of ownership. Internal environment is measured by growth of the organization over the previous three years, centralization of, and responsibility for implementation of, management development. It is our contention that these comprise important, though not exhaustive, contextual factors influencing the policy, method, amount and effectiveness of management development provision in a given firm. A third cluster of potential importance is that relating to career management; the existence of a planned career structure, succession planning and a policy of appointing managers for a career (rather than solely a job).

The first attempt to examine the determinants of management development by statistical methods, by Mangham and Silver in their major survey in 1985, noted: 'The high level of variability within size groups . . . reflects the poor explanatory power of the size variables. There appears to be a high degree of variability in the amount of training between companies which cannot be explained away by structural features of the company such as size, industry, etc.' (1986: 35). Our findings support this. While there is undoubtedly a contextual effect on management development it should not be assumed to be dominant.

Policies (processes). It might also be assumed, as depicted in figure 2.2, that management development policy will be a derivative of human resource policy more generally, but this again may well not be true. Indeed the term 'development policy' may be something of a misnomer since a large proportion even of organizations well outside the small business classification do not have an explicit policy. It may therefore be more reliable to infer strength of policy from what is done rather than what is stated (see Fox and McLeay 1991). Nevertheless, the mere existence of a written policy is an important indicator and we have therefore used it to create a 'policy' cluster, along with the priority given to management development by the organization and the extent of its perceived responsibility for it *vis-à-vis* that of individual managers. Policy, however, needs implementation, and the processes and methods by which this is done are of great importance for the outputs and outcomes of the system. Indeed process is an area which we feel has been badly neglected in the existing literature, whether this be systems of appraisal or some other form of training needs analysis or choice of training method.

Practice (outputs). The range of activities and the amount of time spent on them can vary considerably from company to company, department to department, and manager to manager, as well as from time to time. Possible outputs of management development might be better trained and developed managers, designed to bring the portfolio of competencies closer to the desired optimum or for some alternative goal such as bringing the managerial culture into line with some revised business objectives. In our analysis we focus on two main dimensions of management development practice: the volume, as measured in average training days per manager and the type of development undertaken. We should, however, note that not all development is necessarily under the aegis of the organization; managers can undertake it outside the organization either by themselves or through an agency such as a professional institute.

Impact (outcomes). While the impact of management development on both the organization and the individual can be wide-ranging, it often proves very difficult to measure the bottom-line or other performance impact of this investment. The successful management of change, decreasing turnover of key staff, improved productivity or quality of service may all be tangible outcomes of judicious management training; added to these are the softer, but by no means unimportant, outcomes such as enhanced job satisfaction or organizational commitment. And finally, even if no identifiable improvements can be seen, there is the question of whether things might not have changed for the worse without the development. In our analysis we define outcomes by assessing whether management development has achieved its objectives (an internal measure of the training system), the perceived impact of management development on the organization (an external measure), and for participating managers, how satisfied they are with the development they have received personally. We accept that these are not ultimate or ideal measures by themselves, but feel that they were the best available given the status of our respondents.

So far we have looked at management development at the level of the organization, since this is the main subject of this book. But there are two other levels which must be noted and which involve a similar cyclical model and similar considerations. The individual manager brings a background and a bundle of predispositions, aspirations and expectations which will affect the management development experience. Managers have become increasingly concerned about their careers, more insecure about the future, and more aware of the need for development, whether through the employer or externally on their own initiative. It is arguable that there is a similar cycle of context, policy and processes, activities, and impact as for the organization, although with somewhat different factors, and a diagram reflecting these issues in a career context is presented in figure 10.2.

Similarly, while we are not as interested in the role of the state in management development as in those of the organization and the individual, it is nevertheless an important player in the provision of infrastructure and context as well as of significant policy dimensions. Earlier discussion of human capital and labour market theories showed the fallacy of ignoring the contribution of the national system, both in a comparative context and within the national framework. Chapter 4 is devoted to this topic. Here we simply note that a similar cyclical framework can be painted for the state as for the organization and the manager.

Conclusions

This chapter has reviewed the background theories which underpin management development. In particular, we noted the differing insights provided by human capital, labour market, learning and organization theories. We then examined some of the considerations and goals governing an organization's attempt to set policy for management development. This led us to note the increasingly important role of competencies and the tensions between viewing management development from a shareholder and a stakeholder perspective. While prescriptive advice and partial empirical studies of management training interventions have been plentiful, attempts to build coherent management development theory have been rare. Informed by the best of the literature and taking a contingent, systemic approach, we put forward a 'working' model of management development at various levels, primarily at the level of the organization, but with some reference to parallel models for the individual manager, and state. The intention has been to identify the main factors which are widely thought to have a causal role in management development, with a view to explaining more fully its determinants in an organizational setting.

Several of the succeeding chapters will be devoted to analysing this model in more detail. Before we do that, it is necessary to take a step backwards in time to review the UK historical context which led to the system of management development as it existed in the mid-1980s.

3

The Historical Background

INTRODUCTION: A VERY BRITISH PARADOX

There has been a paradox in Britain in respect of management in that although it was the first country to industrialize, it has been the last amongst the developed nations to recognize management as a distinctive economic role, requiring a body of knowledge and standards, and, for the purposes of this book, a means of development for its greater efficiency. Rather more than a decade ago, two authoritative studies (Constable and McCormick 1987; Handy 1987) finally revealed the depth of British weakness in this central focus of industrial efficiency. Even now, at the beginning of the twenty-first century, Britain's oldest and most prestigious university is only in the process of setting up a fully fledged business school. This book deals with the state of management development in Britain in the late twentieth century, but this in itself is not enough if there is no sense of how we arrived at the present situation. Any analysis of management development must therefore begin with the paradox above and with a historical perspective. How did the country fail so badly to organize itself in such an important area? This is the question we examine in this chapter, and we do it by taking three main dimensions of the issue up to the mid-1980s. First, we examine the broad socio-economic context of management, albeit briefly, because it is worthy of a book in its own right. Second, we review the different ways in which management development was pursued, using Handy et al.'s (1988) three approaches of corporate, academic, and professional, and adding a fourth, the contribution of consultants. In this middle section we also examine the emergence of a body of knowledge around which the development could be provided. Third, we examine the situation as it was in the mid-1980s at the time that Constable–McCormick (1987) and Handy (1987) were pursuing their enquiries.

▶ The Socio-Economic Context

Britain's relative economic decline for much of the twentieth century has frequently been chronicled and its causes debated, with attention primarily being paid to social factors (Barnett 1972, 1987; Wiener 1981; Rubinstein 1994) or economic ones (Caves 1968). In so far as management is considered in these debates, it is seen as a symptom rather than a cause of decline. The wider issue, as expressed for instance by Wiener, is that in spite of leading the first Industrial Revolution, Britain possessed an essentially anti-industrial culture. We do not have the space to review this debate in detail, but there are a number of factors in it which may be argued to contribute to the weakness of management.

One of these was the structure of British industry. Chandler noted in his comparison of the dynamics of industrial capitalism between Britain, Germany, and the United States: 'British entrepreneurs failed to make the essential three-pronged investment in manufacturing, marketing, and management in a number of the capital-intensive industries of the Second Industrial Revolution . . . Most important of all, the pioneers recruited smaller managerial teams, and the founders and their families continued to dominate the management of the enterprises' (1990: 235). This situation had consequences, especially a very late separation of ownership and control and a lack of scale of operation, which meant that there was no strong impetus for a cadre of professional managers based on meritocratic principles to arise. It is not suggested that Britain did not develop large companies, merely that they appeared later, especially compared with those in America and Germany, and that the growth of professional management has been later still.

A second important area is related to the social status of the professional manager. David Granick noted in his international comparison of management:

The low prestige of industrial management in Britain is probably of major importance in explaining the weakness of the role of its top management. The industrial managerial career probably does not attract as highly talented individuals as is the case in the other countries, and those who do select it have their self-confidence diminished by that very fact. Certainly the breadth of training and experience of top managers is far less in Britain than elsewhere. (1971: 370)

Thirdly, in the wider society, vocational education very much played second fiddle to academic education, with its strong preference for theory over practice. While other countries also had a low level of social mobility within industry, Britain was unusual in the extent to which the school system perpetuated social class structures. Moreover, the public schools (and only to a somewhat lesser extent the grammar schools and universities) were dominated by a humanistic, and especially classical, view of education. They also tended to have a contempt for industry, preferring aristocratic or at least professional values. In so far as wealth was important, it tended to focus on mercantile and London-based activities rather than industrial and provincial ones.

As an outcome of all this, the most comprehensive analytical evaluation of British economic performance in a comparative context is probably the Brookings Institution's survey *Britain's Economic Prospects*. This measured everything that could reasonably be measured, noted a substantial productivity gap, and without suggesting a full explanation came to the conclusion that: 'somewhere in this area of management knowledge, competence, and vigor, may lie an important part of the explanation for the productivity differentials' (Caves 1968: 275–6). These are foreign views, which lend objectivity, but there are many British voices too (Jones and Barnes 1967; Political and Economic Planning 1966).

This view of the inadequacy of management as a factor in Britain's lack of competitiveness took a long time to emerge or percolate through to either the industrial or public consciousness. This in turn meant that the various routes by which managers might have become better developed for their roles were themselves feeble and without strong support for much of the century. We now examine them.

▶ Corporate Training and Development

In the period up to and into the twentieth century management learning took place through practical work in companies. As generations of owning families became established, the argument that managers are born (from the established family background) and not made became more widespread. While experience might be useful, training, and especially education, were seen as unnecessary and indeed irrelevant. Management was seen as an art honed by years of practical experience. For the family members who went into the business, there was an apprenticeship which emphasized learning by doing. This experience was self-reinforcing; thus when the younger family members reached director status, they too did not see the value of education. At a lower level, management was not a recognized occupation. In larger and more structured organizations such as the railways, army officers were common because they were among the few who had gained experience of organizing large numbers of staff and operating detailed plans; indeed Black (2000) argues that the soldier–technologist was the basis of modern management, and that the Royal Military Academy at Woolwich was in effect the first British business school.

As a result, before the Second World War few companies took much interest in or made much provision for training their managers. In so far as there was any interest in training, it was in technical and commercial areas, rather than in generic management or people skills. A 1980s review notes that the onus for any development was on the manager:

> In the pre-war years when university graduates were less commonplace in industry, advancement from the shopfloor and technician level into supervision and management or into any better paid work was understood to include what would now be called self-development. It meant that it was not the company's responsibility to tell employees what, when and how they needed to learn in order to get on. It also meant that the situations in which knowledge and skills were deployed were usually different from those in which they were acquired. Much of the learning was done after a day's work. (NEDO 1984: 84)

However, the report notes that even this declined after the Second World War.

In the first half of the twentieth century few graduates were recruited, and when they were, companies seemed not to know what to do with them until they had acquired 'practical experience'; often they did work which a non-graduate could as well have done, and were left to make their own way. And it could be a risky career, especially in the inter-war period, when working conditions were rarely attractive, and the status of industry was low, especially in manufacturing. No wonder that good graduates preferred the Civil Service or the professions. Nor was the antipathy of industry only towards graduate managers; Caves noted that such a pivotal industry as machine tools 'has always distrusted university-trained engineers, and in 1958 employed only twenty-five graduate engineers!' (1968: 303).

One route by which training was initiated in companies was through consultants. Although organized consultancies were late to develop in Britain compared to the United States and even France and Germany, when they started work from the late 1920s they realized that it was necessary to train managers and others in the new methods being introduced. Sometimes, although not often, this led to continued training. Although there were only five substantial consultancy companies before the 1960s, when the accountants began to be involved, their total impact was not inconsiderable; a conference in 1961 was told that there were 10,360 man-weeks of management training in 1960 provided by the consultants, and that the cumulative number of companies which had been helped to set up their own management training operations was 341. They also tended to be more popular with companies than other modes of training. A major study of the mid-1960s reported that 'many of the courses provided by consultants, for instance, are well supported in sharp contrast to the weak attraction of the longer courses with a higher "educational" content that the colleges and universities offer' (Political and Economic Planning 1966: 265). Other important contributions by consultants were lectures, books, pamphlets and articles. Indeed in the absence of business schools before the 1960s the consultants were the main source of initiative in the management development field, and have remained a significant contributor to management development ever since. Indeed Ferguson (1999) has argued with some merit that they deserve attention as a separate fourth stream to be set alongside the three being considered here.

Turning back to the companies, if the tradition of personal self-development declined after the Second World War, more companies did become involved in training. On the one hand, companies began to develop their own in-house training and graduate development programmes. Unilever was a leader in this area with its Unilever Companies Management Development Scheme. There was also an expansion in the number of private training colleges, of which there were estimated to be about 60 in 1965 (Whitley et al. 1981). Even so, Political and Economic Planning (1966: 87) provided an estimate that 'of the 450,000 managers in industry today, less than 1 per cent have received any form of external management training; among larger companies it has been estimated that about a fifth have a systematic training scheme, while among the smaller ones there are hardly any.'

Yet by the 1960s there was a growing awareness that change was needed. The more proactive attitudes of government in the mid-1960s resulted in the passage of the Industrial Training Act in 1964 with its Industrial Training Boards (ITBs) and the setting up of the Central

Training Council, which provided two reports on the principles, policies and practices recommended for managerial competence. Brech notes that the second of these

> formed a landmark in the progress of Britain's concern for managerial advancement by reason of promulgating for widespread application the policies and practices of management development that had hitherto been the prerogative of the relatively few corporations, companies, and firms. Moreover, for approved successful applications of these policies and practices grants could be gained in part to offset the ITB levy. (1997: 382)

Such grants were especially used in the provision of externally provided short courses rather than qualifications or internal programmes. However, Leggatt, in considering these developments, concluded: 'The practices of the majority of companies leave much to be desired in the diagnosis of education and training needs, in clarifying the objectives of training policy, and in evaluating training programmes' (1972: 164).

But although there was progress into the 1970s as more companies came to recognize the need for management training, we must finish this section with a particularly scathing criticism of the situation in this period by Crockett and Elias (1984), using the 1975–6 National Training Survey. They found that managers were drawn mainly from the 'shop floor', that is from supervisory, craft and operative occupations, and that only a small proportion of the inflow into managerial occupations originated in the educational sector; the proportion of graduates in the sample was therefore extremely low. Even where they did exist, 'managerial qualifications at the graduate or postgraduate level do not appear to raise earnings'. Moreover 'we found that the majority of firms do not train their managers for the jobs they hold, other than the usual Cook's Tour of the establishment. We analysed the provision of vocational training throughout the careers of the managers in our sample but found little evidence of a relationship between training and earnings.' Their conclusion followed from these findings:

> If British managers are criticised for their lack of education and the low priority placed on managerial training, could this mean that the education and training which can be supplied to junior and middle management in this country is considered irrelevant by the senior management who regulate its demand, either directly by granting leave of absence, or indirectly in terms of the rewards to those who participate in managerial education? The lack of any clear relationship between vocational,

'on-the-job' training and the earnings of managers, together with the low priority firms place on the training of their managers represents a weak point in current 'supply-side' strategies designed to improve economic performance in the UK. (Crockett and Elias 1984: 42)

▶ Management Education

There is a strong argument that the British universities were recalcitrant in introducing management as a subject until the 1960s. But this is only part of the story, because there had been efforts to do so much earlier which were not successful. There were attempts at Birmingham and Manchester to start management degrees at the turn of the century (Whitley et al. 1981), but in both cases there was little support from local industry in financing the programmes, sending their own sons, or recruiting graduates. What W. J. Ashley, the first professor at Birmingham, called 'the remarkable conservatism and inaccessibility to ideas', won the day, although Birmingham, together with Edinburgh, the London School of Economics and Liverpool, did continue to offer a B.Com. degree focusing on the economics of business. More practical management studies were confined to the technical colleges, and a few, such as the Regent Street Polytechnic, provided part-time courses for practising managers, but generally without being able to attract those with the ability to be senior managers. So why was British industry so reluctant? A comment by the London Chamber of Commerce about the LSE degree may have some general relevance:

> The great majority of employers are not anxious to employ University men or women. They prefer to recruit their staff at the age of sixteen or seventeen, as in most cases the actual experience of office routine is more valuable to the employer than general commercial knowledge. Any responsible posts which cannot be filled by the promotion of men or women already on the staff, are given to applicants of business experience. . . . While there can be no doubt that the Bachelor of Commerce has a good general background for business work, it is of little value to the employer until a man has had some practical experience. (Keeble 1982: 108)

In October 1945 the Ministry of Education appointed a committee under Lyndall Urwick to advise on the educational facilities required for managers, and its report, issued in 1947, led to the creation of certificate and diploma courses in the technical colleges, under the aegis of the British Institute of Management Education Committee. There seems to have been no thought of a prestigious postgraduate degree such as the MBA, by this time well established in the USA, nor of persuading the universities to become involved. In the event, the certificate and diploma were again not attractive to companies or managers and by the 1960s only 810 certificates and 640 diplomas had been awarded. Even when the diploma was converted into the DMS as a postgraduate-level qualification and taken over by the Council for National Academic Awards (CNAA) for the non-university sector, numbers did not increase significantly. Part of the problem was employer resistance, but another was the lack of prestige of the providers. However there was a flourishing private sector, led by Henley and Ashridge, and a number of universities provided non-qualification programmes.

In general, up to the 1960s there was an introverted complacency in the university world about the nature of disciplines and knowledge, and no sense of responsibility for the world of work. So students did not see industry as an attractive career, compared to the situation in the United States, where the top universities, such as Harvard, Chicago, and Stanford, operated business schools from very early in the century or before, and the best students saw industry as intellectually and socially acceptable, or in Germany with its *Handelshochschulen* (colleges of commerce), or France with the *grandes écoles*. Indeed, by the mid-1960s Britain had still not reached the point reached by these other countries by the end of the nineteenth century.

The main impetus for the spread of management education in the post-war period came not from industry or the universities but from the creation of the Foundation for Management Education in 1960. This was largely the brainchild of John Bolton, himself a Harvard MBA, but was also driven by various industrialists and MPs; of the latter Sir Keith Joseph was perhaps the key figure. At least the FME managed to raise the profile of the area and bring it before the Robbins Committee on Higher Education (1963). However, Robbins was distinctly uncertain about teaching managers or prospective managers, noting that it was 'a subject of considerable perplexity, and opinion is divided on what methods of training are appropriate' (1963: 127). Nevertheless the report did recommend setting up at least two major postgraduate schools, and this led to the establishment of the Franks Committee to examine ways to activate these recommendations, with the result that the London and Manchester business schools were launched in 1965. Industry did provide a considerable amount of the funding by setting up the Council of Industry for Management Education to raise money for these and later other business schools.

Even the new business schools did not have an easy time with industry's expectations of them. London and Manchester essentially wanted to recreate the American model of management education, and especially the two-year MBA. Industry for its part did not want the business schools to produce young, academically qualified managers; what it wanted was practical training for existing middle managers, and its use of the schools confirmed this. In contrast to this, it is worth noting Leggatt's view about the role of business schools: 'We share ATM Wilson's view that the principal task of the business schools is not to educate/train large numbers of managers but to carry out "an intellectual R and D job"; that is, to make management science intellectually respectable, such that recruits of increasingly higher standard are attracted into management' (1972: 166).

Nevertheless, the business schools did begin to make considerable headway in the 1970s through four main routes. One was a rapid expansion in the number of overseas students. There was also a very rapid spread of undergraduate degrees in business, initially through the polytechnics and the CNAA, but soon with many universities also joining in. Another important route to undergraduate teaching was through engineering programmes, which as a result of the Dainton Report (1972) were deemed to need an input of management studies. Several of the most prestigious universities originated management programmes in this way. But perhaps the most important aspect of the move forward was that the division between the business schools and industry had moved towards resolution, largely because the schools opened up part-time and, later, distance-learning qualifications which could be taken by existing managers without being absent from work for a year or, worse, two. The existing managers, for their part, were becoming increasingly enthusiastic about such programmes, and many companies doubtless decided on a line of least resistance that if this was what they really wanted they should do it, as long as the time required was largely the managers' own.

▶ Professional Institutes for Management

Professional institutes have played a very important part in British industrial life. The civil engineers were the first to form a professional organization in 1771, and were given a royal charter in 1828. Other institutes for engineers and accountants followed at intervals through the rest of the nineteenth century. But management was not seen by contemporaries as an equivalent occupation. It would be wrong to say that there was no sense at all of an emerging need for a central institute in management, and there were enthusiasts who were known as the 'management movement'. Brech has explored the origins of the Institute of Industrial Administration (IIA) for managers in the aftermath of the First World War, but this did not impact on the vast majority of managers. Indeed at the first AGM of the IIA in 1921 there were 221 enrolled members, but a year later the membership had actually dropped, there was a virtual stop in enrolment and its journal ceased publication in 1923 after fifteen issues (Brech 1997: 24). There were several contributory reasons for the failure of the IIA, including the severe recession of the early 1920s and the lack of dynamic leadership, but an unavoidable conclusion is that there was also a deficiency in demand from everyday managers and employers. Indeed it stood as something of a monument to the resistance of the vast majority to the ideas of the management movement.

The concept of management as an emerging profession in its own right as perceived by the management movement did not go away, and indeed the IIA did not disappear entirely, but progress was extremely slow and within a limited circle. There were also various sectional management societies and institutes in addition to the attempts to form a central institute, and these too played a part in the growth of the management movement. An important period was the formation of three management institutes (Works, Office, and Purchasing) in 1931–2, which launched a joint journal, *Industry Illustrated*. This was a valuable focus for expanding knowledge of good practice, since most of the published material came from management practitioners. This was particularly important because a good deal of empirically based progress was being made in management practice and techniques by the larger companies at this time. But across the management spectrum there was no real momentum to expand membership. Joining was a matter of individual initiative; progressive companies might publicize meetings, but there was no expectation that their managers should join, and there was little marketing to attract any latent demand. As a result, membership of none of the institutes reached four figures until well into the 1930s. Indeed, the very existence of the management-related institutes helped to perpetuate the view not of managers, but of engineers, salesmen, buyers, and accountants who happened to run departments. Nevertheless, the institutes did try to create standards by providing a curriculum and examinations, usually through correspondence courses.

One of the recurring themes was whether management constituted a profession, and if so, what this implied. Urwick, in his pamphlet *Is Management a Profession?* (1954), argued that as education became more extended and democratic, management posts would only be filled by those with higher academic qualifications. Yet in a debate between a profession and increased professionalization which continues to this day management clearly lacked several key dimensions of a profession, such as a considerable teachable component, an impartial public interest perspective, the open exchange of technical information, a code of ethics and community approval of the profession's authority. And the question of whether there was some overall system of knowledge on which its practitioners could draw was very much open to doubt. The great majority of managers never came close to accepting such a position.

In the setting up of the British Institute of Management (BIM) in 1947 there was a clash of perspectives between those who took an elitist conception of managers who had achieved identifiable career success and status in becoming general managers and those who followed the IIA, wishing to provide for a system of managerial growth through professional standards, with a base in qualifications, education according to a body of knowledge, and training. The BIM was not necessarily against professional standards as such, but the chairman, Sir Charles Renold, laid down two fundamental convictions: (1) 'that professional qualifications in general management are desirable only in so far as they can establish themselves with industry as significant indications of capacity to manage, i.e. to undertake general management responsibility; and (2) that an assessment of personal qualities is an indispensable element in the granting of professional qualifications in general management' (Brech 1997: 501). These effectively meant that achievement was to be the key attribute, and that it was to be measured by industry, not by qualifications, which must have played a part in diminishing the demand for them. The term 'general management' was an additional problem, since from contemporary and indeed present-day perspectives it meant the upper level of management involved in co-ordinating activities and responsible to the board of directors. This was inevitably a restricted concept of management and denied the role of lower levels below general management, and the role of younger managers, even if rising in the hierarchy. It therefore also denied the wider concept of management as a profession and roles in functional areas of management. Perhaps as a result, the BIM only achieved a slow inflow of the 'founder members' it saw as its base; by the end of 1949 there were only some 500, as opposed to some 1,500 'associate members' who did not carry voting rights; nor did the BIM have a local branch network.

This elitist position created a difficult relationship with the IIA, although the two did amalgamate in 1958, and this was paralleled by relations with the other, specialized, management societies, irritated by the BIM's proposal in 1948 that they should become 'local management associations', which would have reduced them to second-class status. Although the amalgamation of the BIM and the IIA did finally occur in 1958, relations with the other institutes, by now numbering into double figures, remained problematic, and they formed a joint body of their own, the Co-ordinating Committee of Professional Management Organizations. Thus while the early assumption had been that there would be a common body of knowledge about management, and indeed the functional institutes had accepted this even up to the national syllabus launched by the Urwick Committee, the institutional implications were not followed through.

In its early days the BIM did not provide management development, although it did give information and advice on other development schemes, but from the late 1950s a demand for seminars on current management practice became obvious, and regions and branches began to respond. In 1963 it produced guidance on the setting up of in-company management development schemes. But a central BIM management development unit was not started until 1974. Thus while there was eventually a professional institute for managers, it cannot be said that even by the mid-1980s it provided a clear framework of development for either education or training such as many of the professional institutes in other occupations did.

Indeed it is necessary to finish this section with the observation that the most important professional institute for management was not the BIM at all, but rather that of the chartered accountants. If management did not have a qualification structure which was credible to industry, the accountants certainly did. Indeed Matthews has argued 'The main reason for the accountants' success in reaching the top . . . is that the accountant's articles was probably the best and until very recently one of the few ways of acquiring a formal management training in Britain' (1998: 73). Moreover, he argues that, far from being merely 'financial functionaries', their training as auditors could give them unique experience of the wider workings of business. Furthermore, this wider experience derived initially from auditing is closely connected with their emergence as a dominant force in consultancy. Not only does Britain have far more accountants as a proportion of the labour force than other countries, but an increasing proportion of them have gone into industry, where they have steadily increased their role on boards of directors as well as adding professionalism to the financial function.

Britain has of course a very wide range of professional institutes, and it is not possible to do justice to all their contributions to the development of management as an outcome of their professional roles. Harvey and Press (1989) do for instance draw attention to the standards of mining engineers in the late nineteenth century in spite of their lack of university education, and give credit to these standards to the education and regulation provided by their professional institute. Other examples could doubtless be adduced and the cumulative impact on management could be significant.

▶ The Development of Management Thought and Practice

In trying to bring together these various routes for developing managers, how far could it be said that there was a body of knowledge and principles which provided a framework for developing management as an occupation and emerging profession?

In the development of the Industrial Revolution there was inevitably a need for codifying emerging knowledge, both technical and, as an offshoot, managerial in terms of the techniques appropriate for the particular industry. Books were written, and where the knowledge required was more general, as in accounting, there was a surprisingly large number of textbooks (Pollard 1968: 140). But the focus was on the function or the industry; there was no common body of knowledge about management as such, and indeed there was no sense of an emerging profession and little to link the groups of managers across industries.

Slater Lewis (1896) was the first to write a general text in the main areas then covered by management, that is, mainly production techniques such as production planning, stock control, and costing, but much less on organizational issues. Elbourne's similar book of 1914 was much used in the First World War, and others followed, most of whom were practising managers (Lee 1921; Sheldon 1923), but none of these achieved recognition in the same way as their American counterparts did. They were also mainly concerned with production systems rather than the wider aspects of management. The first comprehensive British book on management to incorporate organizational principles was probably Urwick and Brech (1948).

The new managerial methods expressed in scientific management to a large extent passed Britain by compared with Japan, the United States, and France. In part this was due to the lack of large organizations, in part to the hostility of labour, and in part to the complacency and elitism of the directors of companies. Child (1969) has noted that in the early development of management thought in Britain there were three strands or perspectives, namely management as a technical function, management as a social group, and management as a system of authority. The last of these, and to some extent the second, became concerned with considerations of social legitimation in the wider society, particularly in relations with labour. As a result of these primary concerns, the first strand, that of the technical aspects of management as a function, with all its implications for efficiency and professionalism, was prejudiced by arguments about legitimation. In any case, the implication of scientific management was of a meritocracy and professionalism which clashed with the social class perspectives of the elite, who preferred amateurism based on a classical education and essentially class-based leadership and man-management skills.

A group did grow in Britain after the First World War which pursued the objective of a coherent body of knowledge, operating on scientific principles, and which came to be known as the management movement, but it was always small and beyond the interests or even awareness of the great majority of managers. As Whitley et al. put it, 'The members of the management movement found themselves preaching to a largely unresponsive audience, and were sometimes driven to bitter criticism of employers for their extreme conservatism in the face of new ideas, their lack of interest in business research, and their unbending resistance to management education' (1981: 32).

The only coherent attempt to share experience came through the Management Research Groups, which were set up in 1926–7 by Seebohm Rowntree of the chocolate family, based on an idea he had picked up in the US. These consisted of the confidential exchange of developments in practice among the directors of member companies. In spite of their name, however, they were not concerned with research, and they were not interested in general dissemination.

There was nevertheless a growth of knowledge in techniques and practices in the inter-war period, but it was very much based on experimental pragmatism within individual companies, and was published by being written up for one of the management journals operated by one of the professional institutes. Such journals did not, however, have a wide circulation, and had limited impact. There was virtually no research or even analysis carried out by the university world until well after the Second World War; such research as was carried out in the earlier period was done by the consultants and then in a narrow range of areas mainly concerned with production. Nevertheless, the consultants were probably the main conduits for the development of a body of knowledge, but only with limited impact until after the Second World War.

Whatever the development of practice in some companies, this was not widespread. Thus, even in the mid-1960s, Political and Economic Planning could argue: 'It became apparent that many of the firms visited did not apply even comparatively simple techniques that should contribute to high productivity' (1966: 13). Caves noted on the same issue that 'use of the technique of work study is said to be fifty years behind the United States' (1968: 303).

Thus, even if there had been a willingness to take management development seriously, there was no accepted or coherent body of management knowledge, theory or practice in Britain on which to base it, while those who were writing in the field reached only a small audience.

The Position into the Mid-1980s: Identifying the Problem

By the 1980s the criticism of management development had reached a crescendo, culminating in the Constable–McCormick and Handy reports. One incisive evaluation was by Tom Kempner (1984), who in a five-country study argued that British managers were amateurs whereas their competitors were professionals. A major NEDO report of 1984, *Competence and Competition*, was instrumental in heightening awareness about the importance of training among British management by comparing the British situation with its three main industrial competitors, Germany, the USA and Japan. This was followed by *A Challenge to Complacency*, a survey by Coopers and Lybrand (1985) commissioned by the Manpower Services Commission to investigate the state of training within British industry. Their report showed that there was widespread ignorance among top management of how their company's training performance compared with that of their competitors; that many senior executives had only a limited knowledge of the scale of resources directed to training within their company; and that training was not seen as an important contribution to competitiveness and profitability, but rather as an overhead to be cut when profits were under pressure.

In 1985 there was a substantial survey and report by Mangham and Silver (1986: 12) on the extent of management training in industry, which they summed up as 'a lamentable state of affairs' in which 'it is clear that a significant proportion of the management cadre in the United Kingdom in 1985 received no formal training of any kind in the skills which many of them, and virtually every critic of our economic performance, regard as important to the nation's success'.

We take the mid-1980s as the heading for this section because the rest of this book essentially starts from the point where the Constable–McCormick and Handy reports of 1987 left off. These were complementary reports, with the former, entitled *The Making of British Managers* being based primarily on the results of four working parties on various aspects of management development in Britain, and the latter, *The Making of Managers*, being a comparison of management development in the United States, France, Germany, and Japan as well as Britain. Taken together, they represent the most comprehensive analysis of management development yet carried out. Both were heavily critical of many features of the British system, or, as Handy argued, the lack of a system by contrast with its main competitors. A quotation from Handy summed up the situation: 'There can be little doubt that, by comparison with the other countries in this study, Britain has neglected her managerial stock. With some notable exceptions her companies have asked too little from their would-be managers and given them too little in terms of education, training, and development' (1987: 13). These reports, taken with Mangham and Silver, constitute a damning indictment. And they came after a considerable improvement in most aspects of management development since the 1960s.

Conclusion

We now return to our dimensions of management development. We have followed each of the approaches from its origins up to the 1980s. By the mid-1980s there was in each of them some considerable progress, but all still had great weaknesses. And as Handy et al. noted of their three routes, 'They are not mutually exclusive, for it is possible to combine any two of them, but nor are they easily compatible, for none really accepts the relevance of the others. The result is confusion' (1988: 169). There was also confusion within each of the groupings. Corporate training had in most cases little structure and was more a statement of intent driven by the initiative of individual managers. There were too many and overlapping academic qualifications, and in the case of the best known, the MBA, there were already beginning to be too many variations in length, content, quality, and mode of delivery for it to have a single coherent image in the managerial labour market. There were also a number of managerial professional institutes, but with different approaches; the central institute had no quality control on entry and no process of evaluation other than achievement. The consultants had had a useful input as a pump-priming mechanism at an important point in time, but training was only a secondary interest for them. As for the final dimension, the body of knowledge, that too was something of a chimera. Much of the content of academic programmes was based on texts developed in the United States, research in Britain could only be described as feeble in its impact on practice, and in the training area there was little idea of the nature of the skills which needed to be inculcated.

Clearly, there was a great deal that required improvement, and the 1980s saw possible solutions being put forward.

Geoffrey Holland (1986), the Director of the Manpower Services Commission, became a leading exponent of the need to take action, arguing 'the most crucial block of all is missing: a serious, systematic, modern and effective system of management development, management education, and management training', and proposed ten objectives over the next decade. Constable McCormick and Handy also provided numerous recommendations, and these were largely subsumed in the initial objectives of a new body which arose out of the two reports, the Council for Management Education and Development, soon to become better known by its marketing arm, the Management Charter Initiative (MCI). To take the story further would, however, take us out of the historical background and into present issues.

4

National Management Development Systems

INTRODUCTION

The focus of this chapter is twofold: the first half sets management development in Britain in the context of other national systems; the second examines the management development system in Britain at the national level in rather more detail. As has already been noted, this book deals mainly with management development at the level of the organization and the individual manager rather than national policy frameworks or management development as part of the educational system. Nevertheless these latter are important dimensions and require recognition.

▶ Comparative National Systems

Management development systems are deeply embedded in the history, culture, education, and labour markets of countries, and are not independent and self-sufficient. There is nothing approaching a single model; indeed, we would fully accept that there cannot be a single model in spite of some trends towards convergence, and that countries need to develop a framework consonant with their history, culture, and educational infrastructure, even though the incorporation of external models may have contributed to any single system. Nevertheless, many of the industrializing countries, with the notable exception of Britain, had seen the origins of a coherent system of management development before the First World War and some degree of consonance between their educational and managerial systems before the Second World War. Even as late as the mid-1980s it was the main finding of the Handy Report (1987) that all the other countries surveyed had coherent and well-established, although different, systems for management development and that Britain did not. We will therefore briefly sketch the history of the other main countries, and these can be contrasted with the historical evolution of management development in Britain described in the previous chapter. In reviewing the main systems and their characteristics we shall follow Handy (1987) in examining the American, German, French, and Japanese systems, but omitting the British system, since the rest of the book deals with this. We recognize that there are many other national systems, but we are merely trying to provide a context for examining the British system rather than carry out a truly international comparison. In the categorization which follows, we have been particularly guided by the work of Handy and his colleagues (1987, 1988), Amdam (1996), and Sparrow and Hiltrop (1994), who in turn borrow a useful schema from Evans, Lank and Farquhar (1989).

The American model

From the time that the United States began industrializing in the 1820s, there have been commercial colleges to train clerks and bookkeepers. Managerial capitalism became important with the emergence of the railroads and the administrative innovations which they required (Wren 1994). Many of the new managers came from the army college at West Point; indeed Congress instructed the army to make its engineers available for railroad projects. West Point's ideas and methods in turn came in considerable part from France and Germany (Spender 1999). Moreover, the emerging industrialists were interested in ideas. It was no coincidence that Joseph Wharton visited both Germany and France and spoke both languages, delivered papers to the American Social Science Association, hired Frederick W. Taylor to reorganize his Bethlehem steelworks on the principles of scientific management, and founded the first business school, the Wharton School at the University of Pennsylvania, in 1880. Other leading universities such as Harvard and Chicago followed around the turn of the century. The early business schools were not very sophisticated by modern standards, but they did give credibility to a vocational orientation in higher education. Moreover, there was a growing demand for the products of the business schools as American industry became dominated in the 1920s by large-scale divisionalized corporations with a separation of ownership from control and a substantial managerial hierarchy.

The American approach gives a high recognition to management as a social and economic grouping, and also to the means of its development. Education is seen as an investment to provide credentials for the market-place and as a way to shape one's own destiny. The universities produce very large numbers of business studies graduates and postgraduates, with some 85,000 MBAs, half of whom already have a business undergraduate degree, and around 250,000 first degrees in business every year. Putting the latter figure into labour market terms means that, if directly translated into new managerial starts, some two-thirds of all new managers in the United States will have a degree in the subject. At a later point in their careers, almost all managers will have both a degree and substantial continuing development. While experiential development is seen as important (McCauley et al. 1994) education is also central to the self-image of managers. Employers frequently criticize business degrees, but use them as a sifting mechanism for recruitment, based on a pecking order depending on the prestige of the university. General education, including a business education, is seen as being the individual's financial responsibility.

The MBA is an American development, and central to how education interacts with industry. It must be noted, however, that there is no single MBA. There are very considerable differences in quality and prestige, and there are very different intellectual models. Thus Harvard is associated with the case system, whereas Chicago believes in intellectual rigour within individual disciplines, more on the French model of the *grandes écoles*. Indeed, the American model risks not being defined as a system at all, being, as Handy (1987: 71) put it, 'uncoordinated, undirected, unplanned'. But all MBAs are based on assumptions of business leadership and general management, in contrast to the German system described below. There have also been important temporal cycles. In the late 1950s, the Ford and Carnegie foundations heavily criticized the American business schools for their 'trade-school' mentality, and demanded more research focus and intellectual rigour. These were duly incorporated, to meet the challenge in the early 1980s that the business schools had moved too far away from the interests of industry by becoming too abstract and detailed and dominated by increasingly fragmented sub-disciplines (Porter and McKibbin 1988). In the 1990s the schools tried to strike a new balance by moving towards a more integrated view of management with more emphasis on the softer skills. There are still many criticisms, such as that research is too abstruse to have an impact on practice and that management teachers have little experience of the real world, while industry is accused of not being clear what it wants from the system (Aaronson 1996). Nevertheless, it has provided a very substantial base of activity for the development of managerial skills. Executive education, both degree and non-qualification, is provided by most business schools, and for some comprises a considerable proportion of their total income.

Company-based management development covers a wide range of activities and a high level of expenditure, and there is a move towards setting up corporate universities, some of them running their own MBAs or other masters degrees. Indeed development is increasingly in-house, geared to the particular needs or strategy of the organization, and based on the softer skills of leadership and group dynamics. Much of the learning in this sense is corporate, and comes close to the concept of the learning organization. There are also massive amounts of managerial literature with which managers are expected to have some acquaintance. The US differs from the other models by having a high level and awareness of mobility in its managerial labour market, and therefore a predominantly external framework for managerial careers and development. But this does not necessarily mean that managers work for a large number of companies.

America has become the main model for copying, especially after the Second World War and with agencies such as the Ford Foundation and the European Productivity Agency actively seeking to extend management development. Even in countries where there was no element of control, such as Britain and Australia, there was an apparently proven model waiting to be taken up.

The German model

Germany was able to achieve a substantial early commitment to the preparation of managers. Locke (1984) has argued that during the growth period of the Second Industrial Revolution, Germany developed a system of management education which complemented entrepreneurial activities, although there had been commercial academies since the eighteenth century. The German foundation of *Handelshochschulen* began around the turn of the century, but unlike the American focus on the MBA and general management, the German approach centred on business economics and specialized tasks. Nor was the German system built on a distinction between undergraduate and postgraduate education; rather, the main output has been the Diplom Kaufmann. But as a result of these two characteristics, business education has not been equated with management education, and law and engineering have also been starting-points for managerial careers. German management, and indeed German industrial society, may be said to start from an admiration of and preference for the professional, whether in management or elsewhere, to be contrasted with the British long-standing preference for the amateur. The concept of *Technik*, the creation of useful objects, closely aligned with engineering, is separated from *Kunst*, the performing and fine arts, and *Wissenschaft*, which incorporates knowledge in the sciences and some of the arts. *Technik* is strongly associated with the cult of the professional, and dominates the development of managers. Higher education, whether through university or polytechnic, provides future managers with vocationally oriented, broadly based, and, by British standards, lengthy studies. Even then, the aspiring manager will typically have a two-year apprenticeship with a good deal of job rotation. There has, however, been a problem of rising graduate unemployment as higher education has increased in scope. There is no degree equivalent to the MBA; although some Germans go abroad to the US, Britain, or to INSEAD in France to obtain one, on the whole the German system does not provide the international perspective that is needed with globalization, and indeed German companies' foreign operations.

But higher education has not been the only route into management; the apprenticeship system has probably been stronger in Germany than anywhere else, leading from apprentice (*Lehrling*) to skilled worker (*Facharbeiter*) to master craftsman (*Meister*). However, there is an increasing academic focus for German management, and this route has become much more rare. Even so, the apprenticeship is not dead, since approximately 15 per cent of those obtaining the *Abitur* or university entrance qualification elect to serve an apprenticeship first and then go to university. This not only happens in manufacturing but in commercial industries such as banking. At the other end of entry to management is the doctorate, which, far from its British association, has been almost essential to reach the upper ranks of management in some companies and industries such as chemicals and insurance. Randlesome in Handy et al. (1988) reports that in 1984 53.8 per cent of the management boards of the 100 largest German companies possessed doctorates.

Once in the organization, some graduate entrants receive no induction, some a limited amount of on-the-job training and job rotation, and a few participate in a graduate trainee programme. After that, the initiative for further development lies with the individual in conjunction with their immediate superior; personnel and training departments have only an indirect role, in keeping with the belief that line functions should be more influential than staff ones. The vast majority of management development is carried out internally by in-house training staff, brought-in specialists, or senior managers. There is a reluctance among the larger companies to send staff on open public courses. As a result, very few of the universities offer management development programmes, although there are private organizations which operate courses for medium-sized and smaller companies. But much more important at this latter level are the chambers of commerce, which have an important role in all training, from initial vocational training through apprenticeships up to management development. Even so, small businesses in Germany as elsewhere are reluctant to avail themselves of management development, and for the usual reasons of lack of time and suspicion of relevance.

Germany has a low level of mobility of managers for a number of reasons, including strong regional identities, paternalistic companies, and non-transferable benefits such as holidays and pensions. Earnings also tend to be reasonably standard for similar jobs, which reduces the incentive for movement. Another dimension is that the importance of *Technik* means that people tend to stay in the same occupation once they have entered it. Interestingly, strong internal labour markets are seen as a problem rather than an advantage.

In the Scandinavian countries and in the Netherlands, the German influence was strong before the Second World War. The first business schools in Scandinavia came after the foundation of German-style technical universities, so that engineers have again had an important role in the managerial hierarchy. Even so, it must be noted that Sweden's first higher education school in business, the Stockholm School of Economics, was founded in 1909, followed by the Gothenburg School in 1923. The foundation of both schools owed a great deal to private funding and the interest of the industrial world, a strong contrast with the situation in Britain at the time, and owed only a limited debt to the German model. In the Netherlands business schools were founded according to individual leadership approaches, but within an overall German-style higher education framework. Nevertheless, it might be argued in broad terms that there is a north European approach to management development.

The French model

France has long had a strong centralist and elitist focus, and this carries over into the development of managers. From the setting up of the École Polytechnic in 1749, the *grandes écoles* were created quite separately from the universities to provide the administrators and engineers necessary to run the state apparatus, and the tradition of their dominance in French life has extended to industry and commerce. The more specifically industrial École Supérieure de Commerce was set up in 1820 and the prestigious École des Hautes Études Commerciales in 1881. They obtain the best students and are highly elitist and competitive, with studies strongly based on mathematics; management, like other occupations, is primarily an exercise of the intellect. Their scientific approach was influential in the US through its impact on West Point as the source of early American management. There is indeed an argument that there is a neglect of the human skills in spite of the intellectual approach to problem-solving. Their graduates form a very powerful network across industry, commerce and the public sector, and also tend to be self-perpetuating in their social composition. Engineers tend to occupy the majority of top management posts in French companies, even in non-technical industries such as banking and finance, although their position of supremacy is now being challenged by the growth in the number of business schools which began in the 1960s. The universities also play a role in the education of managers, since the numbers in the *grandes écoles* are limited, but tend to be treated with suspicion by employers, who think of them as sources of left-wing ideas and revolt. However the universities have been trying to vocationalize their courses in line with industry's perceived needs.

Organizational management development is part of the wider training system. A training tax is levied on all companies employing more than 10 people, and at a rate of 1.2 per cent of the wage bill. Companies with more than 50 employees must draw up a training plan which is then discussed with the works committee; minutes of the discussion of these must be included with submissions to the local tax authorities. This can be seen as burdensome for smaller companies, but can be important in larger ones, especially where there are strong trade unions. In addition, individuals have a right to training leave of up to a year, financed from the training tax. All this provides a considerable stimulus to companies to engage in training. They can do their own training or contract it out to the local chamber of commerce or business school, or to a private training company. Often the decision is economic; it pays to train large groups internally, but small groups or individuals are most economically trained externally. The large companies in France with more than 2,000 employees, according to Handy et al. (1988), spent on average 3.36 per cent of their wage bill, considerably more than the law required. Training departments, however, do not have much influence or prestige in French industry; rather, departmental managers have the main responsibilities in this area and are often actively involved in training. Lower-level management development programmes are generally concerned with the acquisition of specialist skills, perhaps because the *grandes écoles* are seen as being too generalist and intellectual, and it is felt that what their graduates require is essentially practical skills. There is relatively little training for those at the top of organizations.

There is only a limited amount of managerial mobility, with perhaps more at the top than lower down. The *congé* or training leave is sometimes seen as a means by which managers can gain mobility, and for that reason it is distrusted by companies, unless, of course, they want to encourage managers to leave in a shakeout. It is not widely used in most companies, partly, companies argue, because the necessary training is provided anyway. But the continuing professional development of managers is seen as of increasing importance, preferably from an industry-wide perspective tied to some portable credentials and taking account of pressures towards globalization. The French are more international in this sense than the Germans.

It has been argued by Nioche (1992) that there is a Latin model of management education consisting of France, Italy, and Spain, based around the disciplines of law and economics. There is an interesting example in Italy of the failure of an American-style business school, set up with Ford Foundation and Harvard Business School support, as well as the support of some key Italian industrialists such as Adriano Olivetti. IPSOA was founded in 1952 and closed in 1964. It used the American case method and an inductive approach which sat ill with the Italian university establishment, which strongly preferred a deductive approach. Although there were also arguments about its management and personality clashes, it helps to show the difficulty of introducing new formats. On the other hand, the success of INSEAD, which was founded in 1957, shows the opposite.

The Japanese model

Of the countries discussed here, Japan was the last to industrialize. By the time of the onset of the Second Industrial Revolution around 1870, Japan had only 5 per cent of its labour force in manufacturing and these in family firms. Even so, the Tokyo Higher Commercial School was founded in 1875, later to evolve into the Tokyo University of Commerce and then Hitotsubashi University. From the start its curriculum was strongly influenced by the local business community, who were very happy to hire its graduates (Nishizawa 1996). After the Russo-Japanese war of 1904–5, a number of higher commercial schools and commerce faculties were created. Then, after Taylor's *Principles of Scientific Management* appeared in Japanese in 1912 (Wren 1994) there was a managerial revolution, replacing the family firms and providing the basis for the modernization of Japanese industry in the 1920s. Training for all was one of the keys to higher productivity, improved work methods, and harmonious relations with the labour force. Japan, in other words, had a reasonably strong and early start in the integration of academic and practical management.

Japanese managers are the products of a very competitive educational system at all levels from early school to university, and education is held in high regard, as indeed is success in industry. The universities are geared to the needs of an advanced industrial society, and there is considerable emphasis on technology, although business studies are becoming more widespread and acceptable, especially in the service sector. There are almost no postgraduate business degrees, although more Japanese have been taking MBAs abroad. Within the big companies, which dominate the economy, there is however a very careful recruitment process for future managers from the leading universities, so that those entering form an elite pool and top management is almost entirely dominated by university graduates. Managers are seen as key assets by companies, and as with other aspects of corporate policy, the perspective is a long-term one. Gow (Handy et al. 1988) notes a number of characteristics of Japanese management; those especially relevant to the development process include internal labour markets, lifetime employment, long-term planning perspectives, and extensive on-the-job training. The social tradition of commitment to the family and the organization, and the acceptance of authority, also have an influence, so that individualism is much less pronounced than in Anglo-Saxon cultures. Japan uses many important dimensions of corporate learning, including the very important one of mentoring as a formal requirement of every manager.

Overall, the development process is more integrated into the career and is more of a package with the career than is the case in Britain. Thus Storey et al. (1977: 223) note 'the apparently anomalous finding that British managers often reported more training than their Japanese counterparts'. The explanation was that training is much less of a distinct, separate activity in Japan. On-the-job learning starts with extensive induction courses and job rotation associated with mentoring. Although there is an experiential dimension, learning is planned and structured; many companies actually have a formal manual for on-the-job training. The elaborate *ringi* system of decision-making lays itself open to on-the-job learning, and constant performance monitoring is a further feature which makes managers aware of the need for development. It is also important that managers have a good deal of multi-functional experience early in their careers through the prevalence of job rotation, so that they can appreciate the organizational perspective. The outcome is competent generalists rather than specialists.

There is also off-the-job training, both provided by the organization and pursued by individuals at their own expense. This latter has become more important in the recent past, and in many respects equates with the sort of life-long learning that British governments have tried to encourage. There has been increasing emphasis on development for the higher levels of management. Japanese managers tend to be very well read in terms of business publications, and in foreign languages as well as Japanese. The professional management associations also run extensive correspondence courses, and chambers of commerce and the SME (Small and Medium-Sized Enterprises) Agency are important in the small business sector. Assessment/appraisal is an important part of Japanese managerial life. However, some elements of the Japanese system are either limited in scope, that is, they are not characteristic of the small company sector, and some, such as lifetime employment, diminished in the recession of the 1990s.

Towards convergence?

All countries are trying to reduce the financial responsibilities of the state with the onset of mass higher education, and management development is an area which the state will see as being market-driven. At the same time it has a strong interest in the quality of management as a key input into economic competitiveness, and for SMEs almost everywhere, and in the less developed countries for all managers, there is still a willingness to pay for interventionist policies. And even where they are market-dominated, management education and development are everywhere becoming a major consideration for all stakeholders. Globalization and the spread of the multinationals are creating common expectations of managers across the world, and corporate cultures are arguably becoming more influential than national cultures. There are of course still differences. German, French, and Japanese management models start with a preference for the technical in early education and sometimes later. Continental Europe also gives a strong role to the chambers of commerce. Britain and the United States have less technical focus and less clear-cut supportive institutions. They also have a greater focus on external rather than internal labour markets. But the general trends are similar. All the models expect something from the individual manager in terms of self-development over and above what might be done by the organization. All five countries favour development beyond the initial education and induction; in Germany and Japan it is more formalized, especially in the large companies, than in France, the United States, and Britain. All the countries have problems with management development in small businesses, but perhaps most in Britain because of the low level of general education. We would argue that there is a significant trend towards convergence, admittedly mainly because an international over-lay is appearing, driven by the large multinationals and the increas-ing ubiquity of the MBA, which operates on top of existing national systems. But the national systems are exhibiting the same trends.

In concluding this section of the chapter, it is an open question as to whether any model can be said to be better than another, so long as it is coherent and can provide both continuity and change. It might be noted rather cynically that when the post-war economic hegemony of the United States began to be challenged in the late 1970s and 1980s, its management development system also began to be challenged. In turn, the merits of those of Japan and Germany, which were the main challengers, began to be championed. Now, however, those two coun-tries are going through something of an economic relapse, and their management development is no longer seen as quite as attractive.

▶ British Management Development at National Level

It is by no means easy to obtain a snapshot of management develop-ment in Britain at the national level, in spite of the Constable–McCormick and Handy reports of 1987 both saying very clearly that it was important to be able to monitor events and progress over time. There are relatively few sources for monitoring longitudinal training and education developments for either individuals or organizations, as Tamkin and Hillage (1998) discovered in their attempt to provide indicators with which to monitor the situation. Moreover, although there are important policy dimensions, many of these are derived from wider education and training policy rather than being explicitly for management. We will start with a review of the policy milestones before examining practice through the various providers and institutions.

The policy framework

Inevitably, management development must be seen in the context of national policy for training and education more generally. Before describing these, however, we need to identify some of the main mile-stones in the policy framework, which has been one of a changing infrastructure and with it, funding, systems, and policy itself:

- In 1963 the Robbins Committee on Higher Education created a basis for expanding the higher education system, including paving the way for London and Manchester business schools. The Franks Committee followed in the same year to make the proposals for their creation more explicit.

- In the late 1960s a range of industrial training boards (ITBs) were created as a result of the 1964 Industrial Training Act, with a power to collect training levies from employers. Policy was thus based on a sectoral and compulsory approach. As reported in chapter 3, these were important in stimulating company training and especially the use of short courses.

- In 1973 a new central agency, the Manpower Services Commission (MSC), was created and most of the ITBs were disbanded.

- In 1986 the MSC was replaced by the Training Agency and a new competency-based approach was introduced through the National Council for Vocational Qualifications (NCVQ). This sponsored national occupational standards and vocational qualifications (NVQs) to relate to them.

- In 1987 National Training Awards were introduced.

- In 1988 the control of training was taken back within the Department of Employment and operated through the Training Education and Enterprise Department (TEED).

- In 1988 a White Paper, *Employment for the 1990s*, introduced a decentralized approach to training with the creation of 82 Training and Enterprise Councils (TECs) in England and Wales, and 22 Local Enterprise Councils (LECs) in Scotland.

- In 1991 the Investors in People (IiP) standard was introduced. At the local level, IiP is promoted and assessed by the TECs. IiP has four main criteria for an award: the existence of a written business plan and information on how employees will contribute to achieving it; regular meetings between line managers and employers on training needs linked to business goals; evidence of induction training and continuous development of all employees; and evaluation of training against business goals. It also favours the use of competency frameworks within these criteria. To achieve recognition requires a considerable effort on the part of all employees. Nevertheless, the 'kitemark' has proved popular, and in 1998 there were well over 11,000 company recognitions, with 36,000 commitments, covering nearly 50 per cent of the labour force.

- In 1995 the Department of Employment was merged with the Department for Education to form the DfEE in order to bring under one roof a range of different policy responsibilities.

- In 1997 two major reports, those of the Dearing Committee on Higher Education and the Kennedy Committee on Further Education, had an underlying theme of how the tertiary education system could be realigned to have a more explicit focus on the needs of the economy.

- In 1997 the Qualifications and Curriculum Authority (QCA) was created to replace the NCVQ and the Schools Curriculum and Assessment Authority and provide an integrated policy framework for all qualifications.
- Also in 1997 a series of 37 National Training Organizations (NTOs) was set up to provide sectoral integration for training by setting standards, promoting qualifications, and providing labour market and skills information. In management, the MCI came together with its small firms equivalent to become the Management and Enterprise Training Organization (METO).
- In 1998 a Green Paper, *The Learning Age,* announced the government's intentions in the area of learning, with a particular focus on life-long learning, and introducing two initiatives, the University for Industry and individual learning accounts to enable people to take responsibility for their own learning.
- In 1999 another White Paper, *Learning to Succeed,* disclosed yet another institutional framework. Its main recommendation is to create a national and between 40 and 50 local Learning and Skills Councils for England. The national council will have a budget of some £5 billion (of which about £3.15 billion is for further education) and will be responsible for strategic development, planning, funding, management and quality control of post-16 education and training (including further education but excluding higher education). It will take over the funding of workforce training from the TECs and also of the further education sector. It will also advise the government on national learning targets. Once legislation has been introduced, it will start operating in April 2001.

There has thus been movement between national, sectoral, and local levels for primary responsibility, while there have also been numerous changes in institutions. This lack of continuity in a policy framework has been paralleled by a similar lack of continuity in organizational training structures and policies, and these together must bear some responsibility for the uncertainty still surrounding training and development. These policies have also been criticized for creating 'a jungle of job creation and training schemes' subject to vested interests calling for increased amounts of taxpayers' money (Shackleton 1992: 8).

The infrastructure of training policies has not for the most part been directly concerned with management, although it has had some indirect significance. The IiP standard has been perhaps the most influential of the various interventions in that it requires a commitment to purposeful training for the whole of an organization. Thus although management development was recognized as of national importance, and increasingly so following the series of White Papers on competitiveness beginning in 1994, the main approach in the late twentieth century was exhortatory rather than proactive. Thus in the National Development Agenda 1996 one of the sub-aims was the achievement of competent and high-quality management. So how was this to be done? The document noted:

For 1996/7, development activity will concentrate on the following areas:

- helping intermediaries (including TECs, ITOs and Business Links) become more effective in supporting management development;
- illustrating innovative uses of the Management Standards and/or innovative ways of implementing competence based management development;
- providing a range of information and learning materials aimed at the various participants (and potential participants) within the management development market;
- encouraging Business Schools to make their courses more competence-based;
- developing standards for management consultants;
- encouraging the adoption of consortia approaches to management development within small companies, including collaborative arrangements to help support and facilitate the implementation of management NVQs;
- exploring ways in which the Management Standards and work based upon them can enhance the Investors in People process. (DfEE 1996: 43)

While this might be considered a worthy set of objectives, it suffered from being low-key and lacking either a carrot or a stick with which to implement it. In addition, as can be seen, there was a heavy emphasis on using the 'Management Standards', the management occupational standards associated with functional competencies and NVQs. Moreover, the document went on to say that the responsibility for implementation was to be indirect: 'MCI is seen as the Department's main intermediary in the Management Development area as well as being the lead body for management. For this reason much of the work listed will either be carried out by MCI, or be channelled through them.' The MCI (Management Charter Initiative) had started life as the Council for Management Education and Development in 1987 following the Constable–McCormick and Handy reports, and became the industry lead body for management, responsible for developing its national standards. This detracted from its original and industry-led focus in the late 1980s of bringing together all the players in the management development area and made it into a promoter of a particular dimension of national training policy which won only very limited support from both the providers (especially the business schools) and the customers (industry, especially large-scale industry, where companies preferred to develop their own competency frameworks). There have been a number of these 'players' concerned with management development: the Institute of Management (IM), covering management in general and a dozen or so other institutes concerned with functional aspects of management; the Association of Business Schools (ABS); the Association of MBAs (AMBA); the Foundation for Management Education (FME); the Association for Management Education and Development (AMED); and other more general but influential bodies such as the Confederation of British Industry (CBI). But while there has been no lack of institutions dealing with the subject, they have shown no real ability to work together.

But early in 2000 a new body, the Council for Excellence in Management and Leadership (CEML) was created, which brings management development right to the centre of national policy. The CEML is a non-executive body composed mainly of leading industrialists, and has an ambitious remit and plan of work. The remit covers:

- identifying issues for management and leadership in England, and the key stakeholders who need to take action;
- articulating a vision of management development for the future through developing a management development strategy for the UK. This will incorporate leadership and address in particular the needs of small firms. It will draw in the contribution and expertise of management councils in Scotland, Wales, and Northern Ireland;
- reviewing the quality, relevance and support for management education and training across a range of management issues;
- monitoring progress on issues identified by the Council as in need of action; and
- reporting annually to government and stakeholders on the progress of those responsible for taking action.

The plan of work for the first year is to include the following:

- the production of a management strategy;
- an examination of the way management education is organized and delivered in the UK, focusing particularly on:
  - business school provision for smaller firms and the capacity to teach entrepreneurial skills

- improving the quality of business school graduates
- enhancing the international standing of business schools (including considering the case for a world-class 'virtual' business school);
- a review of institutional arrangements, particularly the extent to which the emerging post-16 infrastructure supports or inhibits management development;
- consideration of the possibility (and practicability) of establishing a research council for management education;
- the production of a report on the key actions needed to address deficiencies in management education in England.

It is of course far too early to predict the success of the new body, but it creates a framework and capacity for action which have never been available before. We now proceed to look at the contributions of the various providers, even if the requisite information is limited.

Educational provision and qualifications

This section is not intended to be a major discussion of the management education system but rather a presentation of statistical categories to help explain its contribution to management development overall. Even this is surprisingly difficult due to problems in classification and measurement for different groups and qualifications. The total numbers in higher and further education have expanded dramatically. In 1962–3, at the time of the Robbins Report (1963), there were 216,000 students in full-time higher education courses, with a further 117,000 part-time students, of whom the vast majority were in the further education sector. In 1997–8 there were some 4.4 million students, of whom 2.3 million were part-time, a more than tenfold increase over the thirty years. Of the total, 1.9 million were in higher education and 2.5 million in further education. There is, however, a big difference between the full-time and part-time ratios, with a majority of further education students in part-time education while the vast majority of higher education students are full-time. Higher education alone has expanded to the point where over 30 per cent of 18-year-olds are participating, to say nothing of a very rapid increase in the number of mature students. This very substantial number of students in whatever category at least meets one of the main recommendations of the Handy Report (1987), which argued that a key need for the improvement of management was much more general education.

The number of management programmes and students in the educational system has risen far faster than any other part of education.

Table 4.1 Increase in number of qualifications in business and financial studies

	1975	1985	1996–7
Undergraduate			
Universities	560	1,250	29,600
Polytechnics/colleges	1,080	3,250	
Postgraduate			
Taught			
Universities	1,150	2,400	19,000
Polytechnics	700?	700	
Diploma in Management Studies	1,800	1,800	
Research		300	300
Sub-degree			18,900
HND	3,900	3,900	
Total academic	9,190	13,600	67,800
NVQs in management (1997–8):			
Level 3	13,969		
Level 4	3,122		
Level 5	588		

Sources: 1978, 1985: Constable and McCormick (1987); 1996–7. These data were obtained from the DfEE on 0114–259–3787.

Partly this is driven by student demand; *The Learning Age* (DfEE 1998) noted that 40,000 managers were studying for MBAs, as compared with 18,000 four years previously, and an annual output of some 1,200 a decade previous to that. Clearly there has been a very rapid rate of increase, which constitutes one of the key components of progress in management development as a whole. Table 4.1 illustrates the rate of increase; although there are various problems with the precise definition of the statistics in each of the three periods, it can be seen that the order of magnitude has changed so much as to make fine detail unnecessary. Beyond the numbers themselves, there are two other important shifts. One is that the standing of the qualifications has improved, with a much higher proportion being at Masters level. The second is that the universities have become much more involved, and even the most prestigious are finding it to be a popular subject; thus the new management degree at Oxford attracted more applicants than any other Oxford degree in 1998, a far cry from the lack of programmes or student interest in the 1960s.

All the above is very positive. However, and very importantly, the figures above are flow statistics and are put into context by the very limited educational achievements of the whole stock of managers as given below. The DfEE's 1997 Labour Force Survey identified the highest qualifications obtained by managers and administrators as follows:

Degree or above	21.5 per cent
Higher education below degree	11.2 per cent
GCE 'A' level or equivalent	26.8 per cent
GCE 'O' level or equivalent	21.2 per cent
Below 'O' level or equivalent	2.0 per cent
Other	7.2 per cent
None	5.8 per cent

Putting it a different way, the 1998 Labour Force Survey identified 6 per cent of managers and administrators as having a highest qualification at NVQ level 5, 32 per cent at level 4, 21 per cent at level 3, 21 per cent at level 2, 15 per cent below level 2, and 5 per cent with no qualifications at all. This was on the basis of a survey of some 3.453 million managers and administrators, representing 15.1 per cent of the employed labour force. This limited level of education of the whole population of managers must be taken into consideration when noting the rapid increase in those taking degree-level qualifications. The percentage of managers with a degree according to the Labour Force Survey in 1985 was just over 12 per cent, so there has been a 9 per cent increase over the 12-year period; thus if the management population is becoming better qualified, the overall pace of this is clearly not rapid, although it may be accelerating. But a more optimistic way of looking at the figures is that, taking Constable's and McCormick's assumption of a 30-year career for managers, the ratio of 1986 was 90,000 annual entrants to an annual qualifications output of 12,600, indicating (very crudely, because many qualifications are obtained when people are already in work) that some 14 per cent of entrants had a qualification. The equivalent percentage in 1996–7 was 59 per cent (an output of 67,000 compared with an annual rate of entry to management of 115,000). Taking the Constable–McCormick estimates for 1975, an optimistic estimate of qualifications output would have shown a percentage of less than 10 per cent, with output biased much more to lower-level qualifications such as the HND. Thus a crude ratio analysis shows a massive improvement over the 10- and 20-year equivalent figures. And this is only taking the business and management qualifications; many graduates in other disciplines have also moved into management. Even so, although there are no directly comparable up-to-date statistics with Britain's main competitors, it may confidently be said that Britain is still at a disadvantage in respect of the educational qualifications of its stock of managers.

Vocational qualifications

Vocational qualifications have not had an easy time in gaining acceptance. Nevertheless, there has been significant movement in the recent past, with an increase of over 90 per cent in the numbers of NVQs awarded between 1993–4 and 1996–7, while awards of GNVQs have risen almost fivefold over the same period. *The Learning Age* (DfEE 1998b) reported that 100,000 people were working towards management vocational qualifications, as opposed to 40,000 four years previously. Perhaps more important has been the contribution of the occupational standards to the overall move to an acceptance of competence as the basis of analysing managerial skills.

Training in perspective

In broad terms, training can be split into that supported by government and that paid for by employers. Government-supported training, mainly delivered through the Training and Enterprise Councils, provided around half a million starts per year throughout the 1990s; however, relatively little of this has been directly relevant to management, although there are some management trainees in the Modern Apprenticeship programme. Far more important for managers is training paid for by employers. In 1993, the latest comprehensive figures (IFF 1996) for the cost of all training courses and supervised on-the-job training to employers was £10.6 billion, or double the expenditure of the new Learning and Skills Council, and almost half as much again as that spent on all higher education. The average costs of training per employee were £589, although there were no explicit figures for the amount spent on managers. In the 1998 national training statistics (DfEE 1999a), however, the percentage of managers shown as undertaking job-related training was only a little higher than the average for all employees. Tamkin and Hillage (1998) have done some valuable preliminary work in trying to set up a framework of indicators in the management area, although unsurprisingly they found considerable difficulties in monitoring changes in the amount, content, and impact of development. More recently the Management Charter Initiative (1999) has produced an initial set of indicators; as it develops over time, this should be a most valuable tool.

This book is primarily about development in the organization, so our perspectives on this area are not provided here. One area which should be covered, however, is non-qualification development external to the organization. According to Osbaldeston (1987) the supply of post-experience, short-course management education amounted to

68,500 participant weeks for general management and 62,500 weeks for specialized courses, both on open programmes, giving a total of 131,000 participant weeks. This was a major increase on the 10,360 weeks provided by consultants in 1960. In 1994 the Cannon Report (Institute of Management 1994) estimated that the total number of participant weeks was around 290,000, based explicitly on the same criteria as Osbaldeston, showing that this form of development more than doubled in less than a decade, and bearing out the predictions of a significant increase in demand by the respondents to the Osbaldeston survey. Since then there have been no major surveys in the management area and information is very limited; an important survey in 1993 noted that private training providers supplied 30 per cent of all externally purchased training days (IFF 1996), but this covered all training, and may not reflect the proportion for management. There appears to have been a considerable number of new entrants, many of them managers who have retired early. As Tamkin and Hillage (1998) found in their attempt to survey data collection on management development, many of the organizations such as professional institutes or trade associations that might be expected to hold such data do not do so, at least not in a format suitable for analysis. Moreover, many of the existing data sources had considerable flaws, such as discontinuities or incompatibilities between data sets, or an inability to identify the quality of training. Moreover, these only dealt with amounts of development; much more difficult still were sources of data on outcomes.

The management professional institutes

The role of the professional institutes in management development is considerable, but by no means easy to define precisely; *Management Development to the Millennium* could only say that 'there have been suggestions that this sector has increased its contribution but in a disconnected and fragmented way' (Institute of Management 1994: 46). As noted in the previous chapter, Britain has a wide range of professional institutes, and some of them have long had a role in the management of their area. Increasingly, however, even those institutes which concentrate primarily on functional skills are recognizing that at the higher levels of their profession management skills are necessary. They contribute in four main ways: through their own qualifications; through the direct provision of development; through influencing and sometimes providing vocational qualifications; and through influencing the curriculum of the profession when it is taught elsewhere. The Constable–McCormick Report (1987) put forward as one of its recommendations that management-oriented institutes should adopt the proposed diploma as part of their qualification requirements, but this has not been followed through. At much the same time there was a considerable debate about a professional status for managers through the concept of 'the chartered manager', but this was not implemented in practice. The idea, however, may still have some future relevance.

Conclusions

So what does all the policy framework and increase in development numbers add up to? Where does Britain stand now at the national level? Certainly Britain does not now lack institutions or recognition of the importance of management; both of these can confidently be said to be superior to anything that has previously existed. The new Council for Excellence in Management and Leadership promises more co-ordination and leadership in the area than has previously been available. But there are still weaknesses. The commitment to life-long learning and continuing professional development is more of a commitment than a real framework. In particular, while there is a recognition that much learning takes place in informal and self-directed ways, there is a focus on qualifications, which are not easily able to take account of non-formal learning. And while there are various national learning targets, soon to be taken over by the new Learning and Skills Council, there is not one for management, in spite of a consultation paper in 1996 to enquire how this might be set. Part of the problem relates to the issue of what should be measured, i.e. something more than inputs, and part to how the measurement should be carried out. The idea of a National Record of Achievement for individuals, which would reflect and record learning, has also not made much headway.

As a result of these gaps, it is difficult to ascertain how the quality of management in Britain is changing. This question then became the subject of a broader survey by the Institute for Employment Studies for the DfEE (Tamkin and Hillage 1998), which sought to establish a framework of indicators which could monitor the progress of management development. In developing a possible matrix, they used the four stages in the cycle which we outlined in the previous chapter, namely inputs, processes, outputs and outcomes. But, as noted earlier, they had great difficulty in identifying appropriate sources, although a national and local set of indicators has now been published (Management Charter Initiative 1999).

As a result it is difficult to relate British management to that elsewhere. For several years in the 1990s, governments of both parties have published White Papers on competitiveness, intended to give both an economic evaluation of Britain's performance in relation to its competitors and to set a policy framework for the supply side of the economy. At one level, as the White Paper *Learning to Succeed* (DfEE 1999b) noted, the Gross Domestic Product per worker in the UK lags behind the US by almost 40 per cent and behind France and Germany by around 20 per cent. It identified the major deficiency as being at intermediate and technician levels of the workforce, but successive White Papers on competitiveness have also identified problems with management, with the most recent still noting: 'Management skills have been identified as a key constraint on productivity' (DTI 1998: 33). As this and the setting up of the Council for Excellence in Management and Learning recognize, there is still work to be done in the area.

5

Demand for Management Development

INTRODUCTION

Demand for management development is a necessary precursor and complement to its supply. Nevertheless, demand is an ephemeral concept to measure and in practice difficult to isolate and to disentangle from supply. Indeed it has been argued that, by and large, the number of students taking courses is the only available statistical proxy for demand (Stoddart 1987). Almost universally, supply can much more easily be identified and measured than demand, and uncertainty surrounds the response to the launch of almost every new product.

Demand as a concept can be disaggregated into several dimensions which are relevant to management development:

- Effective demand, which equates to supply which is taken up.
- Expressed demand, which is not fulfilled, as where a manager asks for development but it is not permitted.
- Latent demand, where managers would go on a particular development programme if there were one suitable, or where demand is in very general terms, lacking focus or specificity.
- Somewhat different but related is need, where managers need training to be effective but don't demand it or get it. The

demand is not from the managers, but from others, usually policy-makers, on their behalf. In this sense need has almost always been much greater than any measure of demand. Even need, however, may not be recognized; for much of the twentieth century there was not only little demand but little recognition of any need for management development.

A second preliminary consideration is what the parties want from development, at least in general terms. Lindley (1991) has provided a useful list of what the individual wants from training; the items are not specific to management, but are nevertheless also relevant to managers:

- certification based on the achievement of agreed standards rather than forms of time-serving;
- flexible training suited to the needs and circumstances of the individual;
- access to training unrestricted by age, sex, and length of service;
- recognition of training by employers and other labour market institutions;
- broadly based initial training for young people which would include elements of education and industrial training which would be mutually reinforcing;
- correspondence between the standards of competence achieved by young people and adults beyond the stage of initial training;
- provision of opportunities for training and education throughout working life to enable people to adapt to changes in employment patterns.

Such a list perhaps implies a level of homogeneity of demand which is not intended. Stoddart rightly argues that 'different motives and career patterns are served by different modes of manager development. Variety in modes of provision is therefore imperative' (1987: 110).

A similar list for employers would probably include the following:

- providing employees with the skills necessary to do their jobs;
- providing development for future expected skill requirements;
- providing an acceptable level of recognition of employees' aspirations for their own future careers and development;
- access to the external labour market when the required skills can be more cheaply obtained from this source;

- protection from having trained employees poached by other employers.

A final preliminary aspect of demand is to note that the objectives of individual managers and organizations do not always, or perhaps even usually, coincide, as the two lists immediately above imply. Differences can be both in terms of objectives and methods, such as who pays the costs, the types of skill acquired and how this is done, and poaching already trained staff. At one level, each party would prefer not to have to pay the costs of skill acquisition. At another, each may also want rather different types of development; the individual wants it to be as general and portable as possible, whereas the employer generally prefers it to be immediately job-related. Even if the employer does need general skills, he would like to be able to hire them in the external labour market rather than have to train his own. On the other hand if the employer primarily operates an internal labour market, he is going to be willing to invest in the skills of his workforce, but not want them to decamp elsewhere with these skills.

This difference in perspective has been particularly acute in the case of formal qualifications, and especially in relation to the MBA. Many managers see the MBA as a means of changing their employer, or at least their job function, and even if this is not the case many feel that their employers are not interested in their academic progress and that their new skills will not be adequately recognized. For their part, many employers have distrusted the MBA not only because of the potential loss of managers, but also because it does not appear to provide the skills they need, at least in the short term, and also because MBA graduates often seem to have unrealistic expectations of promotion (Ascher 1984). Both sides have a problem here. If the employee does not seek out such portable qualifications, there is the danger of being seen as unemployable elsewhere later in his or her career. If the employer accepts training, the danger of losing expensively trained staff is great.

This chapter examines the nature of demand from both individual managers and organizations in three time periods. First, and briefly, there is an examination of demand before the major surveys of the mid-1980s. Second, and using as a benchmark the working party reports of Constable and McCormick (1987) as the most extensive evaluation of the demand for management development yet carried out, we examine the factors involved in changing demand in the last decade or so. Third, there is a preview of future demand.

▶ The Historical Context

Why did demand take so long to become established in Britain? It is always convenient to blame the supply-side institutions, companies, professional institutes, universities, and government for not creating an earlier and better infrastructure for management development. But this leaves the open question of why there was not more pressure from managers themselves.

In Britain the issue of demand for management development was particularly difficult, because until well into the twentieth century there was little understanding about the nature of management, the skills required for it, or how such skills were acquired, and therefore about the desirability of education and training. There was only a slow development of the organizational structure and the separation of ownership from control that were necessary for the growth of a cadre of professional managers. There might be an acceptance of a need for instruction in technical or commercial knowledge, but, as noted in chapter 3, management was seen as a natural skill; experience would be sufficient to improve the existing personal qualities engendered in the manager by the public school system and family background. Not only was there no tradition of learning in any other way, but there is little evidence that the average manager recognized any personal deficiencies which might be improved by training beyond the technical, non-generic aspects of the role. No doubt there were those who did have such feelings, but such demand was latent rather than effective. We have seen in chapter 3 that there was little demand for membership of management-related professional institutions, that the few degrees offered were not popular, and that ideas such as scientific management which might have generated a demand for development were not taken up in Britain.

After the Second World War, although management development was coming to be recognized, in practice little was done to encourage demand; indeed, as we have seen, the BIM's membership requirements militated against it. Given the difficulty of achieving professional status, the relatively low social prestige of managers, with no educational status to replace it, and the poor relationship between training and earnings (Crockett and Elias 1984), it is not surprising that managers did not appreciate the desirability of development. Moreover, there were no role models or clear ladders by which they could advance themselves. All this was exacerbated by the functional compartmentalization of most managers which prevented them from seeing their generic management role as important in comparison with their functional duties.

Even with the creation of London and Manchester business schools, these supposedly high-prestige institutions were not overwhelmed with applications, and Manchester struggled for numbers until well into the 1970s (Wilson 1995). However, the business schools as a whole expanded in number and size in the 1970s, which suggests that there was some growing demand from managers. In particular, the new part-time and later distance-learning programmes fitted much better with the needs of practising managers and undoubtedly enabled much latent demand to become effective.

Even so, when Mansfield et al. (1981) examined the views of BIM members in 1980, training was not an issue thought worthy of consideration in the survey, quite unlike the situation when the survey was repeated a decade later. But in 1990, when a similar BIM sample agreed vigorously with various statements about management development, the authors noted:

> This almost totally unanimous support for management training and corporate support for such training is the strongest set of attitudes assessed anywhere in either of the two surveys and clearly indicates the importance that the typical British manager now places on this. . . . It would be very surprising if this degree of support had been present at the beginning of the 1980s . . . On the evidence of the attitudes expressed by this sample, and the extent to which they had individually been trained in the last year, it would seem that there has been a radical change in the United Kingdom in attitudes to, and the practice of, management training. . . . Training clearly has an enormous intrinsic value as judged by the views of the British manager today. (Mansfield and Poole 1991: 35)

This trend was confirmed by Warr (1993), again using a population based on the BIM. His survey, however, dealt much more explicitly and comprehensively with training than Mansfield and Poole's. Attitudes were very positive about training generally, and only rather less so about provision in their company:

- 81 per cent said they would be more effective managers if they received more training.
- 89 per cent reported that the business environment was changing so rapidly that managers needed more training than in the past.
- 83 per cent said that organizations ought to require all of their managers to undertake some training every year.

A third report was *Management Challenge for the 1990s*, which can be dealt with briefly through a single quotation:

All commentators agree that the demand for Management Education, Training and Development by individuals from external providers is growing. The figures that can be presented most easily relate to management education and in particular to course admissions. Although these provide ample evidence of rising demand it must be recognised that the number of individuals admitted to courses is constrained by course availability – so to some extent the figures reflect supply rather than demand, and may understate the actual demand by individuals. (Deloitte, Haskins and Sells 1989: 19)

What unites these reports, coming shortly after Constable–McCormick and Handy, is that attitudes were becoming more unanimous about the need for development. They certainly make sense as a stepping-stone to the period of our own surveys. In this decade, the situation was transformed. Why this was so we shall now proceed to discuss.

▶ Factors in Increased Demand for Management Development

We would argue that there was no single driver but rather a wide range of factors accounting for the increase in demand, of which the key ones are:

Continuing momentum. As we have seen, from the mid-1960s there was a gradual increase in demand. This momentum was building up to a point where the conditions were ready for a take-off in the mid-1980s. While this take-off was dramatic, as de Tocqueville so well understood, most revolutions occur when change is taking place anyway.

Competitive environment. The recession of 1980–2 was notable in that it had a significant impact on managerial and white-collar employees whereas previous recessions had tended to be felt most by blue-collar workers. Sadler and Barham (1988: 49) note 'the 1980–82 recession may come to be seen as a watershed in the history of management training and development in the UK. The recession concentrated attention as never before on weaknesses in British management and on the deficiencies of UK organizations vis-à-vis their foreign competitors.' Revans (1980) argued that for organizations to remain competitive, the rate of learning must be at least equal to and preferably greater than the rate of external change. This message was beginning to be recognized.

Critical mass. As the amount of development grew, so it became more apparent to those who were not developing, among both employers and managers, that they were in danger of falling behind their competitors. Whereas those who came early into the development process did so out of a desire to gain an advantage and thus for aggressive reasons, those who came later were more concerned not to fall behind and therefore did so for defensive reasons.

Managerial insecurity. As we shall explore further in chapter 10, managerial careers have changed considerably in the last two decades, and perceptions of them perhaps even more so. The recession of the early 1980s was the first in which white-collar workers, including managers, lost their jobs in substantial numbers. As a result of that and other factors mentioned in this section, attitudes have changed. Few managers expect to have a career for life in any given organization, and most recognize that they must prepare for change before it overtakes them. This has helped to generate the concept of a 'contract of employability' with employers, in which the managers are developed with a view to being employable in the external labour market.

Rate of return to development. Looking back, it was one of the most alarming features of management development before the 1980s that there appeared to be a very low rate of return to management development and therefore little incentive to undertake it. We have noted in chapter 3 that Crockett and Elias (1984), using the 1975–6 National Training Survey, were puzzled by their finding that 'there is no significant relationship between the earnings of managers and the duration of vocational training of all types of their work history'. More recently, this situation has changed considerably. The Association of MBAs, in their 1997 *Salary and Career Survey*, note:

> The clear evidence of the survey is that the salaries of the students rise with graduation. The average rise for all respondents is an outstanding 42%; when adjusted for salary inflation the figure is still 27%, making the rate of return on investment impressive. The impact of the MBA is strongest among those who change job following qualification. For this group, overall salaries rise 59% unadjusted, 43% adjusted. Those who remain with their existing employer see a significantly lower increase at 16% unadjusted and only 3% adjusted. (AMBA 1997: 8)

This suggests that the main increase in earnings potential is generated by the higher level of mobility which the MBA provides, rather than its contribution *in situ*, although many of those staying put saw other benefits or increased responsibility, or used it as a means of changing their functional area of responsibility. Other studies (Forrester 1985) have also indicated that there were significant gains in salary at least from taking the more prestigious MBAs.

Self-reinforcing demand. The more education and training that people undergo, the greater their demand for more (Rigg 1989; Skoulding and Peppercorn 1987). This is very much the message from our own surveys, and particularly from the AMBA 1997 survey. As more managers have had training, and as more have gained qualifications at all levels, so the numbers recognizing the value of development have increased, with a consequent impact not only for themselves, but in creating the critical mass effect previously noted.

Better-developed senior managers. In the earlier periods, few if any senior managers had themselves any experience of development other than on the job. As a result they tended to feel that if they could be successful without any more formal development, so could others, and therefore gave little support to development. However, when the first generation of senior managers who had themselves had more formal development came to top positions in organizations, they were much more favourably inclined to support and indeed sponsor it. Not only did this increase demand from the employers, but it also gave encouragement to managers by providing them with role models of success as well as making development available. We found this to be an important factor in our comparison of 1986 and 1996.

Structural change. As a result of structural change in organizations, demand for management development was generated in order to respond to the new conditions. This is not to say that structural change had not occurred in earlier periods, but from the mid-1980s onwards the pace and extent of change accelerated. Delayering, downsizing, outsourcing, globalization and similar modes of change created new, more flexible, methods of working with wider spans of responsibility, fewer promotion opportunities, and greater use of projects and team-working, all requiring different skills (Coulson-Thomas and Coe 1991). Especially where such changes came in wave after wave, with little respite from a stable state, demand for more flexible managers and therefore for development was clearly generated.

Technological change. Another important type of change which accelerated from the mid-1980s was technological change, and especially of course IT-based systems. These required of managers quite different sorts of skills, both manual, as with keyboard skills, operational, as with the new requirements for information and knowledge management, and organizational, as with new communication and control systems. Again, this generated a demand for development, and indeed regular updating to acclimatize to new types of software or communication. Gallie and White (1993) noted that there had been a skills revolution in the last five years at all levels, such that 63 per cent of skilled manual workers and 70 per cent of non-manual workers reported that their work required increased skills. This was mainly due to the rise in use of computers, although an increase in monitoring and social skills was also reported.

Labour market change.   Associated with the discussions of career change in chapter 10 is change in labour markets. There are debates about the extent of this change, but it is noticeable that at least some of the most consciously career-based companies, such as Unilever and ICI, have moved towards bringing in at least some senior managers from the outside rather than depending almost entirely on their internal labour market. Even the Civil Service now expects that its senior managers should have had some exposure to external industrial or commercial experience. More generally, employers have learned to live with their ambivalence towards qualifications, as we shall see in chapter 8. Managers therefore need development and preferably qualifications in order to compete in the external labour market. Ascher (1984) found that those doing a full-time MBA were overwhelmingly doing so in order to improve job opportunities, either directly, or through changing career direction. More recently the improvement of job opportunities has again shown up as the key driver behind MBA studies in the 1997 *MBA Salary and Career Survey* (AMBA 1997); following at a distance were: to obtain a business qualification, for intellectual stimulation, to obtain generalist rather than specialist skills, to increase salary, to change career direction, and to increase self-confidence.

Widening of demand.   A rather different labour market aspect of management development has been its widening. This has been particularly true among professional groups, where a managerial dimension has been discovered that was unrecognized or ignored in earlier periods. Law, medicine, surveying and the like now recognize that managerial efficiency can be an important dimension of professional success. But there has also been a move downwards into supervisory and even manual categories as new roles take on at least some management responsibility.

Recognition of responsibility.   Individuals have become much clearer as to their own responsibility for their career and their own development, even though companies may still provide the infrastructure and the financial support. Companies, however, have also become aware of their side of the responsibility.

Better supply. The very considerable expansion of the supply of management development has itself contributed to an expansion of demand. Moreover, training has become more accessible locally, more competitive and, especially, has introduced more flexible modes of delivery such as part-time, distance-learning, and computer-based methods. As we saw in the previous chapter, at the under-graduate level there has been an enormous expansion of supply to make the largest single degree category; this could not have happened without commensurate demand. What is more, the quality of the students is equivalent to most other degree courses and rising; much less is heard now about bright people not wanting to enter management.

Government exhortation. The British government had been con-cerned with training since the mid-1960s, and had important institu-tions, first the industrial training boards and then the Manpower Services Commission from 1973. But concentration tended to be in areas other than management until the director of the MSC, Geoffrey Holland, gave a lead in 1986 with ten policy objectives, as was noted in chapter 3. More recently, management quality and development has been an important issue in governmental attitudes, as reflected in the series of White Papers on competitiveness.

Defining targets for management development. Targets are a way of trying to define need. It is easy to be cynical about targets, and many companies would rebut any perception that they have been influenced by them. But there has for the last fifteen years or so been a widespread acceptance that a reasonable amount of time to give to management development is five days a year, and it would be surprising if that has not had some impact in the light of our findings on the amount of training as reported in chapter 8. The 1987 Constable–McCormick Report, *The Making of British Managers*, and its associated working parties, provide the first attempt to define need in any concrete terms. At the time, about 12,300 people received a formal education in management at levels ranging from the HND to postgraduate degrees, while the report identified 90,000 annu-ally requiring first-line manager training/education, 35,000 need-ing middle management development, and 17,500 needing training to the most advanced level. In other words, something more than a tenfold increase in provision would have been required to meet this approach to need. As noted in the previous chapter, however, although various training targets have been set, there has not been one for management.

Publicity for the issue. From the early 1980s there was a widespread expression of concern about training in general, and by the middle of the decade this had come to have a special focus on management, with the three main reports on the subject followed by the setting up of the Council for Management Education and Development. It was a period when it would have been difficult as either a company or a manager not to be aware that management development had become a national issue.

Organizational policy development. This was also a period when organizations expanded their policy framework in the area. Written statements of policy helped to give recognition to development, internal procedures such as the growth of appraisal helped to create a workable system, and a more permissive attitude to individual interest in qualifications and training more generally helped to unlock latent demand and transform it into effective demand. Better training objectives also played a part in the changes in organizational policy. The rise of the competency movement, both in terms of the British national occupational standards and the more behaviourally based frameworks originating from the United States following Boyatzis (1982), has enabled demand to be much more clearly focused in more specific training activities and thereby increase demand through recognition of greater effectiveness.

Other sources of change in demand. There are various other factors in changing attitudes to development. The belief that managers are born not made and the assumption that training could be cut at the least sign of recession were both diminishing at this time. The internationalization of companies was probably another factor, both in the sense of foreign companies bringing practices to Britain and of British companies needing to compete externally.

▶ Constraints on Demand for Management Development

In spite of the growth in demand, there are nevertheless constraints, and these were also examined by Stoddart (1987), who divided possible constraints into personal and organizational. Some may have diminished since 1987, but are still likely to have relevance.

Personal

Career evidence. Individuals who see their career as disappointing despite management training or successful without it may share a feeling that it is irrelevant. Perception of others' careers may indicate that management training does not guarantee success or that it is not required for success, and may suggest there is little payoff from training. Interviews for the Stoddart survey illustrated the importance of personal example in career planning; the tendency to model oneself on others could be subtle and indeed unconscious, as well as deliberate.

Lack of a trigger. Appraisal is often a trigger for development, but if there is no appraisal or if those responsible for carrying it out do not link the appraisal with development, training will not have a starting-point. In the Stoddart survey (1987), 37 per cent reported not having an appraisal scheme and 32 per cent said that it made no contribution to their use of training opportunities. 'However, individuals working in large companies offering career paths which are well mapped out, with developed training schemes and formal appraisal, saw the system as a whole carrying the responsibility for career. Appraisal schemes here did have a major role in initiating the decision to undertake management training' (1987: 60).

Ego-defensive resistance. It is sometimes difficult for an individual to admit that they have training needs, either because they have low self-confidence or low self-esteem, maybe through a legacy of failure or because they cannot engage in realistic self-appraisal.

Ideologically based attitudes. Where there is a belief that managers are born not made, or that the only valuable development is experiential, training is therefore not seen as a useful activity.

Age. Negative attitudes can be connected with a generational dimension, in which the individual feels too old (or too senior) to need training or that 'you can't teach old dogs new tricks'. Training has typically been concentrated in the early years of a career (Chapman 1993) and has been connected with career dynamics (Schein 1978) so that different types of training are required at different stages of the career.

The home–work relationship. In the survey 59 per cent of those who had unfulfilled plans for management development quoted difficulties of fitting the workload with family or other personal commitments as a reason affecting their ability to go ahead with the development. The home–work relationship is often a particularly difficult problem for women. Even for men, however, many managers are already carrying workloads which impinge on the balance between work and domestic life, and not infrequently both partners are working and faced with the need for such a balance.

Supply problems.   Areas such as distance, inappropriate timing, costs, perceived relevance, or academic pressures were given as reasons for not undertaking a course in management education.

Organizational

Fear of poaching or turnover.   Many companies have not trained because they fear that their investment will be lost if the individual leaves the organization, whether they are poached by a rival or personally taking the initiative to leave.

Training as a threat to others.   Superiors can feel very defensive and that their own competence as managers is being called into question if their juniors attend training that they have never had, and this makes them discourage it. This can be exacerbated if the initiative for management development resides in the individual superior rather than the organization more widely. This personalization of opposition to development was a common feeling amongst members of the discussion groups. Stoddart noted (1987: 122): 'Our findings offer some indications of a stratum of "stationary" middle managers whose occupational culture is strongly resistant to formal manager development and who on occasion not only frustrate their subordinates' career development plans but also undermine their efforts to capitalise on the skills and competencies acquired through formal training.'

Company culture.   Such an anti-development ethos can also reside in the organization. Indeed, in Stoddart's discussion groups, strong company support for development was often portrayed as examples of a rarely experienced ideal.

Cost and constraints on staff.   This was particularly a problem for small companies, but also a common rationalization for larger ones with tight cashflows and where covering for the loss of people for any amount of time put pressure on operations.

Criticism of quality of training provision.   Training was often seen as too academic, and not close enough to the real world to be immediately applicable.

Lack of accessibility or availability. This could still be an important consideration in the 1980s, but with the development of vast amounts of materials and growth of flexible provision, either locally or by distance learning, this is less easy to justify now.

The increase in development activities over the last decade that will be described in succeeding chapters clearly means that the constraints on development have been outweighed by the pressures to undertake it. Several of the constraints noted above are almost certainly less relevant. It is also possible, however, that new constraints have arisen which are not on the list, such as increases in work pressures.

▶ Conclusion: Demand in the Future

Most of the findings of the surveys associated with Constable and McCormick pointed to a higher level of demand in the future, and so it has proved. Moreover all the signs point towards a continuing increase in demand, although not necessarily for the same package of skills. One perspective on what competencies industry wants in the future came as part of *Management Development to the Millennium* (Institute of Management 1994). The three most important were: strategic thinking (78 per cent); managing and responding to change (75 per cent); and an orientation towards total quality/customer satisfaction (67 per cent). There was then a large drop to the next three: financial management (46 per cent); facilitating others to contribute (44 per cent); and understanding the role and contribution of information and IT (42 per cent). But while these and other answers suggested skills, the document also notes that attitudes were even more important:

> Executives seemed to be suggesting that in a competitive world where product lead or technology edge can only ever be short lived, managers must not only have the right attitudes, but that these attitudes have to be constantly in tune with a changing internal environment and a chaotic business environment. We were left with a sense that the acquisition of specific skills, whilst being important, is an insufficient solution to the complex problems of the future. (Institute of Management 1994: 57)

As a result, the report tried to define necessary mindsets and the ability to encompass apparent contradictions, namely: long- and short-term; local and international; task/functional and process/ behavioural skills; internal and external; individual and team working; action and reflection; operational and strategic.

If these changes are what industry saw as desirable, individual managers also see that the future will not be like the past. Also in *Management Development to the Millennium* (Institute of Management 1994) 86 per cent of respondents believed there would be an increased need to acquire new work-related skills in the period to the millennium. This demand came from all sectors, age groups and levels within organizations. When asked about the key issues from an individual perspective, 92 per cent mentioned transferability of skills to support job mobility, 84 per cent said that individuals would increasingly take responsibility for their own learning, and 81 per cent said that accreditation of learning would be increasingly important. Worrall and Cooper (1997) backed up these findings with almost 90 per cent of respondents saying that their need to acquire new skills would increase over the next five years, with the belief being most pronounced amongst junior managers.

In our own surveys there was also a strong indication of increased future activity, as will be reported in the succeeding chapters. We have noted that organizations anticipate that the amount of training in the future will be greater than at present, that management development will be a higher priority, and that it will come closer to their conception of optimality. More widely, there is a growing trend for organizations to set up their own 'corporate universities' in the USA with signs that the idea will also take hold in Britain. At the individual level the main indications come from our survey of MBAs (Thomson et al. 1998, especially chapter 6); indeed one of the key issues which the survey set out to explore was the perceived needs and expectations of the respondents for further development. Most had participated in a good deal of development in addition to and since their MBA, and the assumption was therefore that many MBAs would want to continue this indefinitely. Even so, we were surprised at the extent of expressed intention to pursue further development: 92 per cent had such an intention, and this was uniformly high with little difference between the various breakdowns. Even those at director level, who might have been expected to feel that they did not need further development, wanted it. Of those who said not, the only reason with any support was lack of time. Virtually nobody thought it was not necessary.

Continuing with the MBAs' views of their future intentions, the respondents are prepared to spend a substantial amount of time on their own development, in fact more than they are currently spending, and a considerable amount of their own money, with a mean of around £500 per annum. The main reason for further development is keeping up to date in a changing environment; the main skills sought are general management skills, although people skills come next quite a long way ahead of financial skills; and there is a range of perceived routes to further development and ways of undertaking these. Only 29 per cent wanted further qualifications, which is perhaps not surprising since the MBA is the highest generally recognized management qualification. Most MBAs want to follow a mix of modes of development rather than a single one. Some two-thirds also wanted some form of recognition of their learning, obviously in the expectation that it would have some sort of career payback over and above the possession of an MBA. Just how to achieve this recognition is less clear, which is not unexpected since a coherent national framework for continuing professional development did not and indeed does not yet exist. Nevertheless the trend is certainly towards such a system, whether provided by professional institutes, the educational system, or a further development of government policy for life-long learning. Whatever the mechanics, demand will certainly increase. Indeed, if anything emerges from the survey, it is that not only is an MBA by itself not enough, but that there is a strong demand for ongoing development. It might be argued that this MBA group represents a particularly unusual group of managers and cannot be taken as representative, but the results are not dissimilar to the other evidence in this section.

This review of demand concludes the background chapters. We now move on to the group of chapters dealing with management development in the organization, substantially based on our surveys, and starting with issues of policy and responsibility for development.

6

Strategy, Structure and Responsibilities

INTRODUCTION

This is the first of several chapters that will draw primarily on our survey findings in order to evaluate management development practices in organizations. In this current chapter we examine the first stage of the model presented as figure 2.2, and more specifically the right-hand segment labelled 'policies'. In particular, the chapter addresses three interrelated issues: first, the link between management development and business strategy; second, the question of the consequences of organizational structuring; and third, the question of who is responsible for management development. This agenda takes us into the related areas of the kind of priority which management development is accorded and the way in which responsibility for management development is allocated across organizational roles. It also introduces empirical evidence of the strong–weak policy spectrum presented in chapter 1.

▶ Business Strategy and Management Development

While in general terms it is widely assumed that management development must (or should) be in some way interconnected with business strategy, there is very little literature and even fewer empirically grounded studies which explore this linkage, as is evident from the review in chapter 2. There is a huge literature addressing aspects of learning styles, types of training provision, and so on, but the literature on the wider business meaning of all this managerial development activity is sparse. Arguably this lacuna in the literature reflects the reality of practice on the ground; thus Seibert et al. (1995) refer to the association between business strategy and management development as 'the weak link'. In those instances where the linkage is addressed there is rarely a sound empirical base to the normative stance that is usually adopted extolling the strategic use of management development for competitive advantage. For example, Osbaldeston and Barham (1992) argue that management development is a major strategic tool and 'should' be integrated in business strategy. They further contend that management development 'should' be central to business strategy and that learning 'should' be a cherished organizational value. But studies demonstrating the precise nature of this link and especially the processes involved are very rare indeed.

In one of the few research-based studies, Seibert et al. (1995) report on a survey in the USA of 22 'leading firms' including such luminaries as Apple Computer, AT&T, Digital, Du Pont and Xerox. A key finding was 'an admission on the part of the respondents that [this] link between business strategy and executive development strategy is especially weak' (1995: 550). Nevertheless two companies in particular (3M and Motorola) were shown to be overcoming the weak link by conducting management development in a way which contributed effectively to business strategy. This was achieved by ensuring an outwardly focused rather than an inwardly focused orientation to management development. Business issues were taken as the driver for management development. Each new strategic initiative simultaneously triggers a management development activity. Moreover, the ideal is described as going further – not only ensuring that management development supports the business strategy but that it becomes an integral part of business activity to achieve business results. The same point, though in a more prescriptive manner, is also made by Berry (1990), the organizational development director of Coca-Cola. And a European case where management development was used as a strategic tool driven by the needs of the business is described by Cannon (1995).

One aspect pertaining to the link between management development and business strategy that did become increasingly common in the 1980s concerned the understanding of management development as a device to bring about organizational change and in particular to engineer 'culture change'. Thus, Lippitt (1982), for example, talked of management development as 'the key to organisational renewal'. This link between culture change and management development has been particularly noticeable in the finance sector, but there were also several celebrated cases such as Jaguar, British Airways, Lucas and Courtaulds which were reported as achieving turnaround attributable at least in part to a radical change in management culture. Management development has also been used as a tool to effect and deliver specific business agendas, such as 'total quality', innovation, cost reduction, staff retention and 'profitability through excellence' (Alexander 1987; Tate 1995; Nagler 1987; Wagel 1987). Companies increasingly declare that their training activities are to be seen as explicitly linked with establishing and embedding company values such as 'existing for the customer'. Management development may also be used as a means to forge a common identity following a take-over, merger, or demerger.

In the early 1990s, the concept which above all laid strong claim to a direct linkage between human resource development and business strategy was that of the 'learning organization' (Senge 1991; Pedler et al. 1991; Garratt 1994). These bullish accounts of the critical centrality of organizational learning made claims to a direct and powerful link between it and successful business performance. For example, Garratt (1994: ix) claims to have identified 'healthy results linking improved business performance directly to continuous learning in the organisation', although in contrast, research by Raper, Felstead and Storey (1997) revealed that even organizations more than averagely active in training and development fell some way short of approaching the claims of the learning organization. But the idea of the learning organization, although subject to strong critical challenge, served to focus attention upon the idea and importance of learning and development as a business-critical and therefore strategic area of concern. However, to a considerable extent the enthusiasm for the learning organization has been replaced by that for knowledge management (Scarbrough et al. 1999).

Despite these various attempts to clarify the linkage between management development and business strategy the nature of that relationship remains relatively obscure. The theme, although clearly vitally important, is evidently in need of much greater empirically grounded attention. Our surveys offer two approaches to this issue.

Table 6.1 Business strategy and management development

Scale 1–10	All (%)	MBAs (n = 450)			Client managers (n = 120) (%)
		High impact (%)	Medium impact (%)	Low impact (%)	
1–2	25	16	11	35	15
3–4	20	11	15	27	22
5–6	25	17	43	20	29
7–8	22	46	26	10	27
9–10	6	11	4	6	7
Mean	4.79	6.05	5.54	3.90	5.18

1 = does not reflect business strategy
10 = fully reflects strategy

The first approach came from a question which we put to the 'consumers' or recipients of management development. We asked the MBA graduate panel and the client managers' panel the extent to which they believed their organization's management development policy reflected its business strategy. Answers were on a scale of 1–10 where 1 equals 'does not reflect business strategy' and 10 equals 'fully reflects strategy'. The results are shown in table 6.1. The MBAs and the client managers recorded mean scores around midway, but what was also interesting was that, as the table shows, in those cases where there was a closer fit between management development policy and business strategy there was a perceived higher impact of management development activity. It is worth noting at this juncture that this is the first of many findings in the next few chapters which point to the importance of what we term a 'strong–weak' spectrum in management development policies.

Another way to look at the link between business strategy and management development is to assess the factors perceived to be driving the latter. In the various surveys we asked respondents what they judged to be the most influential factors, both externally and internally, that influence the amount and nature of management development activity in their organization. A list of 16 factors was presented, with the list being created from the results of an open-ended pilot question. The results from the surveys of organizations, MBAs and client managers are shown in table 6.2.

The results show the mean scores for the organizations on a 10-point scale asking how influential each factor was perceived to be. For the MBAs and the client managers the question was slightly different, asking for all factors felt to be influential to be ticked and thus

Table 6.2 Influential factors in management development

Factor	Mean for HRD managers (n = 501)	Percentage for client managers (n = 120)	Percentage for MBAs (n = 450)
Business efficiency	7.23	56	42
Company strategy	7.21	64	63
Support of board	6.84	44	32
Ability to do job	6.60	44	31
Company culture	6.38	42	41
Individual potential to progress	6.36	47	38
Customers/clients	6.36	31	16
Structural change	6.25	51	43
Staff motivation	6.02	42	38
Career development	5.98	47	42
Demand from managers	5.89	36	34
Retention of personnel	5.58	24	21
Competitive activity	5.40	18	20
Cost of management development	5.07	29	36
Investors in People	4.54	31	24
NVQs	3.49	7	6

giving a percentage rather than a mean. What is especially notable from the pattern of results is the high ranking achieved by the company strategy factor, in spite of the relatively low association between it and management development reflected in table 6.1. Indeed for two groups represented in table 6.2, the MBAs and client managers, it is far and away the most frequently mentioned, for the former group by 20 percentage points. Moreover, in our regression analysis using the HRD manager sample, company strategy was found to be a highly significant independent variable when taking a written statement of management development as the dependent variable (Thomson, Mabey and Storey 1998). In broad terms the three groups agree on the ranking of variables, although structural change and career development are seen as more influential by the customers of management development than they are by the HRD managers as providers. Demand from managers is ranked lower by all three groups than we would have predicted, while the cost of management development is also not seen as particularly influential. Finally, the external policy variables, Investors in People and NVQs, are ranked low overall, although they tend to be a statistically significant influence in our regressions, indicating that where they do have an influence it tends to be an important one.

Table 6.3 Existence of a written statement (HRD managers, n = 501)

	Yes (%)	No (%)
All	43	57
Size by no. of employees		
100–299	24	76
300–499	34	66
500–999	46	54
1,000–4,999	54	44
5,000+	60	40
MBA panel	44	55
Managers panel	38	52

Formal management development policy

We asked all respondents whether their organization had a formal written statement or series of statements covering management development policy. As shown in table 6.3, 43 per cent of the HRD managers sample, 44 per cent of the MBA graduates and 38 per cent of the client manager sample answered 'yes' to this question. As expected, larger organizations, measured both by employee numbers and revenue, were more likely than small or medium-sized enterprises to have such policies. The significance of the existence of an explicit policy in this area is revealed in this and subsequent chapters. Its importance is indicated by the fact that companies which had formal and explicit policies for management development undertook significantly more management training than did companies without such a policy. As is further expanded in chapter 8, HRD managers in companies with a management development policy reported on average 6.5 days of training per manager per annum compared with 4.6 days in companies without a policy. From these and similar findings we came to realize the existence and importance of what in this book we refer to as the 'strong–weak spectrum'. This, as we will reveal throughout the book, refers to a consistent pattern of results which suggests that companies which express and demonstrate serious policy intent with regard to management development tend to be those which also have the most extensive engagement with actual management development practices and which experience the most satisfactory outcomes from that activity.

Evidence drawn from each of the different panels pointed in the same consistent direction – commitment to management development in the shape of a formal policy appeared to be highly significant. The

Table 6.4 Statement and impact of management development on the organization (HRD managers, n = 501)

Formal statement	High impact	Medium impact	Low impact
Yes	49	43	22
No	51	56	78

amount of training and of other types of development appeared to depend more on the *choice* of an organization to give priority to management development and to provide the resources to make it happen than on the range of structural variables such as organization size, sector, ownership or centralization/decentralization. Regression analysis carried out on what we term the 'policy cluster' of variables confirmed the crucial importance of strategic choice (see appendix 2 for details of the regression equations). Four 'clusters' of variables were used in the regression equations, including independent variables such as industry sector, ownership and size of organization; internal organizational variables; and a career cluster of variables. The equations assessing the policy cluster proved to be the most persuasive, consisting of the existence of a policy statement, the degree of priority accorded to management development, and the acceptance of organizational responsibility for it. The single most important variable influencing dependent variables such as the amount and impact of training was whether a written statement existed. To illustrate one of these relationships, table 6.4 indicates the extent to which the existence of policy statements was associated with the degree of impact which management development activities were judged to be making.

These data again suggest that the extent of management development is influenced by managerial choice. Likewise, if we look at the small business panel a very similar pattern is evident; further details can be found in chapter 11. But for the moment it is also worth observing that where there was a formal policy statement the average number of training days was 7.4 compared with only 3.2 in organizations with no policy on this matter and 4.0 where there was an informal policy.

Apparently paradoxically, in our one-to-one interviews, senior managers in large corporations tended to marginalize the importance of formal policies. The message appeared to be that written management development polices and manuals were somewhat sceptically viewed as mere statements of intent; procedures were given much lower credence than heretofore: action, facilitation and subtle interventions were the new canon. In expressing scepticism about the value of formal policies, the large company interviewees were articulating much of the current conventional wisdom about the nature of modern organizations. Traditional models of management development which were designed to service the needs of corporate hierarchies have come under scrutiny. Downsizing and delayering, along with new technology, have been seen by many as signalling major threats to the managerial occupations and to middle managers in particular (Kanter 1986; Goffee and Scase 1986). The apparent paradox may be explained by the fact that the largest corporations were arguably in a very different phase of a cycle from most other companies, and that while they have been downsizing and decentralizing they have been doing so from a position where management development was already institutionalized. Indeed the main reason we wanted to talk to this group directly was to see how their comprehensive written policies of 1986 had changed. By contrast the great mass of medium-sized as well as smaller enterprises has, according to our findings, been moving in the opposite direction by institutionalizing management development provision from a position of low acceptance of management development – and, as the great body of our survey data would suggest – are benefiting from that. The overall empirical evidence from our various panels suggests that this latter is the wider picture.

We now turn to a closer examination of the other elements in the policy cluster.

Priority accorded to management development

How much priority was accorded to management development in UK organizations in 1996? How did it compare with the state of affairs a decade previously? To measure priority we used a 10-point scale where 1 stood for low priority and 10 for high priority. The results are shown in table 6.5. The overall mean score for the HRD managers was 6.02. The MBA panel and the managers' panel recorded mean scores of 4.74 and 5.20 respectively. This ranking of HRD managers taking the most positive view followed by client managers, with MBA graduates the least positive is a pattern which is repeated in replies to several of our other questions. What is the implication of the means reported? They clearly indicate less than strong approval of the degree of priority; to put these into perspective, useful points of comparison are available with the past and the prospective future. Interestingly, our HRD informants expected priority to increase in the future from an overall mean of 6.02 to one of 7.21. When asked conversely about the state of affairs ten years ago, the same respondents judged that the priority

Table 6.5 Priority given to management development

	HRD managers (%) (n = 501)			MBAs (%) (n = 450)	Client managers (%) (n = 120)
	Now	10 years ago	Future	Now	Now
1–2	7	34	2	24	12
3–4	15	29	4	22	24
5–6	33	20	20	21	33
7–8	34	6	54	27	25
9–10	11	2	19	4	5
Mean	6.02	3.45	7.21	4.74	5.20

1 = low priority
10 = high priority

given to management development then was in fact much lower, with the mean score being only 3.45. This again is part of a pattern whereby the respondents saw the present in a more positive light than the past, but expected the future to be more positive still. Returning to the present, there was some variation depending on the size of the organization, but perhaps not to the extent that might have been expected; the mean priority score for companies with over 1,000 employees was 6.38, while for companies in the size range 100–299 it was 5.48. Foreign-owned organizations tended to accord a higher priority to management development than did British organizations.

We also looked at the association between a claimed 'high priority' accorded to management development and the amount of actual training occurring. Where management development was given high priority there were, on average, 6.9 days of manager training per annum compared with just 2.7 days in organizations with a low priority given and 5.6 days where a medium-level priority was judged to exist. Also, in small businesses, where high priority was attributed to management development, the average number of training days was 6.6 compared with just 1.5 where low priority was reported. Readers are also referred to table A2 in appendix 2 where an equation will be found which has the priority given to management development as the dependent variable. In another relationship, low priority, as might be expected, seemed to correlate with low impact. We also found from the HRD managers' sample that 55 per cent of organizations with low impact also rated the priority given to management development as low (i.e. between 1 and 4). The client managers' sample confirmed the association between priority and actual impact. Thus among those reporting 'high impact' of management development some 67 per cent of client managers judged that priority was also high, whereas only 17 per cent of those in this category judged the priority to be low.

Organizational or individual responsibility for management development

We also examined whether responsibility for management development was driven more by the organization or by the individual. Again a 10-point scale was used. At one extreme, responsibility solely by the individual was represented by a score of 1, while at the other extreme, total responsibility by the organization was accorded a score of 10. The results are shown in table 6.6.

The interesting point about this set of results is the migration towards the middle band. Somewhat surprisingly, given the widespread discussion of 'self-development', there is a marked decline from the 25 per cent attributions to the individual with the main responsibility ten years ago, to 8 per cent presently – and declining further to 5 per cent in the future. Respondents seemed to perceive a much greater balance of responsibility in the future. There seemed to be some evidence here of a reacceptance by the organization of its role in management development; the balance was once more being tipped back. It is interesting to note, however, that the MBA graduates were more likely to perceive responsibility as resting with the individual whereas members of the client manager sample were somewhat more likely to endorse the assessments made by organizational spokespersons and view responsibility as shared between individuals and organizations.

Using cross-tabulations it was found that the overall tendency was that in those organizations with explicit policies the organization made

Table 6.6 Responsibility for management development

	HRD managers (%)			MBAs (%)	Managers (%)
	Now	10 years ago	Future		
1–2	8	25	5	35	19
3–4	12	15	16	29	27
5–6	42	16	46	20	31
7–8	30	19	27	14	19
9–10	8	14	6	3	5
Mean	5.71	5.07	5.63	3.83	4.73

1 = total individual responsibility
10 = total organizational responsibility

the running. In the organizations without explicit policies individuals were left to make the running. This pattern of results was also confirmed by the client manager sample. They reported that in the absence of a policy statement, responsibility was far more likely to be left to the individual. Conversely, responsibility for management development was far more likely to be accepted as the responsibility of the organization in those instances where a formal policy on development existed.

▶ Organization Structure and Management Development

The association between organizational structure and business strategy has long been recognized as important (Chandler 1962; Channon 1973; Goold and Campbell 1987). Chandler explained the emergence of the divisionalized structure as a way of freeing up the corporate centre so that it could plan for the long term. Goold and Campbell traced the growth and diversification of the largest companies in the UK. With diversification came structural change towards divisionalization and the associated devolving of some degree of responsibility to business units and/or divisions. Large companies may have five levels of 'general manager': profit centre; business unit; division; group; and corporate headquarters. This raises the question as to the role of the various levels and their relative degrees of influence. In general, where divisionalization did occur, one of the functions most likely to be retained at the centre, if only in vestigial form, was management development.

As noted, even in the diversified and decentralized organizations one of the functions most likely to have some reserved status at the centre has been management development. Following the restructurings and downsizing episodes of the 1980s, the erstwhile large central management training and development departments characteristic of the large corporations such as British Telecom were frequently cut back, with in-house training programmes curtailed or outsourced. The associated career paths upwards through tall, stable hierarchies were also undermined. Companies such as Courtaulds, with hundreds of profit centres, dozens of businesses, and a range of divisions left as much of the initiative to business units as possible and at the centre focused on reviewing business unit plans and proposals. Notably, however, they also retained at the centre some oversight and role in the education and development of management. Similarly, at Unilever the corporate centre maintained a key role in management development, seeing it as part of the 'corporate glue', a phrase to which we will return. The senior management cadre was seen as part of the corporate resource rather than being 'owned' by the constituent businesses no matter how devolved they might be.

In practice, as Storey, Edwards and Sisson (1997) discovered, the residual management development functions at corporate level in many of the largest UK companies in the 1990s were often isolated, much reduced in size and often uncertain about their role and influence. Their very presence was in some conflict with the prevailing ideology which celebrated devolved accountability to business units. For example, business unit managers were reluctant to impair unit performance through the loss of a top team player or a key contributor at the whim of some corporate management development planner. Likewise, corporate management development directors found it very difficult to impose corporate-wide standards and procedures such as appraisal, induction programmes, career planning procedures, job rotation, management training programmes and so on. In general, corporate management development directors found it necessary to tread cautiously and to win commitment and gain 'buy-in' from the various business units, many of which would have their own dedicated management training and development specialists.

Following a couple of decades of corporate change, therefore, management development in the largest UK companies has become a function which has had to justify its existence, has in large measure devolved itself into the various businesses and, at corporate level, offers its services rather more in the mode of 'internal consultants'. In some organizations this involves an actual or quasi-internal market arrangement, and an increasing proportion of corporate specialists are able (or find it necessary) to offer their services, at least part of the time, on the open market.

Some of these shifts in structural arrangements occurred as a result of cost-cutting exercises during downturns in the business cycle. Thus, for example, much retrenchment in corporate management development took place around 1990–1. In such circumstances management development in Britain is peculiarly prone to chopping and changing compared with other countries such as Japan which over many decades have managed to sustain a relatively consistent approach to management development. The continual churn in management development programmes and provision in Britain has been described as the problem of 'programmitis' (Storey et al. 1997).

Such shifts are by no means entirely viewed as negative by the key participants in British management development. As our interview programme with 18 senior corporate managers confirmed, these remaining top players tended to argue that the fundamental shifts during the past decade or so had been necessary and positive. They tended to disparage the old-style corporate manuals with their top-down directives and standard programmes. In the new, flexible, environment it was judged necessary to have highly adaptable and tailored interventions and 'facilitated support'.

These observations emphasize the shift towards what Dore (1989) terms the 'market-oriented' as opposed to the 'organization-oriented' approach to business management. These two ideal types can be summarized as follows. The market-oriented type is characteristic of the British case. It is marked by high labour turnover, remuneration based on the going market rate, competitive entry to firms at all levels, and motivation based on individual interest. The underlying facilitating conditions are short-term profit as the dominant objective, a reliance on equity capital, and firms being regarded as the property of shareholders with a strong market in acquisitions and take-overs. The move is towards an external labour market for managers, and in management development terms this implies a lower level of commitment. In contrast, the 'organization-oriented' type is characteristic of the Japanese case. Labour turnover is low, remuneration is based on seniority rather than a market going rate, there are fixed entry points mainly at lower levels, interpersonal competition is restricted, loyalty to the group is high. The facilitating conditions are: the firm as a community of people with no or very rare hostile take-overs; and the use of bank equity with financiers focusing on long-term growth rather than immediate returns. There is still a commitment to an internal labour market.

The significance of organizational structure and of organizational restructuring was a central context-setting theme discussed at some length by most of our direct interviewees; downsizing, delayering and flatter organizations proved to be key themes of many of the analyses offered by our respondents. It is necessary once again to note, however, the important distinction which has been made in this chapter between the divergent trends in the largest corporations which were decentralizing and informalizing some of their business functions and the medium-sized companies which appeared to be moving in the opposite direction. Hence, before describing the findings from the surveys in the areas of responsibility, it is necessary to assess the extent to which the populations of organizations really have devolved and decentralized management development.

Centralized or decentralized management development?

There are grounds for expecting that the extent to which an organization is centralized or decentralized will influence the conduct of management development. It is of course theoretically possible for a generally centralized organization to operate its management development activities in a decentralized manner. In general, however, this would not occur because one of the functions most likely to be held at the corporate centre tends to be management development. The maintenance of central responsibility for management development offers a number of potential advantages. It enables uniformity of practice, which in turn allows a greater chance of ensuring compliance with at least minimum standards, and it offers the opportunity of building a corporate-wide resource from the senior management cadre. Finally, centralized and standardized management development can help to maintain the 'corporate glue' which holds divisionalized corporations together. On the other hand, the proponents of decentralization in management development would argue that buy-in, flexibility, relevance and responsiveness are all associated much more with a decentralized approach.

In practice, of the 501 organizations in our larger company survey, 42 per cent reported themselves as 'highly centralized' and a further 30 per cent as 'quite centralized'. Thus, 72 per cent were self-reporting as centralized to one degree or another. Only 7 per cent reported themselves as 'decentralized'. Centralization was particularly marked in manufacturing (51 per cent) and rather less so in services (38 per cent), holding companies (36 per cent) and, perhaps most surprisingly, in government organizations (30 per cent). There was, as expected, a size effect: larger organizations were more likely to be decentralized and the smaller organizations were more likely to be centralized. For example, 58 per cent of the 100–299-employee category were highly centralized, compared with just 15 per cent of the organizations with over 5,000 employees. What is most surprising about these results overall is that, despite all the talk in the past decade about 'devolved management' the degree of centralization reported in UK organizations remains remarkably high.

But in this overall context what is the balance with regard to management development? Of the total 501 respondents, 47 per cent said that the overall management development system was 'highly centralized' in their organisations. Only 4 per cent said it was 'highly decentralized'. As with general organizational centralization, the manufacturing sector was the most likely to report centralized management development and government organizations the least. Of particular interest was the association between centralization and judgements about the effectiveness of management development. In fact we found that those respondents from companies which had a centralized approach to management development were more likely to report that the overall provision of training and development was closer to being optimal than did those from decentralized companies. This is an issue to be picked up later in respect of the role of line managers.

Along the same lines, the client managers who reported their organizations to be highly centralized were also more likely to report that their own development was tied to an organizationally defined set of competencies, more likely to have a personal development plan, and even more likely to report that they were better able to transfer learning from development experiences to their jobs. The implication would appear to be that a centralized approach to management development correlates with a more serious approach to management development in practice.

The above set of findings relating to the significance of organizational structure in relation to management development would suggest, by implication, that the allocation of responsibility for management development is also likely to be a matter of some considerable importance. It is to an examination of this theme that we now turn.

▶ The Allocation of Responsibility for Management Development

The way in which management development is carried out depends to a considerable extent upon who is charged with responsibility for it. Some larger organizations have specialist designated roles carrying titles such as Management Development Director. Even in such instances the prime responsibility for management development activity could well rest with the board as a whole, or with line managers, or even with individual managers responsible for their own self-development. The locus of control in management development can also relate to differing conceptions about the way managers learn most effectively. What for one organization might be a well-planned, centrally co-ordinated and cost-effective whole-organization programme will be dismissed by another as mere 'sheep-dipping'.

In the UK a survey by the Institute of Personnel and Development (1999) sought to establish who was responsible for organizational development. It was found that around a third of organizations were making changes to the allocation of responsibility, with movement occurring in both directions. There continues to be a heavy emphasis on devolving responsibility for performance (around 90 per cent of respondents across all sectors reported this) and yet at the same time high proportion (between 80 and 90 per cent) also referred to an emphasis on 'more leadership from the centre'. Around 45 per cent of chief executives in both financial services and manufacturing reported

Table 6.7 Initiation and implementation in management development (n = 214)

	Responsibility for initiation (%)	Responsibility for implementation (%)
Chief executive	21	7
Board	24	8
Central HR/personnel	50	59
Divisional/unit manager	7	25
Other	2	5

Answers add up to more than 100 because some were multiple answers; the table covers answers only from those companies with a policy statement.

a trend towards 'taking back decision making from divisional business units' (1999: 6). While the IPD report captures some of the fluidity in the allocation of responsibility for organizational development matters, it has less to say about where responsibility for management development and related organizational development matters actually resides. However, it noted that overall, 85 per cent of organizations set the strategic framework for HR as a whole in the corporate centre. This is another area where we sought to make a contribution.

In our surveys we made a distinction between who was responsible for the *initiation* of management development policy and who was responsible for its *implementation*. First we asked who had the main responsibility for initiating management development policy. The spread of results is shown in table 6.7. Central HR/personnel with a score of 50 per cent were clearly seen as carrying the main responsibility for initiating management development policy. But if the board (24 per cent) and the chief executive results (21 per cent) are combined, the balance of judgement could arguably be regarded as fairly evenly split. In the 1986 study, of those who did have an explicit policy, 51 per cent said the responsibility for initiating it was located at board level, while 45 per cent attributed it to the personnel department. In broad terms therefore, it could be said that very little has changed here during the past decade: responsibility for initiating management development policy was, and remains, evenly divided between the board/CEO and the personnel department (although it must be remembered that while the 1986 survey was composed entirely of large organizations, the 1996 one took account of medium-sized ones as well).

Another point deriving from the data is that, despite the growth in multi-divisional forms of organization in the UK (Marginson et al. 1988), only a minority of organizations looked to divisional managers to formulate policy in this particular area. Even in organizations with over 5,000 UK employees, only 12 per cent gave this responsibility to divisional managers. It was in the distribution sector that the central HR function was especially important in formulating management development policy.

The HR specialists were, by far, the people who carried most responsibility for *implementing* management development policies. Also, as might have been expected, divisional and unit managers were also mentioned fairly strongly. In smaller organizations the CEO or board was seen as carrying responsibility for implementation. What is most interesting about these results is that, despite the emphasis given in recent years to devolving responsibility to line managers, central personnel/HR was seen to retain such a strong standing. As expected, the incidence of unit or divisional manager responsibility for implementation was most marked in organizations that were more decentralized in general.

Evidence from across Europe (Brewster and Hegewisch 1994) suggests that line managers have been shouldering greater overall responsibility for a range of human resource management functions including management training and development, and there are concerns that the demands on line managers are perhaps too high. They may not be equipped with the skills to handle the development process and they may not in any case accord it a high place on their list of priorities. This suspicion is given credence by the results of various studies which indicate that line managers themselves often accept that they do not have the necessary skills to coach and develop their people, nor, given the degree of operational pressures, do they feel they have the time to take responsibility for training and development. Such findings suggest a reason why, in our surveys, central commitment and acceptance of responsibility for manager development are so strongly associated with the highest impacts (Hendry and Pettigrew 1990).

Resources committed by individuals and organizations

Another way of tackling the question of 'whose responsibility is it?' was to enquire about who was expected to commit resources in order to ensure that management development actually took place. The 1986 survey had difficulty in asking about amounts of money, so we used a rather different approach. We asked a series of four related questions. These probed the proportion of resources put in by the company and by the individual. A scale was used, with 1 representing a state of affairs where resources came totally from the individual and 10 totally from the company. The first three questions asked about resourcing the time needed by managers to participate in internal development activities, resourcing the time needed to participate in external development activities, and the fees, costs and related expenses for external courses. A fourth question asked whether organizational support was given (either financially or through time off) for NVQs, certificates, diplomas, or MBAs.

The time for internal development was overwhelmingly resourced by organizations, with a mean score of 8.0, which should not be surprising. Indeed, so overwhelming was this answer that there was little differentiation even by the policy cluster variables of written statement, high priority, and company responsibility for management development; in other words, even those organizations at the 'weak' end of the spectrum provided the time for internal development. Rather more surprising was a similar response, to a slightly reduced extent, for the resourcing of attendance at external courses, where the mean score was 7.3; here there was rather more differentiation between high- and low-priority companies. Certainly more surprising was the response to the third question, as to whether organizations paid the fees for these external courses; here the mean score was 9.3, with a remarkable 73 per cent saying that the costs were totally paid by the company. In the final question of this series, whether the organization supported managers either financially or giving time off or in other ways in taking qualifications, again there was very positive response: 80 per cent said they supported certificates, 79 per cent diplomas, 58 per cent MBAs, and 49 per cent NVQs. The MBA response was the only one where there was a significant difference between categories; only 38 per cent of the smallest category gave support here, as opposed to 83 per cent in the largest grouping. Moreover, there was a difference in relation to the policy variables, with 73 per cent giving the MBA support with a written statement but only 48 per cent without, and 70 per cent where there was high priority and 41 per cent where there was low priority. Taken overall, these results show a very considerable commitment to supporting managers in their development, whether internal or external.

Another dimension of organizational responsibility is illustrated by the explicit allocation of resources to development. This we measured by enquiring whether a budget had been set aside for this purpose. From the main sample of 501 organizations it was found that 40 per cent did have such a budget while 57 per cent did not; the fact that an organization had no explicit budget did not, of course, mean that it had no expenditure on development. What was most revealing, however, was the significance of having a budget. Those organizations with a special management development budget were also the ones

Table 6.8 Existence of a budget for management development

HRD managers (n = 501)	Yes (%)	No (%)
All	40	57
Policy statement		
Yes	53	44
No	30	68
Priority		
High	52	44
Mid	33	65
Low	23	74
Responsibility		
Company	46	47
Mid	40	57
Individual	33	65

most likely to have an explicit formal policy on development, to report that they accorded high priority to management development and to be the ones which accepted company responsibility for ensuring development happened. These connections are revealed in table 6.8.

Conclusions

This chapter has examined management development policies, priorities and responsibilities. The overall results tend to support a fairly optimistic view of the state of management development in the UK today. Moreover, the importance of top management choice in giving priority to management development and in formalizing that priority in the shape of policies has been revealed. The significance of the 'strong–weak' distinction – that is, the existence of a policy statement, the allocation of priority to management development and the acceptance by the organization of responsibility for management development – is reinforced by the pattern of responses not only from the human resource development specialists but also of those from the other panels. Three main points stand out.

First, the priority accorded to this aspect of management was reported as having increased significantly compared with ten years ago. There was also an expectation that in the future this increased emphasis would continue. In 1986 almost none of the organizations surveyed gave management development as a high priority; by 1996 the figure was 45 per cent. Furthermore, 43 per cent of larger organizations now have a formal written statement or policy concerning management development. This was shown to be rather significant in that a whole series of measures revealed that where there was a priority given to management development and where a formal policy existed there were a number of close associations with the actual amount of training and development and with perceived outcomes from such development.

Second, the balance of responsibility between the organization and the individual had shifted. Some organizations in the past had placed prime responsibility on individuals to look after their own development, others had put this responsibility in the hands of the organization. Our respondents reported that, over the past decade, there had been a migration from these polar extremes to a more balanced sharing of responsibility between the organization and the individual. While the trend was towards a balance of responsibility, central HR is now reported to carry the main responsibility for initiating and implementing management development policy in larger companies according to over 50 per cent of respondents – compared with only 17 per cent ten years previously.

Third, while the existence of formal policies and ring-fenced budgets for management development was only found in just over 40 per cent of the overall sample, where policies and budgets did exist, management development was perceived to have a greater impact on the organization.

Taken together, these three findings tend towards a positive outlook for management development. Nonetheless, as this chapter has also shown, there are ample grounds for caution. While the idea of the 'strategic' importance of learning, capabilities, competencies and knowledge is currently popular, the evidence concerning effective linkage between business strategy and training and development remains rather weak. Moreover, Martin Clarke (1999) has argued that a great deal of the new activity in management development may be delivering dubious outcomes. He traces this to the 'game' element in much management training and development activity.

There are implications for practice arising from this exploration of the link between management development and business strategy, structure and responsibility. Those engaged in management development will need to widen their focus beyond assumed best practice in management learning. Moreover, greater attention may have to be paid to matching business needs. Merely reciting the slogan that in today's environment learning is the only 'sustainable competitive advantage' (De Geus 1988) is not enough. Analysts of the business strategy–management development link suggest that simply stressing learning and development is far from sufficient. Their message, rightly or wrongly, is that the nature of the development is what counts, not the amount. 'Linking executive development to business strategy means organisations can no longer be content just to provide quality executive development activities. If executive development efforts are truly to provide value to an organisation they must be connected to the business strategy' (Seibert et al. 1995: 565).

But the overarching conclusion arising from this chapter must be the way in which our survey data seem to point towards the crucial significance of managerial choice in relation to management development. In those cases where senior management gave priority to management development and where they embedded that priority in formal policies then a whole series of consequences followed. The amount of management development activity was greater, and the judged impact was also greater. In these instances too, organizations had also ensured that appropriate structures were in place and that the allocation of responsibility for designing and implementing management development processes was given greater thought. It is to a closer examination of those processes that we now turn.

Management Development
Procedures and Processes

INTRODUCTION

In this chapter we are concerned with an organization's internal processes of management training and development. This forms part of the second major stage of our model of management development policies presented in figure 2.2. Here we explore the significance of management development processes and procedures: in particular, the way decisions are made about the strategic positioning of training, the way training needs are diagnosed, the way organizations and individuals go about planning and then subsequently reviewing training and development activities. This is an area which has typically been under-researched and undervalued. It is our belief, and we support this with several significant findings from our research, that this element of the model – far from being unimportant – is actually crucial to our understanding of management development. The previous chapter established the undoubted importance of strong and weak management development policies, but what does a strong policy imply for the way management development processes are handled? Here we review what current literature has to say about these questions and analyse our own findings in order to draw conclusions about the characteristics and outcomes of management development processes in UK organizations today.

▶ Mapping Management Development Processes

Figure 7.1 depicts how, at least in formal and espoused terms, development action undertaken by managers arising out of an organizationally driven review process *can* connect to the corporate objectives or mission of the organization. The top level of the figure shows how the training plan is conventionally derived from the human resource policy and plans, which themselves are devised to help fulfil the overall mission and objectives of the organization. Looking at the downward thrusts of the figure, we see, on the left, that the business plan needs to be translated into behavioural requirements, often in the form of a skills audit or competency framework. At a strategic level an organization will periodically review the outcomes of its management training activities, as well as its succession planning and fast-track programmes, in order to assess its managerial capability for achieving business objectives. Well-understood competencies provide a valuable internal and external benchmark as to progress on this front. The second downward thrust comes from the human resource plan. Here the way of procuring appropriate knowledge and skills is specified more precisely. In some cases the organization will not be able to 'grow' these from its internal pool of managers and will therefore need to recruit from the external labour market; however, where possible, talent will be developed and cultivated internally via the mechanisms of appraisal, performance review and reward, recognition and promotion. Finally, the training plan governs the operational aspects of the business and human resource plans: sometimes part-driven by a training needs analysis (TNA), individual managers will pursue personal development plans which lead to participation in an array of training and development activities, formal and informal, on and off the job, professional and vocational, portfolio- and qualifications-led. The training plan will also usually cover career planning and development, which is the subject of chapter 10.

Within this overall framework, this chapter is concerned primarily with the central management development cycle, represented by the thicker arrows in figure 7.1. In particular, we focus on the four key episodes (competency framework, appraisal discussion, personal development plan and performance review) which are highlighted in the figure. Naturally, each of these episodes is developmental in its own right: helping to derive organizational competencies can be highly instructive for sharpening strategic focus; appraisal discussions and performance reviews (especially where these are ongoing rather than

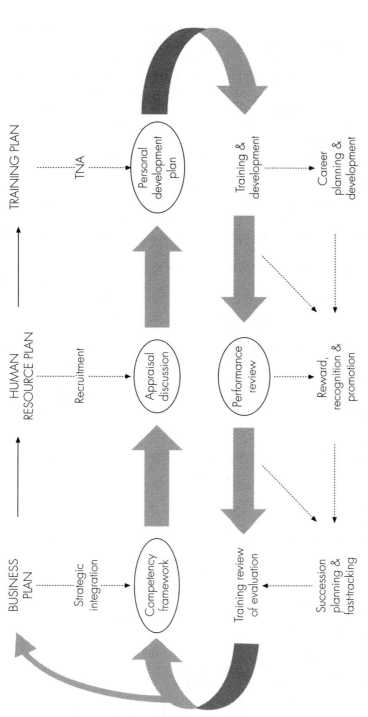

Figure 7.1 Linking the training and development cycle to the organization's mission

annual 'rituals') often incorporate a coaching/mentoring element; and personal development planning invariably helps individuals link their individual learning goals to those of their business unit and/or organization. The following chapter addresses one particular element of the development cycle, namely the amount and methods of training and development, while training review/evaluation and management development processes associated with career planning and development are dealt with in chapters 9 and 10 respectively. Many organizations operate this cycle on an annual basis, with the appraisal discussion as the pivot around which training activities revolve. However, this is a somewhat formal and idealized process, and following the previous chapter, which began to differentiate strong from weak management development policies, we here attempt to understand the reality of this training and development cycle. In particular, we seek to establish how policy translates into action and what elements typify strong or weak management development practice.

The launching-point for the annual management development cycle is identifying the core capabilities required to achieve the corporate mission and expressing this in terms of managerial competencies. Although the precise definition of generic managerial competencies remains controversial, both in concept and content terms (e.g. Reed and Anthony 1992; Holmes 1996), there is growing evidence that competency-based approaches to managerial assessment and development are gaining ground, with results being reported of more successful integration of HR policies (Mabey and Iles 1993), positive links being made with business performance (Shackleton 1992), and the use of competencies to articulate and even modify company cultures (Martin 1995). Naturally, improving clarity about which observable criteria differentiate the excellent from the average performer is a valuable step forward towards strategic HR planning. Gratton (1996), in her study of European multinationals, notes that managers also saw management development as the cultural glue of their organizations, bonding the otherwise loose and separate business entities of which they were comprised.

As we noted in the earlier chapter on management development models, notions of integration, alignment or fit are very much at the heart of strategic approaches to HRM. Based on case-study research in eight companies, Buller (1988) discovered considerable variation in the extent of external integration between HRM and business plans. In the few organizations exhibiting a high level of integration, this took the form of dynamic interaction between human resource planning and strategic planning, with the senior human resource executive seen as a full strategic partner concerned with key decisions, even those which did not always immediately seem to directly involve human resource concerns. In a study of 90 indigenous and foreign-owned Irish companies, Garavan (1991) found a high degree of connection, at least at a formal level, between business strategy and management development: 81 per cent of sample organizations had a written HRD statement and most respondents referred to ongoing modification and review of training plans to ensure they reflected business mission and goals. Despite such reports, we saw in the previous chapter that the empirical evidence for strategically oriented management development remains scant, as do accounts which explicate the mechanisms by which such integration occurs.

▶ Competency Frameworks

We noted in chapter 2 in dealing with human capital theory that the objective of training is a key consideration. It has been one of the problems of British management development that there has been too little focus on what the development was intended to achieve; Mangham and Silver (1986) argued forcefully that the language used to describe managerial activities was quite inadequate for this purpose. However, the arrival of a framework of competencies to define occupational skills has made a very considerable difference. There are of course other ways of classifying skills than through competencies; Katz (1955) suggested the useful division into technical, human and conceptual skills, each of which requires rather different forms of development. But in recent times the concept of competency has become more generally accepted. The concept and definition of competence (or competencies, when referring more to what a person brings to the job) has caused difficulty in recent years because of a range of assigned meanings. Nevertheless, the issue has become an important one for organizations at both a strategic and a human resource level in the last decade or so. There are three particular dimensions we need to examine.

The first dimension is that of core competencies as a distinctive basis of competitive advantage for the organization; thus 'competition between firms is as much a race for competence mastery as it is for market position and market power' (Hamel and Prahalad 1994: 203). Strategy thus created requires other competencies at group and individual level to operationalize it. Hamel and Prahalad define a core competency as: 'A bundle of skills and technologies rather than a single discrete skill or technology . . . It is this integration that is the hallmark of a core competency. A core competency represents the sum of learning across individual skill sets and individual organizational units . . . to actually manage a firm's stock of core competencies, top management must be able to desegregate core competencies into their components, all the way down to the level of specific individuals with specific talents.' Hamel and Prahalad, however, recognize that actually carrying through this deconstruction might not be easy, especially in distinguishing between particular skills and the core competency to which it contributes; moreover 'the subtlety comes when one attempts to distinguish between those competencies which are "core" and those which are "non-core"' (1994: 203). Organizations do not find it at all easy to make these linkages and distinctions; indeed as Hall (1984: 160) has pointed out 'Many organizations invest considerable resources in training and development but never really examine how training and development can most effectively promote organizational objectives.' A further problem is that of bringing together individual and collective competencies; many distinctive and therefore possible core competencies exist because of team-based abilities: 'The problems of recognising individuals' abilities are exacerbated by the fact that people work together in teams where it is difficult to observe directly the contribution of the individual to overall corporate performance' (Grant 1995: 125).

Moving from core competencies to the second dimension of individual competencies, these have been defined as an underlying characteristic of a person which results in efficient work performance (Nordhaug and Grunhaug 1994). Within this, work-related competencies can be said to be composed of three elements: knowledge, which can be defined as specific information about a field; aptitude, which can be defined as natural talents that can be applied in work; and, skill, which is a special ability to perform work-related tasks. These competencies are closely related to the nature of training and the use of internal or external labour markets. Organizations, for instance, will not have an incentive to carry out training if they can just as easily obtain meta-competencies or technical trade competencies from the external labour market, but will wish to concentrate their training on the more organization-specific competencies. Individuals, for their part, will prefer to be trained in meta-competencies or others which can be transferred to the external labour market. This is not to say that individuals will refuse organization-specific training, or that organizations will not carry out training in more general skills, but their general orientation will be in the other direction.

The third dimension of competency deals with how a particular occupation or job is broken down into its component parts, which can be activities or behaviours. This has generated a great deal of interest and development in the last decade or more, but can itself be split into two main approaches. The first uses functional analysis to identify discrete areas of work, each of which can be assessed to provide a mechanism for certifying that an individual is competent in the particular task or sub-task. This approach is very much identified with the British government's occupational standards and the resultant vocational qualifications (VQs) at five different levels, from unskilled to professional, and including management within the top three levels, as outlined in chapter 4. It can be noted that in spite of doubts about the system, it has provided a very important step forward in the analysis of jobs, and therefore has given a focus to the objectives of training that was not previously available. The second approach in the definition of competence starts from a behavioural perspective. This is often associated with the work of Boyatzis (1982), who identified 21 types of behavioural characteristics which he grouped into five clusters: goal and action management; leadership; human resource management; directing subordinates; and focus on others. Many companies and other writers have created modified or alternative frameworks since then, but most have focused on the behavioural characteristics of the person in the role, and not the nature of the job.

Amongst other advantages, competencies can be the spur for the diagnosis and delivery of training within an organization. Competency models identify fairly precisely what a person needs to bring to a given role in order to perform well, and these competencies can be linked directly to business strategy (vertical integration). Once defined in this way, competencies have the potential for creating consistency, coherence and mutual reinforcement across and with HRM policies and practices (horizontal integration). However, functionally derived competencies have been criticized for retreating into narrow vocationalism, crowding out 'any sustained concern with the social, moral, political and ideological ingredients of managerial work' (Reed and Anthony 1992: 60). Indeed, it is not difficult to see how competencies in general can become a senior management device for manipulating the performance, values and self-concept of staff, especially when employed in an assessment, rather than a development, setting. Holmes is one author who notes the inequality of power relations where 'the decision to accord the attribution of competence remains with the assessors' (1996: 97). Clearly care needs to be taken in the way competencies are derived, the breadth of their scope and the purposes to which they are put in an organization.

Turning to our own study, if we were to draw inferences from the HRD manager sample alone, the rationale for management development activity would appear to be reasonably strategic. In response to the question: 'Which skills and competencies is the company trying to develop?', HRD managers referred to people skills and other general management/functional skills most frequently, as shown in table 7.1. However, it is noteworthy that what we might term 'corporate competencies', which cover such things as commercial awareness, customer service, strategic planning and business skills, political awareness,

Table 7.1 Skills and competencies for development (HRD managers, n = 501)

Clusters of skills/competencies	% mentions
People, personal and interpersonal skills	35.0
General management and functional skills	26.8
Corporate and commercial competencies	22.6
Managing change, leadership and influencing	10.6
Personal development, developing and training others	2.5
Others: languages, time management etc.	2.5

networking, risk-taking and flexibility of thought, are ranked third in this list, being cited by nearly a quarter of the sample.

The skills associated with developing self and others receive very little attention. For HRD managers in the small company survey, the order of priority is broadly parallel, with two important exceptions: marketing skills come out on top (38 per cent) and personal development is given much greater importance (19 per cent). One further indication of how seriously organizations take management development can be gleaned from their longer-term strategic plans for developing their management cadres (as indicated in the first column of figure 7.1). HRD managers were asked whether they identified managers with high potential in order to put them on to a fast track for more intensive development. They were also asked whether succession planning was undertaken for existing managers identified to succeed outgoing/retiring senior managers. These two measures were used as a proxy for the degree to which management development was strategically integrated. In table 7.2 we cross-tabulate these two dimensions of

Table 7.2 The association between strategic integration and a strong management development policy and impact (HRD managers %)

	All panel	Policy statement		Priority		Responsibility		Impact on organization	
		Yes	No	High	Low	Company	Individual	High	Low
Succession planning used	60	68	53	67	43	63	45	68	43
Fast-track development used	51	63	42	60	32	53	47	60	35

the management development process against indicators of strong management development policy. It is interesting to note that those organizations with a policy statement according management development a high priority and taking responsibility are consistently more likely to also conduct succession planning and to have fast-track programmes for managers; this is particularly pronounced for management development priority. Perceived impact of management development is also far more likely to be registered as positive where these HR processes are in place.

In order to assess the future requirement and availability of management capability, organizations often carry out a skills audit, or – more recently in vogue – develop a competency framework. Deriving organizationally tailored competencies has become increasingly commonplace in organizations seeking to tie their management development effort into their strategic objectives. This involves collecting data on the capabilities and attitudes necessary for managers to do their job effectively and comparing actual level with desired level of performance. The shortfall in these comparisons reveals both immediate and longer-term training needs. However, organizations are not static: their view as to what constitutes effective performance will alter as they move into new business environments. Sparrow and Bognanno (1993), for example, identify four different categories of competency which help attach a 'shelf-life' to a competency profile for the organization as a whole or to any given career stream or cluster of jobs: *emerging* competencies are those that will require greater emphasis as the organization pursues its particular strategic path; those that are *maturing* are those that are becoming less relevant – perhaps due to technology or work restructuring. *Transitional* competencies are those required of individuals during any change process (for example, high tolerance of uncertainty and the ability to manage stress and conflict). Stable or *core* competencies are those that are central to an organization's performance and so have persistent relevance.

One stimulus to invest in more strategically focused and monitored training, and then to attempt to monitor the impact of this 'closing the loop' as indicated in figure 7.1 is Investors in People (IiP). Even if some of the motivation and somewhat mechanistic methodology associated with IiP has attracted criticism, it is noteworthy that so many organizations and employees are being prompted to consider and assess the strategic value of their development activities and favouring the use of competency frameworks for doing this. Indeed in our regression analysis, IiP emerges as a highly statistically significant influence on the existence of a policy statement, which is hardly surprising since it is difficult to gain IiP status without such a document (Thomson, Mabey and Storey 1998).

During our face-to-face interviews with senior managers, the majority, without prompting, referred to the fact that their organization had devised a competency framework of some kind. This statement from the personnel director at Vickers illustrates the effort, but also the benefit, of persevering with this approach:

> The introduction and acceptance of competencies proved very hard to achieve. It came from top management by a requirement to focus on business priority . . . [the] problem was getting line managers to grasp and accept the competence approach across the divisions . . . it was moved forward slowly and is the basis of Continuous Development Initiative today . . . it rests on the simple premise that a well trained and motivated workforce can only enhance the company's prospects of success.

The comment also illustrates the need for political momentum when introducing management development programmes and activities. Whether derived from competency-based feedback or more traditional training needs analysis (referred to by a number of organizations), successful delivery of management development does not necessarily follow, or depend upon, effective diagnosis. Moreover, we must also recall from the previous chapter that both the MBA and client manager groups generally saw management development as disconnected from their employers' strategic intent.

When it comes to the types of competencies and skills that MBA managers are pursuing, there is a strong interest in updating, deepening and broadening, but of the three, the skills associated with broadening are seen as the most important overall. As table 7.3 shows, those at director level were relatively more interested in updating their skills, while junior/middle managers were relatively keener to increase the depth of their competencies, possibly reflecting the more specialist roles they were engaged in at this management level. In terms of the content of competencies most aspired to, it is not surprising that general management skills come out highest for MBA managers (referred to by 67 per cent), followed by people skills (49 per cent). The interest

Table 7.3 Nature of skills sought by level of manager (MBA managers)

	Means on 1–10 scale	Junior/middle (%)	Senior (%)	Director (%)
Update existing skills	6.32	6.21	6.13	6.60
Increase depth of existing skills	6.81	7.11	6.59	6.72
Develop greater skills	6.85	7.96	8.01	7.90

in interpersonal competencies is possibly due to the fact that conventional MBA courses neglect this kind of experiential development. It is also noteworthy that 33 per cent of MBA managers refer to language(s) as a desired competency, slightly more highly demanded than IT or marketing skills, and well above technical/operational skills.

When asked about their experience of competency frameworks guiding the provision of management training, only 47 per cent of client managers saw management development as closely linked to organizationally defined sets of skills or competencies. As we noted in table 7.2, however, where this *was* the case it was associated with the existence of a management development policy, high priority for and organizational responsibility for management development. Using competency frameworks was also associated with a number of other important management development processes, namely: the use of personal development plans was more prevalent, their line manager was far more likely to be involved in their development, the training activities were far more likely to be rated as relevant to their performance in the job and learning transfer was also more likely to be rated as high. Another crucial relationship was that between the use of a skills/competency framework and the perception that management development was linked to the business strategy of the company concerned.

Certainly one might predict these close associations, but the pertinent fact here is that both groups, those instigating the policies and those experiencing them, draw similarly positive conclusions as to their strategic value. It is noteworthy to find demonstrable support for competency-based management development. Other studies (e.g. Winterton and Winterton 1997) have reported positive outcomes for organizations pursuing this approach, but here we have those on the receiving end responding favourably to development which they deem to be aligned with more strategic concerns. Undoubtedly, the providers and participants of management development differ markedly in their perceptions concerning the extent to which management development is a strategic activity. However, where such activity *is* seen to be integrated with the strategic nature of management development, there is resounding agreement that the outcomes are positive; and the key mechanism for this integration appears to be competency frameworks to provide an appropriate focus for the relationship.

▶ Initiating and Assessing Development

The next part of the management development cycle depicted in figure 7.1 is the appraisal discussion, where the current performance of individuals is reviewed, targets are set for the future and – usually – there is some discussion about development in the job. Raper et al. (1997) conducted interviews across eight case-study organizations in the UK in order to ascertain how far training practices established at company level were operating 'on the ground'. One important trend which they discovered was the widespread devolution of training and development activities to line management and the increasing use of work-based training, not dissimilar to the 'integrated managerial/ opportunistic' type of management development as predicted and advocated by Mumford (1993). Among the forces found to be responsible for this were: restructuring, leading to the need for rapid training to undertake new responsibilities; changes to the product market leading, invariably, to a need for greater customer awareness; efforts to shift culture and improve quality with an increasing premium upon 'soft skills'; and retraining following the introduction of new technologies. Interestingly, this list of strategic triggers for increased human resource development activity is very similar to that uncovered by Pettigrew et al. (1988) almost a decade earlier.

Managers' performance can be reviewed in a number of ways apart from appraisal discussions, such as via development centres, 360-degree feedback or less formal methods. Research findings suggest line manager involvement in diagnostic and development activities is growing and valued on two counts: their role in providing feedback on performance and the fact that such feedback and career planning advice is credible because it is coming from someone who is (usually) connected to the organizational power nexus (Mabey and Iles 1993) and/or a carrier of important cultural information (Preston 1993). Raper et al. (1997) found an extensive use of appraisals as a means of identifying training needs, especially for management staff. However, such reviews are by definition evaluative and often linked to remuneration and promotion possibilities, which is not always compatible with the 'unfreezing' necessary for personal development. In contrast training needs assessment is a process of assessing an employee's mastery of certain skills in his/her present job for the purpose of general self-development rather than for a particular job or set of tasks. A survey of training needs assessment practice across ten European countries shows that the emphasis given to different methods varies widely (table 7.4). It can be seen that the most favoured way of determining training needs in the UK is via performance appraisal, and, apart from Sweden, this is the greatest use of this method across Europe. In contrast, devising training from analysis of the business plan is relatively infrequent.

Increasing numbers of in-house and externally run skills-building programmes incorporate 360-degree feedback (from subordinates, peers, senior colleagues and possibly customers) as a precursor to

Table 7.4 Training policies across 10 European countries

Most important method of analysing training needs	Switzerland (%)	West Germany (%)	Denmark (%)	Spain (%)	France (%)	Italy (%)	Norway (%)	Netherlands (%)	Sweden (%)	UK (%)
Analysis of business plans	10	12	27	30	41	39	39	20	36	22
Training audits	19	39	19	8	0	9	1	31	1	16
Line management requests	36	36	44	45	0	35	35	19	18	20
Performance appraisal	21	10	8	8	N/A	13	22	24	38	35
Employee requests	9	3	2	9	31	4	2	7	7	6

Source: adapted from Holden 1992: 17, 19.

Table 7.5 How is management development triggered?

	HRD managers (n = 501) (%)	MBA managers (n = 450) (%)	Client managers (n = 215) (%)
Performance appraisal	79	33	40
Self	N/A	70	54
Informal discussion with boss	N/A	N/A	48
Training programme/TNA	N/A	16	16
Business school/AMBA	N/A	16	N/A

N/A: Category not asked

management development because such feedback – when sensitively handled – can be a helpful catalyst for real learning and 'represent a major organizational transformation towards greater empowerment of staff' (Alimo-Metcalfe 1998: 43).

Whatever diagnostic approach is adopted, the outcome is usually a more thoughtful set of development targets for the individual and specified training activities, perhaps incorporated into a personal development plan. This then is the catalyst for ongoing training, development and learning opportunities, but it is also where many organizations fall down, and managers find themselves undertaking training and development which – no matter how well designed and delivered – remains uncoupled from the organization's strategic priorities.

In order to examine this important pivot in the management development process, we asked managers about the ways in which management development was triggered. This question was framed slightly differently for each of the sample groups, but the results are displayed in table 7.5 to aid broad comparison.

When asked whether their organizations had regular formal performance appraisal, 81 per cent of HRD managers said yes and only 19 per cent said not, although the latter response went up to 31 per cent in the manufacturing sector. For those companies using formal appraisals, 98 per cent stated that individual development needs were reviewed at appraisal, resulting in an overall percentage of 79 per cent, as shown in table 7.5. Regular use of performance appraisal was also associated strongly with management development policy, priority and responsibility, as well as with higher ratings for the impact of management development.

Client managers gave a somewhat different view of what triggered their development activities. Overall, acting on one's own initiative to organize training and development activity emerged as the most frequent trigger for training used by over half the sample, closely followed by informal discussion with the boss. As table 7.5 shows, appraisal with line managers was only mentioned by 40 per cent of the sample. Thus there is a considerable gap here between the perception of HRD specialists as to the significance of appraisals in determining subsequent development and the perception of those managers on participating in this process. The relatively low significance attached to appraisals as a trigger for development is mirrored by the MBA sample. As might be expected from this group, a much higher proportion (70 per cent) initiate additional learning 'entirely by self', with only 33 per cent referring to company appraisals as the trigger for management development. It seems, however, that top teams are becoming more aware of this shift, with 30 per cent strongly agreeing (and only 7 per cent strongly disagreeing) with the statement 'management development is now driven more by managers themselves seeking personal development'.

Although the use of appraisal as a means of diagnosing training need seems to be less widespread than claimed by HRD managers (and more in line with the 35 per cent reported for the UK in table 7.4 above), table 7.6 shows that this process – where it is used – nevertheless corresponds with elements of strong policy and is associated with higher-impact ratings of management development. The same is true of training needs analyses: this means of determining training is only referred to by 16 per cent of client managers, but the perceived impact on management development where this method is adopted is seen to be twice as great as where it is not used.

Table 7.6 The association between how the management development process is managed and a strong development policy and impact (client managers %, n = 125)

	All panel	Policy statement		Priority		Responsibility		Impact on organization	
		Yes	No	High	Low	Corporate	Individual	High	Low
MD guided by appraisal with line manager	40	56	28	53	31	60	32	49	36
MD informed by training needs analysis	16	29	9	21	16	33	7	22	11

▶ Personal Development Plans

Research has shown that organizations adopt a wide range of mechanisms to help managers determine their training and career development paths, yet those with least perceived validity (career reviews, relying on information on job vacancies and career paths, informal mentors and fast-track programmes) are the most commonly used (Mabey and Iles 1993). As noted by Woodall and Winstanley (1998) however, more recently organizations have been more inclined to adopt structured career development tools like assessment centres, career planning workshops and psychometric testing to assess and develop high-potential managers. Typically the output from these is a tailored plan of action for the individual manager which prioritizes development needs and sets up a plan of training activities to address them. Earlier we discussed preferred ways of diagnosing training needs, but how and to what extent do they become consolidated into meaningful personal development plans (PDPs)? This has been found to be a crucial, yet potentially weak, link in the management development process of many organizations (Mabey and Iles 1993). While organizations might be good at conducting institutional-level training needs analyses, the translation of these into development priorities (see figure 7.1) at an individual level is often less than satisfactory. Likewise, we have already seen that the occurrence and effectiveness of appraisals is limited, and this suggests that individuals rarely walk away from such discussions with clear plans for personal development.

There are many reasons why this might be so. The manager may be suspicious of the organizational purposes of appraisal and ensuing actions (Townley 1993; Newton and Findlay 1998); the manager may be doubtful about the peer and manager ratings upon which the training actions are predicated (Furnham and Stringfield 1998); there may be situational constraints which hinder the personal development planning process (Maurer and Tarulli 1996). More pragmatically, the manager's line manager may be ill equipped or motivated to oversee and encourage their subordinate in the implementation of their PDP. Evidence from 12 European countries suggests that the responsibility for training and development by line management is growing, both in identifying training needs and in making – or contributing to – policy decisions concerning HRD (Holden 1994). This underlines the central role of line managers in the effective integration and implementation of human resource strategies. It is they who interpret and communicate the business plans and attempt to link – at an operational level – the human resource policies to strategic business goals; it is they who operate the procedures and monitor the performance; it is they who devote time and departmental resources to individual and team development; it is they who, in many ways, influence the subculture of their department or business unit. Yet this involvement creates a tension: 'it puts considerable strain and responsibility on the line manager to perform the role with increasing efficiency, not only in carrying out effective monitoring but also ensuring the information is relayed back to the HR central function, which can act as a guide to overall HR policy within the organization in terms of being regionally, nationally and globally strategic in the formulation of HR plans and management succession and other strategic policies' (Holden 1992: 19). As noted in the previous chapter, line managers are not always equipped or committed to carry out this role.

For these reasons, we explored in more detail than most other studies the ways in which diagnosis of management training needs is translated into action. We discovered that for 46 per cent of client managers their development had arisen from some kind of PDP to a greater or lesser extent; this was more likely at junior and middle-manager levels and in larger organizations (over 5,000 employees). Furthermore, where there was first-hand experience of this management development process it appeared to be highly influential in shaping the individual's experience of training and development: the use of PDPs was strongly associated with employers adopting sets of skills/competencies and greater line manager involvement, both of which might be expected to lead to a well-framed set of development objectives. The relevance of training and the transfer of learning were also rated highly by those who had PDPs, as was the ultimate impact and success of and satisfaction with management development.

Table 7.7 reports the association between PDPs and elements of a strong management development policy. The now familiar set of positive associations emerges, especially pronounced for organizations putting a high priority on management development: use of PDPs is twice as likely where a high priority is given. The results also show that a high degree of line manager involvement is associated with the organization having a formal management development policy and it being given a high priority. There also appears to be a connection between line manager involvement and a shared (rather than a solely corporate or solely individual) responsibility for management development, competency-based management development and a higher than average use of personal development plans. Given that each of these features of the management development process would normally imply discussion with one's line manager, this pattern of relationships makes sense. Finally, where the individual's line manager is seen to have a greater involvement in development the impact of management development is registered as almost twice as high. Once

Table 7.7 The association between how the training process is managed and other aspects of management development policy and outcome (client managers %)

	All panel	Policy statement		Priority		Responsibility		Impact on organization	
		Yes	No	High	Low	Company	Individual	High	Low
Use of personal development planning	46	50	47	69	34	67	43	63	40
Line manager involved in MD	37	51	26	53	18	37	28	49	25

again, the constituents comprising what we might term a 'strong' management development process are beginning to emerge.

▶ Performance Review

Following on from the manager's PDP and ensuing development activities (the subject of the next chapter), there is usually some kind of performance review, either formal or informal, where the organization gauges interim progress towards training goals. While the literature on career planning and development is extensive (see chapter 10 for further discussion of this aspect of management development), there is little empirical work on performance review *per se*. Based on a study of 524 organizations Baruch and Peiperl (1997) identified five groups of organizational career management practices, most of which implied certain kinds of performance review. For instance, 'active planning' was characterized by performance appraisal as a basis for career planning, career counselling by the direct supervisor/HR department and succession planning. These activities correlated highly with organizations described as having 'dynamic, open and pro-active climates' (1997: 42).

Apart from questions concerning the occurrence of appraisals (which usually include some discussion of past performance), we did not ask directly about performance review. So, in our search for what constitutes 'strong' and 'weak' management development practice, two proxy measures are used: first, what commitment do organizations make to management development activity, and, second, what roles do managers play in their own and others' development?

The Commitment of the Organization to Management Development

In chapter 6 we reviewed the changes in the initiation and implementation of management development policy in overall terms during the decade 1986–96. One finding was that the relative responsibility of divisional and unit managers increased from 7 per cent at initiation to 25 per cent at implementation. Naturally, the respondents, who are HRD specialists, are likely to hold a fairly positive view of their degree of influence over management development: they attribute 48 per cent of initiation and 59 per cent of implementation to the central HR department. More surprising is the relatively low degree of responsibility accorded to line management, even at the implementation stage (25 per cent), when we might expect a much heavier local involvement in the way management development was being delivered. When we turn to the client manager survey, we find further support for this interpretation. Here the question concerned line manager involvement in management development activity (rather than policy), specifically briefing, monitoring, debriefing and so on. More than a third (37 per cent) rated this involvement as very high or high, but, on the other hand, half of the sample saw their line managers as uninvolved. The fact that no less than a quarter of this sample saw their line managers as having no involvement whatsoever is an interesting revelation, and begins to explain why so many see their development as something they feel it is necessary to initiate, as we saw above. It also suggests that some of the predictions of more extensive line manager involvement in management development activities, reported in the literature, are somewhat premature.

In the previous chapter we referred to the amount of resources committed to development by individuals and organizations. The amount of time allowed for training activities and the extent to which they actively support portfolio- and/or qualifications-based development is one fairly reliable index of an organization's commitment to management development. This is reported by HRD managers in table 7.8, which shows a high proportion of organizations allowing company time for internal development (73 per cent) and slightly less for external development (64 per cent). When it comes to qualifications, support for certificate- and diploma-level training is most popular, followed by well over half (58 per cent) supporting MBAs and just under half supporting the pursuit of national vocational qualifications (NVQs). The pattern of association between these aspects of organization support and elements of strong management development policy is almost exclusively positive, but not as pronounced as for

Table 7.8 The association between company support for management development and other aspects of management development policy and outcome (HRD managers %, n = 501)

	All panel	Policy statement		Priority		Responsibility		Impact on organization	
		Yes	No	High	Low	Company	Individual	High	Low
Company time for internal development	73	77	74	80	69	83	53	74	77
Company time for external development	64	65	61	67	56	66	53	65	53
Support given for:									
NVQs	49	55	45	58	28	52	46	53	35
Certificate	80	86	75	84	67	77	74	80	71
Diploma	79	86	75	85	60	74	75	82	69
MBA	58	73	48	70	41	52	56	62	47

other management development processes reported above. Supporting NVQs and MBAs, in particular, appears to be strongly associated with giving management development a high priority, and, in the case of MBAs, with having a management development policy statement. Somewhat predictably, responsibility for management development is seen as broadly shared in the case of certificates, diplomas and MBAs, indeed in the case of the latter two the responsibility shifts slightly to the individual manager.

The Roles Played by Managers in Management Development

On the second question relating to the nature of their participation in the development process, the MBA respondents were asked what personal role they performed in developing other managers. Given that these managers were likely to be at – or moving towards – senior levels in their respective organizations and, by definition, were taking their own development fairly seriously (by investing time and energy, and usually finances, in a masters qualification), this sample is a good test of the kind of developer roles undertaken in UK companies. The percentages of overall involvement across the 450 managers in this sample are not far removed from those discussed above. Between 31 per cent and 42 per cent had some kind of developer role (or roles), which tallies with the figure of 37 per cent of client managers viewing their line managers as involved; the 30 per cent who saw themselves as having no developer role is also comparable to the 25 per cent of client managers who saw their bosses as having no personal involvement in their development. We noted earlier that only 40 per cent of client managers regarded the appraisal as a significant trigger for management development, and the percentage of MBA managers rating this as a personal role in developing others is approximately the same. This lends further weight to the conclusion that the HRD managers' view of appraisals as a way of determining development needs is optimistic. Appraisal discussions may indeed provide a valuable way of deciding future training, but this kind of joint diagnosis is happening for less than half of the managers we surveyed, not the 80 per cent believed by HRD specialists to be benefiting in this way.

We then asked all MBA managers to judge how important was their role in developing others when weighted against their overall responsibilities. The scale offered was from 1 = no importance, up to 10 = very important. The mean score was 4.06, suggesting that they viewed their management development responsibilities as only moderately important. Only 6 per cent of the 450 managers rated it as 9 or 10 on a 10-point scale of importance, irrespective of organizational size or sector; the stark message seems to be that in the British culture managers do not generally consider management development as one of their key responsibility areas.

This corresponds with findings from another of the relatively rare studies analysing the processes of management development. Storey et al. (1997) found that in-company education, training and development had acquired an even higher profile in Japan in recent years, as firms looked to strengthen their competitive capability; in contrast, British firms were found to be moving away from structured internal labour markets towards individual activity and concepts such as employability, with 'development' becoming the property of the individual manager. Previously, organizations would provide development opportunities and long-term career paths, absorbing much of the anxiety that individuals might otherwise face. It seems that in the UK career development is now becoming the responsibility of employees, who are expected to network and push themselves forward if they want promotion (McGovern et al. 1995). However, a study of three major organizations undergoing large-scale change in the UK found that, because of pressures on business, allocating time for managers to attend courses was very difficult. Further, those who did attend training were frequently unable to put their new skills to work, due to the demands of the business. What development opportunities there were seemed to be the preserve of knowledge workers, with the consequence that the majority of employees viewed the idea of employability with scepticism (Stiles et al. 1997).

Conclusions

At the outset of this chapter we noted that relatively little is known about the internal processes of management development in organizations. The *strategies* devised for developing managers and the *policies* introduced to govern knowledge acquisition and skills enhancement are typically – though not always – publicized and highly visible. Often there is some kind of training policy document or training plan and more than one individual able and willing to articulate the strategic intent of management development for their organization. Such ingredients lend themselves to reportage, and in the past such indicators have been taken as proxy measures for the health of management training activity. In contrast, how an organization interprets and turns these same strategic policies into processes on a day-to-day level is far more opaque, more open to question and more difficult to establish. Yet it is here that the difference between success and failure is likely to occur. No matter how elegantly planned and positioned corporately, the benefits of well-trained managers come from the grass-roots *practice* of management development. The literature that exists in this area provides clues rather than answers. Building on these clues, our study goes some way to exploring the reality of implementing management development. First, by asking respondents to reflect on the 'how' of management development: how it comes to have priority, how training needs are discerned, how involved line managers are in management development and how well management development connects with wider organizational strategies. Second, by comparing the view of those who devise the management development strategies with those managers who participate in the training which is provided.

Following our identification of what constitutes strong management development policy in the previous chapter, here the ingredients of what we might term strong management development processes have emerged. In line with other studies (Patterson et al. 1998; Pettigrew and Whipp 1991), there will be a recognition that management development plays a strategic role in helping to fulfil an organization's mission and corporate plan by 'delivering' apposite skills and capabilities in a timely fashion.

For HRD managers, at least, the tangible evidence for this typically resides in a number of key elements: some kind of succession planning, the use of appraisal for determining development, the provision of time off for internal/external development and organizational support for qualifications-based development. Those managers participating in, rather than providing, management development reported an incidence of these indices of strategic training processes which was more modest than that reported for similar measures by the HRD managers. Nevertheless, where such processes *are* in place they consistently associate with the strong policy dimensions on the one hand and with perceptions of a positive impact of management development on the organization on the other. So, for example, organizationally defined sets of skills and/or competencies appear to be indicative of other training processes (line manager involvement, relevant training and learning transfer); the drawing up of a personal development plan seems to be pivotal in managers reporting their training as a positive and satisfying experience, and is also closely associated with favourable ratings of greater line manager involvement, job-relevant training and high learning transfer. Indeed, impact of management development is rated four times higher by client managers when management development is perceived to be closely linked to business strategy, and twice as high when the individual's line manager is closely involved.

As noted, figure 7.1 represents a somewhat idealistic picture. It assumes strategy-making to be a rational and cyclical process, when we know that in reality it is far more subject to political and personal agendas, more emergent and fluid. It assumes that even if the dominant strategic logic can be pinned down, the appropriate management development policies to support its enactment will be self-evident. It also assumes a consensual, rather than a conflictual, view of employment relations where employers and employees alike will recognize what is required to achieve competitive edge and will work industriously towards these goals (the unlikelihood of this remains one of the criticisms of competency frameworks, for example). Despite this, it does help to contextualize our discussion of the cycle of management development in organizations.

chapter 8

Management Development: Amount and Methods

INTRODUCTION

In the previous two chapters we looked at the policies and processes adopted by organizations in the arena of management training and development. Here we move on to explore the actual activities that comprise management development practice, and in particular the amount and type of management development (see figure 2.2). In terms of the management development cycle (figure 7.1) this represents the one link we did not address in chapter 7. This part of the system is crucial in three respects. First, many accounts of training interventions, and particularly management training, are written from the perspective of those responsible for designing and delivering such programmes. Consequently they tend to focus on intent rather than outcomes, on rhetoric rather than reality; when results are published they are usually more descriptive than critical. Second, it is well known that the quantity and quality of management training in the UK has traditionally been poor; thus there is a need to take stock of current activity at a grass-roots level. Third, there has been a natural bias in the literature reporting management development to concentrate upon programmes and activities and to neglect less formal, but nevertheless highly important informal, management development activities. For all these reasons, an analysis of the perceived quality, volume and type of management development currently being undertaken in UK organizations is most timely.

In this chapter we review what is currently known about the amount of management development being carried out in UK organizations, the balance of methods that are typically adopted to deliver this training and how such management development activities are viewed by different stakeholders in the training process. We report our own findings from UK organizations on these matters, and – where possible – contextualize this within the wider literature.

▶ Amount of Formal Management Development

How much formal management training is being reported?

The primary means of measuring how much management development was being undertaken was to ask HRD managers for the amount of formal training as an average annual number of days per manager across their organization. This is a fairly impressionistic measure in the absence of detailed records in almost every organization, but its virtue is that: (i) it is readily quantifiable; (ii) it allows comparison with other surveys of management training conducted in the recent past; and (iii) it permits important longitudinal analysis and comparison with the state of play in the UK a decade previously.

The mean amount reported by the HRD manager sample as a whole is 5.5 days. We shall see in chapter 11 that the mean in our survey of small businesses is 4.6 days, combining to produce a (very crude) mean of about 5 days across what amounts to the vast majority of the economy in terms of industrial and size groupings. This represents a broad achievement of the target of 5 days a year which has been put forward at a national level over the last decade or so. However, these averages mask the extremes: in the larger company survey 24 per cent of organizations provide only 2 days or less formal training each year, in contrast to the 18 per cent which provide 10 days or more for each of their managers in an average year.

There are several ways of reflecting on these findings: by comparison with the past and prospective future; by comparison with other

Table 8.1 Amount of formal training reported by HRD managers (n = 501)

Days	Now (%)	10 years ago (%)	Next 3–5 years (%)
None	4	15	1
1–2	20	36	8
3–5	40	23	38
6–9	12	4	21
10–14	11	4	14
15+	7	2	12
Not stated	6	16	7
Mean	5.5	3.1	7.3

research; by comparison with our own MBA and client manager surveys; and by examining causal factors, including regression analysis. We will take these issues in turn.

Table 8.1 also shows the amount of training in the past and future compared to the present as reported by the HRD managers. It can be seen that there is a very substantial increase from the amount reported as having been undertaken 10 years previously to that being undertaken at the time of the survey, and then there is a further substantial anticipated increase in the future. Accepting that these are broad estimates the figures nevertheless point towards real change taking place, with more intended in the future. Our data for 10 years previously, showing 51 per cent doing two or less days per year compare with Mangham's and Silver's (1986) report that 'somewhat over half of all UK companies appear to make no formal provision for the training of their managers'. It should be noted that in the corporate survey for the Constable–McCormick Report (Thomson 1987), companies had forecast that they would significantly increase the amount of training carried out, and this appears to have been vindicated. The only comparator with these longitudinal figures is from the Price Waterhouse Cranfield Survey (Brewster and Hegewisch 1994), which found in general support of these trends that 61 per cent of British companies had increased the amount they spent on management training over the last three years after allowing for inflation, whereas only 9 per cent had decreased the amount and in 23 per cent it had remained the same.

The same survey is also a point of comparison with the current figures; with data from 1992, it reported the following: 1 day or less – 7 per cent of companies; 1+ to 3 days – 28 per cent; 3+ to 5 days – 36 per cent; 5+ to 10 days – 22 per cent; 10 days or above – 7 per cent. This produces a mean of just over 5 days per year, which fits very

Table 8.2 Amount of formal training (days per annum) compared

Days	HRD managers (n = 501)	MBAs (n = 450)		Client managers (n = 125)	
		All managers	Self	All managers	Self
None	3	10	4	12	9
1–5	65	45	39	42	46
6–10	12	30	17	33	23
11–15	8	4	7	5	12
16+	10	2	6	4	8
Not stated	3	5	27	3	2
Mean	5.8	4.8	6.4	5.2	6.2

closely with our findings, and those of Mansfield and Poole (1991). Indeed Mansfield and Poole go further to say that as well as some 5 days spent training in employers' time, managers spend some 3 days training in their own time. Deloitte, Haskins and Sells (1989) and Warr (1992) also reported increases in management development activity since the gloomy conclusions of Mangham and Silver (1986), Constable and McCormick (1987) and Handy (1987). Similarly in the small business sector the results from the Kingston project (Curran et al. 1996) parallel our findings. Thus, our findings seem to be corroborated in the conclusion that more managers are receiving more training on a regular basis than in the past.

The next point of comparison is with the customers of management development, the MBAs and the client managers. Table 8.2 shows the extent of their formal in-company training. As can be seen, both MBAs and client managers reported an amount of training for all managers which was somewhat less than the 5.8 days stated by the HRD managers, but also reported that they themselves did more than either of the overall manager averages. About one in eight MBA managers and one in 11 client managers reported doing no personal formal management development, while at the other end of the scale, just under one in 10 MBAs and one in five client managers did more than 10 days per year. The overall mean reported for MBAs themselves was 6.4 days, which may be explained by their having an MBA and to that extent being likely to have a commitment to self-development. But the client managers also have the same gap, although not as great as for the MBAs. As might be expected, the amount of training tends to increase with the size of organization; also, junior and middle managers did more than the senior levels, but the differences were not great, and even directors in the MBA group reported 4.9 days of formal development per year. Again, we would argue that these data are compatible with the responses of the HRD managers.

Factors influencing the amount of formal training

The final focus of reflection in this area is: what factors are associated with the reported amount of management training? Some of the potential influencing factors did not show up as important. Thus the relationship between organizational growth and training volume was negligible except in small businesses, where there was significantly more training carried out in those organizations experiencing rapid growth. Again, there was little variation across organizations of different size and sector, something that was also found by Brewster and Hegewisch (1994). However, when we turn to internal policy and related variables we find much stronger relationships. HRD managers report that when their companies had a policy statement relating to management development, they also provided an average of 6.5 days' training, while those without only provided 4.6. Even stronger, those companies which reported giving a high priority to management development did considerably more training (6.9 days) than those who gave it only a mid-level priority (5.6) and far more than those with a low priority (2.7). It is nevertheless important to note that even those reporting a low priority for management development are doing almost 3 days per manager per year. The customer groups' responses were similar. Thus the MBAs reported much more personal training (7.4 days) where they also reported that their employer had a high priority for management development than when they reported a low priority (3.9), and a similar pattern was true of the client managers. When we turn to the small business survey, the results are even more discriminating. The question on a policy statement was rather differently worded. Where there was an explicit statement there was a mean number of days of training reported of 7.4; where there was an informal policy the mean was 5.7; where there was only a reaction to need or no policy at all the mean was 3.2. The same pattern emerged for the priority given to management development. What we can therefore conclude on the basis of these findings is that the policy variables are more important than the structural ones, and that in small businesses the same factors are even more marked.

The third variable which is part of our policy cluster was perceived responsibility for the development process. Those HRD managers who felt the company had the primary responsibility provided an average of 6.5 days, while those who saw a shared responsibility provided 5.6, and those who saw the primary responsibility as lying with the individual manager provided 4.8. The MBAs again had a very similar pattern, with 6.3 days reported where the company was reported as responsible and 4.7 where the individual was.

To test our findings further, regression analyses were conducted for the HRD and MBA groups in which the amount of training was taken as the dependent variable and external, internal and policy clusters were used as independent variables to see which might be significantly associated with the amount of training (see appendix 2, and also Thomson, Mabey and Storey 1998). For the HRD manager group, it was found that internal structural factors (number of staff, degree of centralization and a management development budget) and external structural factors (size, sector and ownership) were significantly related to the amount of training, but the most strongly significant predictor was the policy cluster, and within the policy cluster the most significant single variable was the existence of a written management development policy. What this result suggests is that the volume of training undertaken is due more to a decision by the organization than it is to the structural context in which the organization finds itself.

These results mirror those of the MBA managers, except that the regression relationships were even more highly significant than for the HRD managers (see tables A1 and A3 in appendix 2). It might have been expected that the MBA results would differ for two reasons. First, since MBA managers are responding as consumers of the management development process rather than as providers, and secondly, they have not as much reason to be knowledgeable about the management development process as the HRD respondents, who typically had a responsibility for it. As it is, the similarity of patterns of relationships across the two sample groups provides striking confirmation of a key relationship. Namely, the internal decisions made by organizations concerning their management development policy indeed constitute the most influential factor in determining the amount of management development that is actually undertaken. This is all the more significant given the fact that there is high consistency across the same two groups with regard to the *amounts* of management development actually taking place in their respective organizations. Also noteworthy is that, in the eyes of MBA managers, other factors (especially external structure) help to determine the amount of management development undertaken. This is somewhat surprising and shows that these participants in management training are keenly aware of the influence of such factors as organization size, sector, and ownership upon the volume of management development delivered in an organization. These may seem unexceptional findings, but they conflict with the frequently made assertion that training is directly related to size or sector or some other predetermined variable. From both providers of, and participants in, management development, we have demonstrable evidence that organizations have choice about the volume of training conducted, and they exercise it.

Beyond the variables utilized in the regression analyses, there was also substantial differentiation shown for the 'outcome' variables, which are further explored in chapter 9. Where the impact of management development on the organization is seen as being high rather than low, and where the respondent's own satisfaction with management development in the organization is high rather than low, there are close associations with higher amounts of formal development. The amount of formal development was also more likely to be reported as high when the management development system is centralized rather than decentralized. And while we did not directly test the process variables mentioned in the last chapter, we would expect that they would also show up as being associated with the amount of training.

Amounts of informal training

So far we have dealt only with the reported amounts of formal training. We also need to report on three other aspects of the amount of training. It is generally recognized that many managers actively pursue development *outside* their organization, and our findings bear this out. Only 12 per cent of MBA managers said they undertook no management development outside the organization, although at least some of the 6 per cent 'not stated' should be added to this percentage. The mean amount for those undertaking management development on their own was 5 days per annum; for those using a professional institute the figure was 4.2 days; while for those using a business school/ Association of MBAs it was 4.3 days, presumably heavily influenced by those taking a course of study. A mean of more than 10 days a year, excluding any informal development undertaken within the organization, signals a substantial amount of training on an annual basis, and considerably more than shown by the only previous attempt we are aware of to measure this amount (Mansfield and Poole 1991).

When we examine the relationship between this and other variables, it is interesting to note that this is one aspect of management development not strongly influenced by company policy on management training. Presumably this is because company policy issues are not directly involved in the decision to undertake development outside the organization (except perhaps in a compensatory sense of making up for what is not provided internally).

It may be problematic to ask about the amount of formal training in terms of numbers of days, but this is still less difficult than taking into account informal modes of development, which are even more difficult to measure accurately. We did not ask the company representatives about the amount of informal training, but we did ask the customer groups. The specific figures reported are probably too uncertain to be trusted, but members of both groups clearly felt that they as individuals were engaging in significant amounts of informal development, more than the amount they reported in formal development. However, their uncertainty was exemplified by the very high percentages who could not answer the question for managers as a whole – over half in the case of the client managers. Nevertheless, we do want to register that both groups recognized that informal development was significant, at least as far as they themselves were concerned.

Satisfaction with the amount of training

The third dimension was how satisfied organizations are with their overall amount of training in terms of sufficiency or optimality measured against what they would ideally like to have done. To try to take account of these issues, we asked the HRD managers to rate the amount of management development undertaken, including all the formal and informal development, on a 1–10 scale where 1 was a very low amount and 10 a very high amount. Again, as with the number of days, we asked this question for the present, as it was 10 years ago, and as they see it in the next three to five years. As an index of satisfaction with the amount of development, the mean stands at 5.3, implying that many respondents feel that not enough is currently being done. The mean for the future is 7.0, which indicates an intention or at least expectation that considerably more will be carried out, and the mean for 10 years ago is 3.3, reflecting the much lower amount of training that was carried out then. There were some interesting, if not major, differences between structural categories for this scale. In the sectors, HRD managers in government organizations, with a mean of 5.6, reported a higher level of satisfaction, with manufacturing lowest at 5.1. There was also increasing satisfaction by size, and non-British companies see themselves as closer to optimality than British companies, and for that matter they do report higher numbers of days. But once again the big differences are related to the policy variables: a mean of 6.0 with a policy statement and 4.7 without, and one of 6.4 where there was high priority and one of 3.2 where there was low priority.

The most telling finding so far is that the vast majority of firms are investing in training. It can no longer be said, as reported by Mangham and Silver (1986), that there are substantial numbers of even the larger companies who are not training their managers. In the small company sector there are many companies which are engaged in a considerable amount of training, equivalent to the amount in the larger size groupings. Furthermore, respondents indicate that these amounts should increase significantly in the future. Less clear at this point is the strategic contribution of such management development activity, apart from sheer volume. Those companies which reported a centralized control of management development also reported higher satisfaction than those which said control was decentralized. Of other variables, priority, effectiveness and impact all showed high levels of correlation with satisfaction. Regression analysis confirmed the policy variables to be much more predictive than external or internal structural variables, and indeed the difference was more marked than in the case of the *amount* of training.

In this section we have conducted a brief 'health check' on the condition of management development in Britain. How much training and development of managers is going on in UK organizations? Does this activity represent an improvement on the past, and how does it compare with management development in other countries? The overall conclusion is, first, that the volume of reported management development is a great deal higher than it was 10 years ago, and second, that the amounts of management development (as indicated by annual days' training) are broadly consistent across our sample groups. Furthermore, such findings appear to corroborate those of other studies which we have cited in passing, for training generally (Ashton and Felstead 1995) and management training in particular (Warr 1993; Brewster and Hegewisch 1994). Research undertaken to investigate management training provision in eight companies comprising four matched UK–Japanese company pairings revealed that British managers reported more training and valued it more highly than their Japanese counterparts (Storey et al. 1997). However, the researchers go on to say:

> The Japanese managers at all levels were able to describe the training and development systems in their companies, this was often simply not the case at all in the British companies. There were dramatic lurches in the British cases: elaborate suites of training courses were designed and refined for one period, only to be totally disbanded the next. Self-development would be the main emphasis at one time and then it would be more or less disregarded at another. As a consequence, line managers were confused and sometime cynical. (Storey et al. 1997: 206–7)

This finding is helpful because it gets beneath the skin of training days reported to the type of training being undertaken and its strategic significance. Obviously, to understand the true picture of management development in Britain we need to explore such things as the way training is delivered, experienced and evaluated, and it is to these questions that we now turn.

▶ Methods of Management Development

In this second half of the chapter we are concerned with three aspects, namely formal methods, informal methods, and the balance between the two within organizations. We are also interested in indications of the effectiveness of different methods.

Formal methods

The use of different management development methods depends in large part on the strategic outcomes desired. Hall (1984) has provided a useful categorization of four outcomes that, taken together, make up much of career effectiveness, namely training which addresses performance, attitudes, identity and adaptability. The strategies for obtaining these outcomes are: *cognitive* – concerned with altering thoughts and ideas; *behavioural* – trying to change behaviour directly; and *environmental* – altering the immediate work environment of the employee. So, for instance, management development might be conceived to address skill and knowledge deficiencies in the organization as diagnosed at an appraisal discussion or arising from a training needs analysis (see figure 7.1). In a UK study of management development, Parkinson (1990) found improving managers' expertise in such areas as marketing, finance and production to be highest on the agenda of the companies he surveyed, followed by the preparation and experience necessary to fit individuals for senior management roles. Alternatively, training and development may be used to act as a *catalyst* for change and might thus be seeking cognitive, behavioural and environmental change. This approach is frequently associated with organization leaders attempting to orchestrate cultural change amongst their workforce. Using such methods as participative workshops with vertical cross-sections of staff, quality improvement projects, team building, problem-solving groups, and so on, the intention is to cultivate a fresh way of viewing themselves, their internal 'customers' and the market in which they compete (du Gay 1996). Also addressing all three of Hall's types of management development is one with a different emphasis from the others, that of encouraging a *learning climate* in the organization. The focus here is on the learning needs of individuals,

Table 8.3 Methods of formal management development by level of manager (HRD managers %, n = 501)

	Overall	Managerial level 1	Managerial level 2	Managerial levels 3–4	Senior managers
Time off to go on external courses	95	83	85	87	71
Seminars/conferences	94	66	77	92	80
In-company training to develop individual skills	92	89	80	68	44
In-company training to develop organization skills	88	76	78	71	46
External formal qualifications	85	77	72	65	44
Other formal development	15	11	14	19	11
Not stated	2	4	4	5	12

guided by organizational goals and underpinned by the belief that within each member of staff resides latent talent and experiential learning ability. Accordingly, the trend is away from structured, taught courses and towards enhanced opportunities for self-development through such methods as action learning, on-the-job training, career breaks, temporary task forces, or computer-based open learning systems.

In our surveys, all respondents were asked to identify what kinds of formal management development were provided in their organization from a range of methods. In the case of the HRD managers, their responses are depicted in table 8.3. As this table shows, most organizations provide a range of different management development methods for all levels of manager. As far as provision for different levels is concerned, in-company training was provided mainly for junior (level 1) managers, both to develop individual skills and to develop skills needed by the organization. In this category of manager, less importance was given to seminars and conferences, although a substantial number of organizations offered time off to go on external courses to managers at levels 1 and 2. Naturally, these external courses could well be related to gaining individual or organizational skills. At level 2, the balance changes somewhat with a greater emphasis on external courses than on ones held in-company and with an increased usage of seminars and conferences. At levels 3–4 and at senior level, a considerable amount of formal management development appeared to take place through seminars or conferences. However, there appeared

Table 8.4 Method and effectiveness of formal management development

	Amount			Effectiveness (client managers)	
	HRD managers (n = 501) (%)	MBA managers (n = 450) (%)	Client managers* (n = 125) (%)	Mean	Rank
Time for external courses	95	69	78	7.1	2nd
Seminars/conferences	94	47	65	5.9	5th
In-company training (individual skills)	92	56	62	6.6	3rd
In-company training (organization skills)	88	50	61	6.2	4th
External formal qualifications	85	38	40	7.3	1st

* Personally experienced in the previous three years.

to be less training and development provided for senior managers. Cross-tabulations revealed that slightly more organizations carried out formal management training activities when moving up the size gradient, but as so often there was a larger difference when the policy cluster of written statement, high priority, and company responsibility were examined.

So far we have examined only the organizational perspective. Table 8.4 displays the relative use of different management development methods by the MBA and client manager groups and compares this with the usage claimed by HRD managers. Immediately apparent is the discrepancy between what organizations say is on offer and what individuals say is the case. For instance, the number of MBAs claiming that their employers offered external qualifications as a method of formal management development (38 per cent) differs significantly from the view of HRD managers, 85 per cent of whom stated that their organization offered this method. This may be explained by the use of the word 'undertaken' in our question to the MBAs. Most organizations do not 'undertake' external formal qualifications, but they may pay for their managers to undertake them elsewhere or offer them as part of their management development programme.

Even allowing for this difference in interpretation, MBA managers put the availability of formal management development methods between 22 per cent and 47 per cent lower than the HRD managers.

When it comes to their personal experience of such training, the percentages given by the client managers tally more closely with the MBA (albeit at a slightly higher level) than the HRD manager sample. This suggests that either the full range of management development opportunities provided by corporate HRD departments is typically not well communicated to staff lower down the organization or that the top team are giving an optimistic view of what is on offer. Despite this discrepancy, nearly two-thirds and upwards of client managers could point to a personal experience of formal development of some kind in the previous three years, and 40 per cent were pursuing, or had taken, formal qualifications. Availability is one thing; perceived effectiveness is another. We asked client managers to rate the effectiveness of the same formal management development methods on a scale of 1 to 10. The type of management development least experienced by such managers, external formal qualifications, is also the type of formal development seen as most effective; while attendance at seminars and conferences, experienced by nearly two-thirds of all managers, is rated relatively poorly as a means of development. Nevertheless, all methods have a mean rating of 5.9 or higher. This group represents the basic managerial customer, as far as we can claim any such representation, and they seem to be quite satisfied with what they get in this important area of management development.

In the MBA group too there are some very positive connotations. The provision of formal management development opportunities is consistently associated with the strong policy factors; in several instances, the incidence of these training methods is twice as likely where the organization also gives a high priority to, and has a written policy statement for, management development. This is particularly pronounced for opportunities for skills training (both individual and organizational). There is a striking association between the usage of all types of formal training and positive evaluation given to management development. It seems that the more management development an organization carries out across the whole range of formal methods, the more highly managers will judge the impact of such training on the business, and the more favourably they will rate their satisfaction with training. This makes intuitive sense, but empirical support for this connection has rarely been established. It would not be unreasonable to surmise that, for many of these MBA managers, such favourable assessments of their employers' training provision leads to improved commitment to the organization and enhanced personal performance.

Overall, as seen by all three groups, there is a wide range and usage of both internal and external methods of training and development. These data compare closely with the results of the 1986 survey and are

Table 8.5 Use of formal qualifications as a method of management development, 1986–1996

	Managerial level 1 (%)	Managerial levels 2–4 (%)	Senior managers (%)
1986 survey (n = 206)	22	38	20
1996 survey (n = 501)	77	69	44

all the more positive given that the latter only covered very large organizations where training was more likely to be occurring. One area of significant change is in the importance of external qualifications. As table 8.5 demonstrates, external qualifications were rated as having relatively little importance as a method of management development in 1986 across all managerial levels. Ten years later, there appears to be a dramatic rise in the adoption of this method.

It is likely that the main reason for this increase lies in the rapid growth of business schools and management-related qualifications over the past 10 years. This proliferation has in turn been generated by demand from managers for qualifications which are respected in the labour market (Mansfield and Poole 1991). Many of these qualifications, particularly at certificate and diploma levels, have attempted to become vocationally relevant as well as retaining a strong academic focus. At the same time, business schools have been increasing their links with employers to provide qualifications geared to the needs of particular organizations.

Informal methods

In the management development literature there has been a wider recognition in the recent past of the value of informal learning for managers (e.g. McCauley et al. 1994). Fox (1997) is one author who makes a helpful distinction between management learning processes and management education and development processes: 'The latter are a narrower, and more formal, set of practices which are frequently *done to* people by professionals to make them learn, whereas management learning processes cover these and the rest of the learning iceberg – the everyday processes whereby people manage learning and learn to manage' (1997: 32, italics in original). In the introduction to their collection of readings on managing learning from the previous decade, Mabey and Iles observe that:

> Earlier concerns with measuring and assessing have moved to how learning can be interwoven with everyday activities in the workplace. Responsibility for development has been shifting from tutor and trainer to manager-as-coach and trainee ... The focus is now on learning through re-framing workplace problems, self-determined development, unfreezing barriers to learning and understanding what it means to be a learning organization. (1993: 1)

Part of this trend is fed by a growing appreciation of the way adults best learn and revise their preferred ways of working, and partly it is driven by structural changes in organizations. Coincidentally, empowerment, the devolution of decision-making and the dismantling of bureaucracies are all causing organizations to rethink their traditional methods of developing managers. As Smith notes:

> Amongst large employers the delivery of training is becoming decentralised as a result of flattening hierarchies and the greater accountability expected of functional and departmental management. The quality movement has also encouraged greater communication and flexibility in the delivery of training and coaching at the point of work. All this tends to militate against formal training courses. (Smith 1996: 61)

In many ways, informal management development is more difficult to assess than formal development. Informal development can – and should – include experiential and 'accidental' learning which takes place in an unplanned way in the course of everyday work (Mumford 1993). This kind of development embodies, for example, learning through observation of others, or from making mistakes, or as a result of a new job challenge (Kotter 1995). It is difficult for organizations to evaluate how much of this informal management development is taking place and how effective it is. But as Burgoyne (1988) has noted, in the more entrepreneurial organizations development takes place because the whole organization is a perfectly structured learning experience, a live business game, with information, ideas, experimentation, and quick natural feedback on the consequences of managerial actions.

In our survey of HRD managers, the main emphasis in methods of informal management development appeared to be on the learning curve experienced through performing the job, followed by coaching at all levels of management, although decreasing in importance as managers took on more senior roles. As with formal management development, there is a general downward gradient from junior to senior managers in the amount of management development provided. It is, however, difficult to establish the extent to which such activities are planned within the organization and how much they happen spontaneously. We might recall the sceptical comments of Mangham and Silver (1986) here: 'A majority of those who consider that these competencies are capable of development believe that the best way to develop them is in-house through experience . . . we do not know how the experience is provided . . . we have reason to believe that it is relatively unfocussed and somewhat haphazard.' However, the amount of mentoring, coaching and job rotation reported by HRD managers suggests a more considered and structured approach to informal methods than their comment implies; perhaps another sign that things have progressed over the past decade.

As with formal management development, we compared the views of the HRD managers concerning the availability of different types of informal management development with those on the receiving end of these training and development activities (table 8.6). Again, and probably for the same reasons, the 'official' HRD estimation of what informal management development opportunities are available is consistently greater across all methods than that experienced by managers in the organizations of which they are part. This discrepancy is particularly pronounced for coaching, in-company job rotation and job observation. Somewhat similar percentages of HRD managers (86 per cent) and client managers (74 per cent) think there are good opportunities to develop management skills through on-the-job training. For MBA managers on-the-job training ranks highest in terms of availability, but still only registered as such by this sample group and it falls nearly 30 per cent short of the stated availability of this kind of informal training in the eyes of HRD managers. Whatever

Table 8.6 Method and effectiveness of informal management development

	Amount			Effectiveness (client managers)	
	HRD managers (n = 501) (%)	MBA managers (n = 450) (%)	Client managers* (n = 125) (%)	Mean	Rank
In-company job rotation	50	24	19	5.7	5th
Job observation	53	25	27	6.0	3rd
On-the-job training	86	57	74	6.7	1st
Mentoring	55	30	35	5.9	4th
Coaching	74	29	27	6.6	2nd

* Personally experienced in the previous three years.

Table 8.7 The association between informal methods of management development provided by the company and outcomes (MBAs %, n = 450)

	All	Impact		Satisfaction	
		High	Low	High	Low
In-company job rotation	24	40	15	40	16
Job observation	25	30	25	30	22
Learning curve doing the job	57	65	55	61	54
Mentoring	30	49	18	55	18
Coaching	29	52	15	54	16

the explanation, HRD specialists should take note that their view of what formal and informal methods are available for developing managers, is not shared by managers generally.

For client managers, the most prevalent method, on-the-job training, also emerges as the most highly rated, with a mean of 6.7 on a 10-point scale, followed by coaching at 6.6. However, as with formal management development methods, the overall scores exhibit a high level of satisfaction.

MBA respondents were asked similar questions and in table 8.7 we report the association between the incidence of informal management development approaches and the outcome measures of impact and satisfaction. As shown, where the organization provided mentoring, coaching and job rotation, MBA managers were three times more likely (on average) to rate the impact of and satisfaction with management development as high. Less than a third of employers were seen to be providing such opportunities for development, but these results suggest that it is well worth the company structuring informal development of this nature. Not shown in table 8.7 are significant associations between in-company job rotation, mentoring and coaching as methods of management development and the degree of priority given to informal management development in the organization and the existence of written policy statements. These methods sit midway on the formal–informal continuum since, in general, they require more structure and organization than job observation or learning on the job. We can, therefore, differentiate between 'organized informal' management development, which requires more support from the company, and 'accidental informal' (Mumford 1993) with less structure or organizational policy behind it. In all cases, with the exception of learning on the job, both organized and more 'accidental' management development were felt to be significantly more the responsibility of the organization than of the individual.

▶ The Balance between Formal and Informal Development

Current and future trends

One important issue is the balance which organizations perceive between formal and informal development. Historically, managers were essentially left to develop informally by experience, but it is clear that formal means of development have been gaining ground in the recent past. Table 8.8 gives the balance as reported by the HRD managers.

As can be seen, there is a slight preference for informal development, but formal development is more common in the larger companies, although the differences are not great and more than a third of the largest companies apparently have more informal development. There is also a substantial grouping where there is a balance between the two. This balance might be taken as an indication that British industry still has a long way to go in creating proper development systems, or it might be argued that companies are now making efficient use of informal systems rather than just letting it happen. We would slightly favour the latter view, although not denying that there are still many organizations for which management development is not a priority. But there is a strong relationship between more formal training and written policy statements and the extent of priority for management development. Thus where there was a policy statement, 43 per cent reported more formal as against 29 per cent more informal, while where there was not, 28 per cent reported more formal and 48 per cent more informal. In a separate regression analysis we sought to discover the correlates of the balance between formal and informal training

Table 8.8 Balance between formal and informal development by size

Amounts	All (%)	100–299 (%)	300–399 (%)	500–999 (%)	1,000–4,999 (%)	5,000+ (%)
About equal amounts of formal and informal	23	22	27	21	23	22
Considerably more formal	35	33	25	37	40	41
Considerably more informal	40	43	47	40	34	35

pursued by organizations. Significant relationships were found between informal management development and the absence of a written policy statement, and a limited use of appraisals. This indicates that formal training is associated with a more structured system of management development, reinforcing the earlier pattern of findings that the existence of a policy statement is a key variable in relation to the volume of training, a higher priority and so on.

An important issue following from this question of balance is how it will change in the future. The HRD managers were asked whether their development methods would change in the future, and 71 per cent said that they would. When asked what differences they envisaged, the most common answer, at 27 per cent of those expecting to change, said they would move to more formal programmes/external training, while the third largest group, at 15 per cent, said they would move to more informal methods of job rotation, action learning and so on. It would therefore appear that different companies are moving in different directions, and that some at least are deliberately choosing a more informal approach. It is a good sign, though, that those intending to use more formal methods were overwhelmingly coming from those groups with a weak policy framework, namely those without a written policy and with a low priority given to training. In order to fulfil their intentions for the future, 18 per cent said they would be using mentors/coaching, 13 per cent said they would be putting emphasis on self-learning by the individual, 13 per cent said they would be utilizing new technology, and 8 per cent each said they would be using open learning systems and NVQs.

Returning to the question of balance, the 1986 survey showed that, overwhelmingly, companies used in-company training at level 1, moving towards external short courses and in-company planned job experience/rotation at levels 2–4. At senior manager level, the trend towards the use of external courses was continued, with an increase in external short courses. In our interviews with HRD managers, several referred to a shift away from more formal, off-the-job, programmatic, mass training events towards more tailored, on-the-job action learning approaches to management development. Although this was said to be partly driven by costs, there was also a growing realization that the latter could achieve more enduring learning for the individual and potentially greater benefits for the organization. This also implies, of course, that considerable thought must be given to the objectives and process of such development, and is further reassurance of change since the situation described by Mangham and Silver above.

One HRD manager we interviewed commented that 'Management development is very much a process of access to resources and not a brochure of courses.' This is very reflective of the shift in thinking mentioned in many of the interviews. Words like 'menu' and 'tool-box' were relegated to the past, as were long residential training programmes and large departments of in-house trainers. Today's catchwords are 'on-the-job training', 'coaching' and 'tailored career development' for individuals. There are more developmental events than training programmes, one interviewee explained, such as away-days, focus groups, discussions and seminars. On-the-job training is seen as more important, and there are fewer two-day 'jollies'. More-over, organizations referring to these activities were also those giving a high priority to and having a high corporate responsibility for man-agement development as well as having a written policy statement, implying that managers in these companies were not learning simply in an *ad hoc*, opportunistic manner.

Work-based learning

There is a consistent strand of research which suggests that managers learn as much, and potentially *more*, from their day-to-day work, from colleagues, from observing other managers and from other life experi-ences as they do from management training programmes (Davies and Easterby-Smith 1984; Kotter 1995; Dawes et al. 1996). There are several possible reasons for this. Some aspects of a manager's role are best learned on the job, being too complex to be taught through formal methods. Addressing isolated competencies removes the opportun-ity of learning how to employ these management competencies in an integrated way, which is what, in reality, managing effectively re-quires. Furthermore, practising is a key part of competence formation and formal courses rarely provide this facility in a way that fully replicates the workplace.

On a somewhat different issue, when asked about their role in devel-oping others, MBA managers cited the roles of adviser (38 per cent), coach (38 per cent) and mentor (31 per cent). Precise definitions were not given, so it would be wrong to read too much into the differences between these roles. However, all these kinds of personal involvement were more prevalent where the management development system was centralized and where the organization's current growth was rapid; also, as might be expected, the percentage playing these roles increased markedly with seniority. However, for all but the adviser role, their occurrence was greater where the responsibility for management development was shared rather than left to the organization, or indi-vidual, alone. This, then, is one instance where organizational respons-ibility for management development is not an indicator of strong process. Finally and significantly, the impact and satisfaction with management development was far more likely to be positive where managers were seen to be fulfilling the roles of appraiser, adviser, coach and mentor.

Clearly, some respondents were playing multiple roles – acting for example as both appraiser and as coach or mentor. However, nearly one in three claimed no developmental responsibilities at all, although this was largely a function of seniority: among the junior/ middle managers some 55 per cent reported that they played no part in developing others, whereas only 11 per cent of directors and 26 per cent of senior managers answered in this way. It might, nonetheless, be seen as somewhat surprising that fully one-quarter of MBAs in senior management positions said they played no personal role in developing others.

In another slightly different area related to balance, the MBAs were asked to rate three methods of training and development, external, internal and experiential, on a scale of 1–10 (1 = of no importance and 10 = very important). The significant finding here is the very high importance attached to external skills (mean of 7.9), with nearly one-quarter (24 per cent) giving the top rating of 10. These are very high scores and it is surprising to see them almost equalled by the experiential learning overall rating of 7.4 per cent. Indeed, given the fact that the respondents had undertaken high levels of formal cognitive development through their MBA studies, their recognition of the importance of experiential development is all the more striking. After this, the rating given to internal courses is very modest (a mean of 4.9), but is quite comparable with ratings given to other aspects of management development. This could partly be explained by the fact that all respondents had undertaken at least an MBA as an external course, but it should also be noted that in spite of this moderate rating, the respondents still engaged in such training.

When it comes to favoured routes to further development, MBA managers expressed equal preferences for structured learning and unstructured learning outside the company context (both 61 per cent). There is also a demand for courses from professional institutes from 50 per cent of these managers, showing that learning is seen as a multi-faceted rather than single-strand process and reinforcing the need for a coherent continuing professional development (CPD) framework, which is as yet lacking. Of the other possibilities, further business school or academic qualifications appealed to a significant minority (29 per cent).

The majority (between 50 and 60 per cent) identified seminars, reading, professional meetings and self-directed studies as the preferred means of undertaking further development, although again a significant majority (between a quarter and a third) were willing to make the

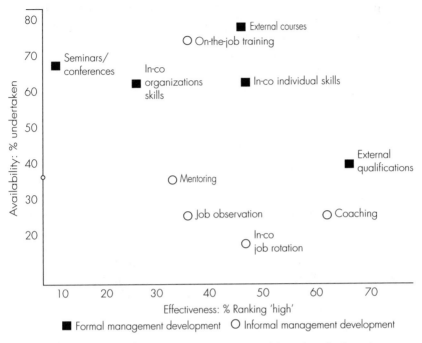

Figure 8.1 An availability/effectiveness quadrant of formal and informal management development

more substantial commitment of 'short courses at weekends, regular learning, distance learning courses and longer training periods'.

While these findings confirm that employers conducting high levels of internal, formal management development are also those organizations with strong policies and procedures governing the appraisal and training of their managers, the perceived quality of management development is quite different from the quantity and the degree to which it is formalized. Figure 8.1 combines the availability and effectiveness ratings for all management development methods, formal and informal. This reveals three features of management development which ought to be informative for those deciding on training policy for their organizations. First, it is relatively straightforward to send managers to seminars and conferences but their impact is low (and indeed their per capita costs are usually high), and more needs to be done to improve the effectiveness of in-company courses which address organizational skills. Second, the high availability of the two formal management development methods (in-company training on individual skills and external courses), and the informal method of on-the-job training is probably justified because each of these types of management development is seen as highly effective by participating managers. Third, the three methods in the high effectiveness/low availability quadrant of the graph represent a strategic opportunity: their effect is seen as very positive by those who have experienced them, especially external qualifications and coaching, yet they are generally under-used.

Conclusions

Earlier we reported cautious optimism concerning the growth and health of UK management training when compared to the situation a decade previously. One legitimate criticism levelled at many of the reports cited to illustrate advances in management education is that they have featured leading-edge companies, typically in the private sector and large enough to be able to afford the luxury of training investment and innovation (e.g. Vickerstaff 1991). In an effort to get beyond the headlines of enhanced training provision at a national level and celebratory accounts of management training interventions, this chapter set out to examine the linkage between management development policy and practice in UK organizations. In particular we have been concerned to tease out findings relating to less publicized and less easily measured methods of informal management training; and we have done this using sample groups covering organizations of all sizes, sectors and geographical location, as well as canvassing the views of different stakeholders in management training activities. The picture emerging can be summarized as progressive when compared with that a decade ago, but with a gap in some areas between the perceptions of the providers and the consumers of management development activities.

Even if management training is both more plentiful in volume and more strategic in orientation, there still remains the fairly self-evident observation that externally inspired and monitored training activity is not necessarily equivalent to learning which can be applied to the job. This point, together with a number of other problematic presumptions in management training, is well made by Cunningham and Dawes (1997). Any extra-organizational attempts to evaluate training and development need to take account of (i) the quality of training – not simply the amount, and (ii) the scope of learning – recognizing that learning is a lifetime activity, fed by all manner of personal experiences and not contained in those of one particular organization. It is here that the recognition of the value of informal learning in the workplace is particularly helpful due to its focus on the process – as against the curriculum alone – of knowledge and skills acquisition. Easterby-Smith and Thorpe (1997) note that the results of research in this area demonstrate that we still know relatively little about the process and content of natural learning. Also, it has been pointed out that learning from the richness of everyday experiences is by no means automatic: 'there is a large potential for error, in large because people leave much of what they are thinking unconscious, implicit and unshared . . . they might not *adequately* frame or contextualise the problem, review their experience, invent a solution, or learn what they need to implement a solution' (Watkins and Marsick 1992: 298, italics in original).

The findings reported in this chapter go some way to answering these questions. We have elaborated the kinds of informal management development activities organizations provide, how these are perceived by managers themselves and the relative effectiveness of these different methods as learning opportunities. It would seem that the model of integrated 'managerial development via opportunistic processes', combining as it does the best features of informal accidental learning processes and the benefits of formal, planned management development (Mumford 1993), has a good deal of currency and value in the organizations we researched. Even more revealing is what we have discovered about two dimensions of management development which have hitherto remained somewhat opaque. First, it has been established that while formal approaches to management development are consistently connected to a pattern of variables which we have labelled 'strong policy': namely, where the organization takes responsibility, where management development is accorded a high priority and where there is a written management development policy, there are also some organizations where this is true of informal approaches. Indeed, in keeping with a trend noted in chapter 6, there appear to be some companies which having once had a formal, comprehensive approach, are now moving away from it. Secondly, it has emerged that these stronger policies will not only lead to enhancements in the quantity of management development in organizations, but also in the perceived quality. This brings important confirmation to a pattern noted by Mabey, Salaman and Storey (1998: 360). In relation to human resource development generally, they noted that 'institutionalized' training, while most visible and quantifiable and certainly preferable to intermittent training, is actually less beneficial than what is termed 'internalized training'. The latter will be less observable to the casual onlooker, but closer scrutiny will show that learning and development *are* taking place at all levels in a more informal and integrated manner. Indeed the skills of structuring and consolidating this kind of learning are fairly sophisticated and are far more likely to lead to the formation of resource mobility barriers for the firm that practises them (Mueller 1996).

It is clear, and all parties agree on this, that when judged by volume alone, there is now a great deal more management development happening in most organizations. Once again, this growth is associated more with internal attitudes towards the topic, such as the priority accorded to management development and whether policies exist to guide its delivery; external factors like size or sector are not the determining factors. There is also a shift in style from more formal, off-the-job, programmatic, mass training events towards more tailored, on-the-job, action learning approaches. This may in part be driven by costs, but we surmise that there is also a gathering realization that the latter achieve more enduring learning for the individual, and potentially greater benefits for the organization. There are, nevertheless, several methods of management development, both formal and informal, which managers themselves regard highly.

9

The Impact of Management Development

INTRODUCTION

This chapter examines the link between management development practice and impact, and how the organizational benefits of management development activities are assessed; it also provides the closing of the cycle of management development as depicted in figure 2.2. The outcomes itemized in the model include financial performance, achievement of objectives, impact of development, satisfaction and productivity. In fact, as we shall see, measuring such things and then relating them causally to management development is notoriously difficult; our surveys had to rely on perceptual measures of outcomes.

As table 1.1 clearly depicts, post-experience training is seen as having an increasingly important role in the creation of future management. Yet evidence for the effectiveness and impact of management development is still relatively scarce. Few would disagree that developing management capability is a high strategic priority for organizations today, yet there remain nagging questions about its value. Management development may be plentiful but is it purposeful? The corporate HRD brochures may be impressive, but how positively is management training perceived by those managers at the sharp end? Can investment in management training be described as strategic and how might the outcomes of management development be evaluated?

But there is also another type of question, namely: what standards of proof are required? It is possible, in the words of the old dictum, to let the best be enemy of the good, and in demanding evidence of high statistical formality, overlook more commonsense validation. Thus Britain's economic record in the first four-fifths of the twentieth century was fairly lamentable at a time when Britain had no coherent system of developing its managers. Britain's economic record has begun to improve in the last two decades, as has the coherence and amount of management development. Given the accepted importance of good management in operating the economy, are the two events not related? Nevertheless, there is a need to at least try to face up to the earlier questions, and we now proceed to do this.

▶ Strategic Assessments of Management Development

Evaluation research

Studies which report the specific impact of management development in quantifiable (or even other) terms are still few and far between. The most comprehensive evaluation of the issue comes from a government-sponsored research report on the business benefits of management development by the consulting company DTZ Pieda (DfEE 1998). To quote from the report's findings:

Impacts of management development (MD) on business performance. Of the 127 firms questioned, some 88 firms identified impacts on non-financial business performance following management development activities. Just under a third of these, however, thought that the impacts were only indirectly due to MD and could have been affected by other factors. The key point on the benefits derived directly and/or indirectly was that not a single firm thought that MD had had a negative effect. The types of impact most often mentioned by respondents were:

Direct Impacts
- improved morale of staff;
- an improved response and greater flexibility shown by managers;
- improvements in quality leading to greater customer loyalty/new business.

Indirect Impacts
- an improved management style;
- better tracking of projects and evaluation of their worth to the firm;
- a greater understanding of the value of training and human resource development in general;
- quantitative measurement of impacts of management development for firms.

Of the total sample, less than a fifth of firms felt that definite, direct and measurable financial benefits could be identified as a result of the MD they had undertaken. When questioned further, only 11 firms felt able to provide a monetary estimate of the impact of MD. Of those firms who could identify financial impacts:

- companies felt that revenues had increased following the MD activity;
- companies identified reductions in cost thought to be due to the MD.

The interesting feature among those firms who were able to provide quantitative measures of the impact of MD is that nine out of the 11 firms were involved in the Investors in People process.

It is important to note that there are a number of problems for firms in assessing the impact of management development, including:

- difficulty in identifying benefits over the relatively short time period following MD activities being undertaken;
- disentangling the effects of MD *per se* from other initiatives and aspects of business that each firm has been involved in over the same period of time;
- measuring or monitoring impacts, particularly financially, due to a lack of systems set up to measure inputs and outputs of MD activities across the firm.

The Pieda survey was carried out in Training and Enterprise Councils and dealt with smaller firms. Nevertheless, the report does reflect the difficulties of identifying what issues are being measured and how to measure them which are general to all organizations.

One rare example of an explicit financial return is that provided by British Telecom, who claimed that a management training programme saved the company £270 million. Managers were asked to estimate the cost of errors made by untrained junior managers. This was quantified as more than £200 million. It included the cost of missing deadlines, failing to deal with customer complaints, poor problem diagnosis and inefficient budgeting. The assessors from the group personnel department estimated that the training had eliminated this waste and added about £70 million to BT's revenue. The evaluation was done by examining performance improvements following each training course. The evaluation took three years, and perhaps most importantly, the company's accountants were satisfied by the formula adopted to quantify improvements (Lee, Coaley and Beard 1993).

Another study also discovered some encouraging support for the value of management development: an in-depth analysis of 16 UK organizations found four to be comprehensively adopting 'management standards' as part of their HRD systems and processes, while a further three had partially adopted such frameworks, and nine had not attempted this or had made little progress in this direction (Winterton and Winterton 1997). Those in the first category shared certain characteristics: management development and other training was competency-based, job profiles or job descriptions related to the competencies outlined in the national occupational standards for management and appraisal systems were designed to support the attainment of these standards. A major benefit identified was the coherent structure which the standards provided for training, management development and personal development (although the standards were not extensively used for recruitment and selection, nor reward and remuneration systems). Gaps in competence, for example, were more readily spotted through appraisal, training needs were specified more precisely in relation to the competencies required for individuals to meet the needs of the organization, and there were clear criteria for human resource planning and career succession. Also, management development was linked to a qualifications framework. Finally, and most impressive, the researchers found a statistically significant relationship between competency-based HRD systems and both individual and business performance.

Further evidence for the positive impact of training comes from two case-study analyses of UK organizations. In both cases repeat staff surveys were used to assess the outcomes of training programmes. In Grampian Health Authority, positive shifts in culture were reported on a number of indices for all categories of staff (except supervisory grades) over the period 1987–90; this was attributed to a range of organization development initiatives, including training in customer care, problem-solving and leadership (Mabey and Mallory 1994). Cannon (1995) used a similar method to assess the outcomes of senior management training workshops and leadership, team and people management skills training aimed at middle managers in a UK bank: over the period 1991–4, six dimensions of organizational climate improved, with the most significant progress being made in the areas of support (for example 'conducting team meetings in a way that builds trust') and commitment ('involving people in setting goals').

A very interesting recent survey (Baruch and Peiperl 1999) has examined the impact of an MBA. The authors asked a sample consisting of both MBA graduates and others of similar status without an MBA about their perceived self-efficacy, i.e. their belief in their capacity to perform a task. Using a range of 18 competencies, they found that the MBAs believed themselves to have a higher level of competence than did the non-MBAs, and they also believed that their studies had contributed to the improvement of their skills to a greater extent than their counterparts. The majority of the comparisons indicated statistically significant differences, and indeed only one competency in the contribution of studies was not significant (interestingly this was interpersonal skills). The authors also noted that the literature suggests a high correlation between efficacy perceptions and subsequent performance.

Standards-based research

If valid conclusions are to be drawn about the strategic contribution of management development, then we need to have a framework, or at least a starting-point, against which performance can be measured. This is one area where recent progress has been made at a national level. Whether overseen by internal assessors, customers and/or third-party bodies, increasing numbers of organizations are seeking external accreditation and kitemarks. Invariably such standards have direct implications for the quality of management training and development. This is certainly true of the Investors in People (IiP) standard. A key criterion for accreditation requires the organization to: 'evaluate the investment in training and development to assess achievement and improve future effectiveness'. This includes measuring the impact on performance, evaluating the achievement of its goals and targets, understanding the broad costs and benefits of training and implementing improvements to training design as a result of the evaluation. A survey conducted by the Institute of Employment Studies compared employers who had gained IiP recognition with those who had not (Spilsbury and Moralee 1995). A substantially higher proportion of the recognized employers had mission statements, business plans, written

HR strategies, and formal training budgets; furthermore these budgets were decided according to their business plans. Although there were no differences in the average number of training days spent per employee on the job, IiP employers registered more off-the-job training per annum.

In a similar evaluation study of IiP, three-quarters of those employers anticipating training benefits said they had achieved them: these included better induction, training being better related to business priorities and changes in the way training was carried out (Hillage and Moralee 1996). They also found 60 per cent reporting improved workforce outcomes (understanding, skills, commitment etc.) and a large majority reporting some direct or indirect improvements in such key areas as quality and productivity or anticipating these in due course. Another qualitative study by Rix et al. (1993) of 24 groups of employers and 19 groups of employees, some committed to IiP and others uninvolved, drew similar conclusions. About half of those committed to or recognized by IiP saw the enhancement in training activity bringing business benefit; for some this was favourably altering perceptions of customers or potential employees; for others it meant strengthening the links in a loosely connected causal chain. None of the firms in the sample had calculated a direct financial contribution to the bottom line, but they all believed that there was a contribution. Also to be noted was the importance of IiP for the Pieda survey reported above, and as well as its statistical significance as a 'driver' of training mentioned in the previous chapter.

Human resource management research

But management development is just one human resource activity among many, and the evidence for the impact of a *combination* of human resource policies/practices is more plentiful (e.g. Fox and McLeay 1991; Arthur 1994; Huselid 1995). In a study of 67 UK manufacturing firms, it was found that the adoption of progressive human resource management practices was a far greater predictor of profitability and productivity than other factors like business strategy, emphasis on quality, advanced technology and R&D. Within this 'bundle', the acquisition and development of skills (selection, induction, training and appraisal) were the most influential of all (Patterson et al. 1998). Such attempts to track the impact of strategic human resource approaches are a step in the right direction, but they say little about the distinctive benefits of investing in strategic approaches to management development (as against other elements of strategic HRM) and even less about on-the-job, incidental, non-programmed skill-formation activities for managers.

In our surveys we chose to rely on participants' perceptions concerning the effectiveness and impact of management development in their organizations. This is less ambitious than attempting to correlate management development activities with more objective measures of firm performance, but has the advantage of isolating the effect of management training in the broader human resource context of other questions concerning recruitment, appraisals, career planning and so on. We now proceed to examine these perceptions and their implications.

▶ Perceptual Assessments of Management Development

There are a number of questions in our surveys relating to the outcomes of development, although not all were asked of all groups.

Achievement of management development objectives

This first question was asked of all the groups: 'How successful do you believe the organization's current management development policies are in achieving their objectives and producing the type of managers it wants?' Table 9.1 illustrates the groups' views on this question, which was based on a 10-point scale where 1 represented low achievement of objectives and 10 high achievement.

As can be seen, most organizational representatives were at least modestly satisfied with the achievement of management development: 41 per cent of HRD managers rated their achievement of objectives as high, and only one in five rated them as low. We should also note that the question had a second strand of producing the type of managers the organization wants, and there is a positive view of that as

Table 9.1 Achievement of management development objectives

Extent of achievement (%)	HRD managers	Client managers	MBAs
Low (1–4)	20	47	53
Medium (5–6)	38	26	27
High (7–10)	41	27	20
Mean	5.86	4.84	4.27

well. There was little significant differentiation by any of the main breakdowns, and indeed the size breakdown showed almost no difference between categories. However, higher scores were associated with the system of management development being centralized in the organizations concerned. It is also worth noting that in the small business survey, given in more detail in chapter 11, those reporting achievement of objectives were twice as frequent as those reporting the lack of it. As with many other aspects of the survey, the main links seem to relate to policy issues such as having a written management development statement, the degree of priority, and responsibility for development.

The overall mean for the organizational perspective is clearly positive, but the same is not true of the two customer groups, with the MBAs being more negative than the client managers. In neither were the structural factors important differentiators, although in the MBA group those who were directors took a more positive view than their counterparts at lower levels. This difference between provider and customer is one that is repeated for other questions. It is perhaps reasonable to expect those whose job is concerned with providing a particular service to want to see that service in a positive light, whereas for the customer groups it is merely a service which can be viewed dispassionately. Perhaps the directors in the MBA group also feel a vested interest, reflected in their more positive view. In the case of the MBAs there is also the likelihood that their experience of management education will predispose them to be critical of their organization's offerings; the client managers may not have the same opportunity of an external point of comparison. Nevertheless, the negative views should not be overstated. Rather more than half of the client managers and only just less than half the MBAs perceive the achievement of objectives as either medium or high. This is not a bad ranking for an area where companies have been heavily criticized in the recent past.

Equally important is the relationship between the customer groups and the strong–weak continuum. Table 9.2 takes the MBA group and shows the very clear association between perceived achievement of objectives and the three variables in our policy cluster.

Clearly the MBAs have a distinct mental differentiation between what they see as a strong and a weak policy framework and the success of the objectives. Perhaps particularly worth noting is the very strong relationship between the achievement of objectives and the degree of priority given to management development; this accords perfectly with common sense, but it is good to see it so plainly confirmed. Overall the positive outcomes of management development are closely

Table 9.2   Achievement of objectives and other variables (MBAs %, n = 450)

	All	Policy statement		Priority		Responsibility	
		Yes	No	High	Low	Company	Individual
Achievement of objectives							
High	20	33	9	41	8	40	11
Medium	27	33	24	34	18	32	22
Low	53	36	67	24	73	29	55
Mean	4.27	5.19	3.54	5.71	3.25	5.57	3.63

associated with the visible commitment to management development of the organization concerned.

Impact of management development

The second question which we asked all three was concerned with impact, namely 'How would you rate the impact of management development on the organization?' on a 1–10 scale where 1 = no impact at all and 10 = immense impact. We did not further define the concept of impact, but assume respondents interpreted it as implying a positive influence. Table 9.3 shows similar patterns to replies to the question about achievement of objectives, but at a higher overall level, even if 13 per cent of the MBAs held that in their organization management development had no impact at all. Again, more than half the client managers felt that management development had a medium or high impact, and almost half the HRD managers believed there was a high impact. As with achievement of objectives there is a clear relationship between the policy cluster variables and the perception of impact, and indeed a table could be created which is almost a carbon copy of table 9.2.

Table 9.3   Perceived impact of management development

Level of impact	HRD managers (%)	Client managers (%)	MBAs (%)
Low	17	38	53
Medium	32	32	23
High	49	29	22
Mean	6.24	5.28	4.37

Table 9.4 Satisfaction with development and association with other variables

Satisfaction with development	MBAs	Client managers	Policy statement*		Priority*		Responsibility*	
			Yes	No	High	Low	Corporate	Individual
Low (1–4)	51	35	20	46	3	69	14	51
Medium (5–6)	21	19	12	20	19	7	16	19
High (7–10)	24	46	67	34	80	24	69	31
Mean	4.4	5.7	6.8	5.0	7.6	4.0	7.2	4.75

* Client managers only

Satisfaction with management development

A third outcomes question was only, for obvious reasons, addressed to the customer groups. This was 'How satisfied are you with the management development training you have received since joining the organization?' In table 9.4, there are two separate elements included, namely the raw scores for satisfaction, and also the relationship with the policy variables, this time taking the client managers rather than the MBAs to illustrate that the same patterns occur.

In table 9.4 there is a substantial difference between the views of the MBAs and the client managers. The client managers have taken a more positive view than the MBAs in previous questions, but this time the difference is marked. Clearly the MBAs have had substantial development experience outside the organization and this has probably coloured their views of organizational training, but the level of satisfaction expressed by the client managers is worthy of recognition. It is easily arguable that they are more representative of managers generally than the MBAs, even though as appendix 1 notes, there was no compulsion to answer the questionnaire in an organization which volunteered for follow-on research. Nevertheless, that almost half expressed high satisfaction and almost two-thirds medium or high satisfaction with the training they had received in their organization is an important finding.

The other component of table 9.4 is the relationship of satisfaction to the three policy variables. The pattern is very similar to that with the MBAs in table 9.2, but the differences are even more marked. If the MBAs can identify relationships, so can the client managers, in spite of being, in all probability, much less well versed in management development than the MBAs. The accumulation of variables associated with a strong (or weak) framework continues, as does the lack of differentiating power of other variables such as size, sector, and growth.

To explore further the reasons behind the assessments of the outcomes, we regressed two out of the three outcome variables against other variables for all three main surveys (larger companies, small businesses and MBAs), and satisfaction with management development only for the MBA group. The results were very similar in each case, although rather different independent variables were used (Thomson, Mabey and Storey 1998; Thomson and Gray 1999; Mabey and Thomson 2000). The most striking results were found in the MBA group regression. All the clusters of variables were significant in each equation, with the exception of the career cluster where satisfaction was the outcome, but in each case the policy cluster had by far the highest level of significance; this latter result will by now not be surprising. It is also interesting that the MBA results achieved a uniformly high level of significance; this suggests that they as a group have a clear perception of the various associations involved in management development, even though they are not as directly concerned with it as the 'provider' groups.

In summary, the results highlight the fact that positive outcomes of management development investment, whether measured by perceived success in achieving objectives, perceived organizational impact or personal satisfaction, can largely be attributed to the way organizations make policy choices concerning the setting up and running of their management training and development processes. Particularly important in this regard is the commitment given by the company to management development activity. Policy statements, high priority, centralized management development systems and responsibility for management development emerge as the key elements of this visible corporate commitment.

Quality of management development processes

A final area by which our surveys sought to evaluate outcomes is in the quality of the processes involved. Research on adult learning tells us that development is likely to be more enduring and effective when certain features are in place: these include the timeliness and relevance of the training, opportunities for learning transfer, mechanisms for review and feedback and reward and recognition for any behaviour/ attitude modification. We asked the client managers to evaluate their experience of these different aspects of their management development, and the results are shown in table 9.5. It should be noted that for this group of questions, although they conform to the 1–10 scale, the high and low performances are reversed, so that 1–4 means high

Table 9.5 Outcomes of learning (client managers %, n = 125)

	Low (7–10)	Medium (5–6)	High (1–4)	Mean
1. How relevant was the development activity to the performance in your job?	14	24	63	3.9
2. To what extent have you been able to transfer learning from your development into your job?	16	17	68	3.8
3. How effectively is your progress against identified development needs reviewed by the organization?	47	21	29	6.0
4. To what extent do the reward and recognition policies reinforce the learning outputs of your development?	62	13	22	7.0
5. To what extent has the business impact of the development been assessed by the organization?	50	22	21	6.7

and 7–10 means low. This obviously also has an impact on the interpretation of the mean.

There are some interesting implications of the results in table 9.5, especially regarding the contrast between answers to the first two questions and the other three. In the first two, almost and just over two-thirds are very positive that the development was relevant to the job and that the learning had been transferred from the development to the job. These results are obviously compatible with the satisfaction, noted above, that this same group had expressed with their training. However, when we move to questions which ask about the organization's response to the training, attitudes change sharply, and the results on the second group of questions are the reverse of those for the first two. Clearly, managers do not believe that developmental progress is reviewed by the organization, that the reward and recognition policies reinforce the training, or that the business impact of the development is assessed. What these results are saying is that organizations are getting it half-right, that the training is relevant and transferred to the job, but that they are not following through on the important second-stage issues. One of these questions raises the commonly articulated but nevertheless difficult issue of how to incorporate the results of training within the recognition and reward system. It would appear from this that the appraisal system, which might be expected to bring these two issues together, is not doing its job properly. The other two deal with an apparent inability to assess the results of training, which, as we noted earlier, is a difficult issue. One of these, the assessment of business impact, does however connect with the question reviewed in chapter 6 about the connection between business strategy and management development, which the same respondents expressed scepticism about. From these results, companies might be accused of not properly closing the loop as articulated in figure 7.1.

Before passing on to the practical aspects of training evaluation, it remains to be said that the same associations occur with this set of questions as did with the earlier ones in this chapter. The existence of a policy statement, a high priority and corporate responsibility for management development are all positively associated with high scores on these five questions. But there are also other interesting associations. Thus there are strong associations with a high score on the impact of management development, and also with two other aspects of process discussed in chapter 7, namely whether the development was linked to defined competencies, and whether development arose from a personal development plan. These latter two factors were said to be part of a 'strong' set of processes, and certainly in the setting of the five process outcomes in table 9.5 they are linked with what might be termed 'strong' outcomes.

▶ Approaches to Practical Evaluation of Management Development

In the chapter so far we have been talking about external research, including our own, into the impact of management development. But what do companies themselves do in this admittedly difficult area? This section examines this issue.

Evaluation models

One of the enduring models for assessing the impact of training is the four-levels evaluation proposed by Kirkpatrick (1958). These are the trainees' reaction, usually collected at the close of a training event; an assessment of learning via a follow-up questionnaire or focus group; impact on subsequent job performance, often reviewed at appraisal; and long-term impact on business, as indicated by such measures as customer feedback, productivity outcomes, attitude surveys and achieving organizational targets. This has been followed by many similar attempts to categorize and measure learning in the workplace. For

instance, a cyclical trainer-centred model for evaluating training interventions (Bramley 1991), a model which tries to take account of more
informal development typical of management learning (Easterby-Smith
1986), and a 'training-for-impact' model which emphasizes the need
for expected outcomes and interpretation of outcomes to be jointly
carried out by trainer, line manager and participant (Robinson and
Robinson 1989). More recently, Kearns and Miller (1993) have also
argued the need to specify bottom-line business objectives in advance
of training activities, helpfully changing the focus from outputs to
outcomes of training.

However, for all the texts and manuals explaining how to carry out
evaluation of training and development, most organizations admit
that investment in human resource development, and especially management development, is still largely an act of faith. Tamkin and Hillage
(1998) report an Industrial Society survey which found that two-thirds
of those questioned rated training evaluation as very important, yet
only a quarter were satisfied with the methods being used to evaluate
training. Frequently, feedback on the effectiveness of management development is not even gathered in the first place. The irony here is that,
though the scarcity of resources usually prompts the trigger for training,
this very scarcity often acts a constraint on the evaluation budget.

Even when evaluation data are available they are often ignored by
the organization concerned. In her book on evaluating the effects of
organizational change programmes, Legge (1984) gives three reasons
why the effects of such change programmes are not evaluated, and
these might equally apply to the outcomes of management development. First, the findings may be weak and/or difficult to attribute
accurately to a given management development 'intervention'. The
problem of measurement becomes more difficult further up the
occupational hierarchy: productivity for production workers is easier
to measure than for managers. The main difficulties lie in the area
of measurement – what is being measured over what period and how
to measure it – and causality – how to differentiate training as a cause
of an outcome which may appear to have many other explanations.
Secondly, evaluation research in organizational settings is likely to have
an inbuilt conservative bias. This is partly because the commissioning
of research itself tends to attach legitimacy to the planned changes
and their goals: the assumptions underlying the initiatives are not
usually questioned (an opportunity for double-loop learning), leading
to a less than radical stance. If the findings *are* at odds with what the
sponsors of the evaluation wanted to hear, they risk being ignored or
rationalized away. The difficulty is that those sponsoring the evaluation
are likely to be the same people who monopolize the resources to be
used for any future initiatives prompted by the results.

Finally, there is the difficulty of closing the loop and demonstrating the value to the business of training and development. Attempts have been made to evaluate the cost benefits of training activity, ranging from fairly sophisticated utility calculations (Smith 1992) to more broad-brush deductions: 'making some quite plausible assumptions some 20 years ago, I calculated that if a one-week residential training course increased a manager's performance by more than 0.5%, it was more profitable for the company to train them rather than not to train' (Everard 1991: 26). But in a sense such equations miss the point in several ways. First, 'Evaluation is about making value judgements as well as technical ones and it is about power, since action may involve, at the least, persuading others of the rightness of one's values first, through to imposing one's values onto them' (Fox 1989: 205). Second, such a method fails to identify the indirect costs of activities related to management development such as problem diagnosis, internal consultancy and *ad hoc* counselling. Third, a systems approach to auditing management development naturally leads to a focus upon inputs and outcomes, which inevitably diverts attention from the important management development processes which include unanticipated outcomes and informal, more covert episodes of learning (Woodall and Winstanley 1998).

Practical approaches to evaluation

More than two-thirds (70 per cent) of HRD managers in our telephone survey claimed that their organization undertook a regular review of management development activities. This compares with a mere 21 per cent of client managers who gave a high or very high rating in reply to the question: 'To what extent has the business impact of your development been assessed by the organization?' However, the HRD responses to the open-ended question as to how this was done varied widely, as table 9.6 shows.

It can be seen that formal, strategic reviews of management development were only referred to in a little over one-quarter of cases (28.1 per cent), although this increases to well over half when combined with other formal methods, including regular feedback mechanisms and other audits of training needs. The more standard means of reviewing management training (questionnaires, follow-up surveys and the like) only receive mentions by 15.6 per cent of the sample. This possibly suggests a justified scepticism as to their value in drawing sound conclusions about the effectiveness of management development activities. More informal methods are not inconsequential, and the responses indicate that an increasingly wide circle of stakeholders

Table 9.6 How are management development activities reviewed? (HRD managers n = 501)

	Mentions (%)
Formal processes	
Strategic plans, management development reviews, regular meetings	28.1
Appraisals, 360-degree feedback, annual reviews	15.6
Questionnaires, surveys, focus groups with trainees	14.1
Training needs analysis, audits, training plans	10.9
Informal processes	
Consultation with line managers, mentors, senior team	18.8
Consultation with training managers, training providers, internal consultants	7.8
Benchmarking, external consultants, customer discussions	4.7

(internal and external to the organization) is being consulted when evaluating development processes. If HRD managers stated that management development activities were not regularly reviewed, they were asked for reasons. The most common replies (33.3 per cent) were comments that this 'was planned for the future', 'not yet established', 'being reviewed' and 'soon to be set up because required by IiP'. As custodians of management development, these HRD managers might be predicted to put a positive gloss on whether and how such activities are assessed for their strategic effect. Yet a further 26 per cent were honest enough to admit that it was a low priority or that they were too busy, and 16.7 per cent preferred 'informal' or 'ongoing' approaches. All in all there is perhaps more happening in the arena of evaluation than anticipated and the methods of review are more diverse.

HRD managers revealed little systematic evaluation of management development, but most were able to refer to more pragmatic, informal assessments. When asked how they went about evaluating investment in management development, the following response from a management development director summed up those made by several case-study organizations: 'We don't really do it. It's too complex. [We] need people on the ground making judgements. We have comments sheets for specific programmes, but this is not about the bottom line. It's an act of faith to be honest. . . . Training days statistics don't mean very much. What I can say is that [management development] is more effective now because it's more focused on business need.' An example of this comes from the management development director at Inchcape describing the outcomes of a senior management development leadership programme: 'Assessment is at the anecdotal level at present. People have said that they have seen improvements, issues have been addressed. In some cases this has happened within the LP [Leadership Programme] by helping to remove the blockages that were dogging their conventional team meetings; these have been resolved and they have put in place a new business strategy and operating plans. Here we have a very tangible impact on the business.'

Conducting evaluation of management development actually comprises a set of choices, influenced by the values and goals of key stakeholders, as Guest and Peccei (1994) have shown in relation to auditing HRM more generally. An interesting approach to differing perspectives has been taken by Garavan et al. (1998). Although theirs was an exploratory study based on fairly small numbers, it sought the views of a range of stakeholders. One key differentiating issue was utilitarianism, espousing the view that development provision should be of immediate value to the organization and the province of senior and line managers, as contrasted to humanism, which emphasizes the priorities of the learner and the long-term contribution of development investment. A similar split occurred with interventionism, with individuals and unions believing that it was the organization's responsibility to develop its human resources, whereas senior managers and HR specialists believed individuals to have primary responsibility for their own development. Other such dichotomies existed between 'centralism' and 'decentralization', and 'traditionalism' and 'continuous development'. Major differences also existed in terms of the benchmarks used to evaluate development success. Senior managers wanted quantitative measures such as increased productivity and flexibility, and optional utilization of human resources. Line managers wanted development to contribute to cost savings within their area of responsibility. Development specialists placed some emphasis on quantitative measures, such as number of training days and enhanced performance, but also had qualitative concerns that development should be of high quality and relevant, and that it should facilitate change. Individual learners on the other hand were essentially concerned with the enhancement of their employability through the level of investment in their personal development, the need for certification and the range of competencies developed. In the context of these differences, evaluation is likely to be as much a political as a technical process. None of this comes as a surprise, but simply serves to underline the importance of taking a pluralist perspective, as discussed in chapter 2 (figure 2.1) when evaluating the impact of management development.

Throughout this book (and particularly in chapter 7) we have tried to give due emphasis to management development processes as well as management development programmes, and we have also deliberately sought to arrive at this pluralist interpretation of management development activities. This is perhaps nowhere more important than in the area of evaluation, so in this chapter we have tried to compare the views of those sponsoring and those participating in management development.

Conclusions

Research to date on the impact of management development leaves question marks against a number of issues. First, while there appears to be an increasing incidence of organizations taking more enlightened approaches to HRM generally and management development in particular, doubt remains as to whether these represent truly strategic interventions. Beaumont, for example, notes that if the key to strategic human resource management is the existence of a 'close, two-way relationship between business strategy or planning and HRM strategy or planning', research suggests that such a linkage rarely exists to any sizeable extent or depth across a wide range of organizations (Beaumont 1993: 4). On the basis of their research, Storey and Sisson (1993) also argue that, even in terms of efficiency, there is a 'massive gap' between rhetoric and reality when it comes to installing such key elements of strategic HRM as training and development, and the integration of human resource practices and business strategy. And a recent review of a range of different human resource initiatives being carried out in several organizations concluded that too often, specific and otherwise well-diagnosed HR initiatives were seen to founder because on the one hand they failed to mutually reinforce each other, and, on the other hand, they underestimated the depth of feeling or miscalculated the intentions and interests at shop-floor level (Mabey, Skinner and Clark 1998). If doubt remains about the strategic nature of HRM generally, then this begs the question of management development too. This, in large part, forms the research agenda of this chapter: to investigate the rationale for management development initiatives in order to tease out the extent to which they support the overall business strategy and are seen to be successful in achieving both corporate and personal objectives.

In summary, our findings highlight the fact that positive outcomes of management development investment, whether measured by perceived success in achieving objectives, perceived organizational impact, or personal satisfaction, can largely be attributed to the way organizations establish and maintain their management training and development processes. Particularly important in this regard is the commitment given by the company to management development activity, with policy statements, high priority, centralized management development systems and responsibility for management development being the key elements of this visible corporate commitment. However, there is strong evidence to suggest that personal satisfaction with management development is also likely to occur when the system and responsibility for management training activities are shared between the organization and the individuals concerned. As with other findings reported in earlier chapters, we found a considerable gap between what organizations think they are achieving through their management development provision (as perceived by HRD managers) and the 'consumer' view of MBA and client managers. However, the reassuring message is that improvements in the effectiveness of management development are not dependent on less controllable, external factors such as firm size, sector or growth patterns. Rather, the data strongly confirm that enhancing the outcomes of management development is in the hands of the organizations themselves, and the way they organize and prioritize their management development processes and systems.

This accords with more theoretical accounts in the HR literature. Mueller (1996) is one author who has tried to assess the relationship between the conventional, strategy-based approach to HRM and the resource-based approach. He argues that corporate success lies, as the resource-based theorists would maintain, in the deeply embedded and hard-to-imitate competencies – or 'social architectures' – that have developed slowly over time and encourage valuable processes of co-operation and learning and 'appropriation'. It is these resource-based aspects of organization, rather than the pervasive and fashionable emphasis upon codified strategic HRM practices, that make the real difference to organizational performance and account for the success of the small number of high-performing organizations. An implication of this proposition, and one reinforced by our analysis, is that any investigation of the effects of management development needs to explore the extent to which such policies and practices contribute to the maintenance and development of these embedded (but often implicit) social architectures.

Plainly, there is a need for more receiving-end research to get 'beneath the skin' of an organization and build our understanding of the purposes and meanings that people attach to management development experiences and activities with which they are involved. Methodologies which rely on inflexible research instruments leave little room for pursuing the unexpected and can take only limited account of context, whereas qualitative methods pay greater attention to interdependencies, settings and complexities of behaviour in organizations because they focus on 'naturally occurring, ordinary events in natural settings, so that we have a strong handle on what *real life* is like' (Miles and Huberman 1994: 10, italics in original). Our own research, reported here and in previous chapters, goes some way to meeting these criteria; for instance, extended telephone interviews allow many nuances to surface that a questionnaire would not, and the comparison of senior management views with those of middle managers, sometimes in the same organization, permits a vital receiving-end perspective to emerge. However, future research would need to adopt other qualitative methods in order to tease out the 'realities' of management development and its contribution as a strategic asset in UK organizations.

Managerial Careers in Relation to Development

INTRODUCTION

The purpose of this chapter is to examine the relationship between managerial careers and management development. As we saw in chapter 5, part of the demand by individuals for management development seems fuelled by career concerns, just as labour market changes have stimulated demand for development and qualifications to compete in the external labour market. Similarly, many organizations have sought to use different modes of development to facilitate different career patterns. Possibilities for conflict between individual and organizational aims may often arise, especially in terms of who 'owns' a managerial career and who is responsible for career development.

For these reasons, we need to explore careers from the perspective of both the individual and the organization. The chapter begins with an attempt to identify the current situation on careers and then proceeds to review the literature on career development from an individual perspective, and then that on organizational career management. This is followed by material relating to careers from our own surveys, with a particular focus on whether different career patterns in different kinds of organization can be linked to the policy framework on career and management development

			Mutual focus			
Organization-centred career management			manager-assisted career planning		Employee-centred individual career planning	
Corporate succession planning	Corporate talent inventories	Development centres	Manager– employee career discussions	Corporate seminars on organizational careers	Company-run career- planning workshops	Self-directed workbooks, CD ROMS and tapes

Figure 10.1 Spectrum of career development activities

– in particular, whether organizations which adopt a particular policy towards careers (such as taking responsibility for career development, career structures and succession planning) can be linked to the development of a 'strong' policy framework regarding management development. After this section we put forward a framework for understanding career development, based on the central model for the book of figure 2.2. A final section before the conclusion looks at the possible future direction of careers.

Career topics have often been studied in terms of specific areas of interest, such as vocational guidance and counselling for initial career choice or succession planning for senior managers. A common distinction is between approaches focused on the individual with their roots in individual psychology, often termed career-planning approaches, and approaches focused on organizational processes and strategies. These have their roots in organizational sociology and psychology, as well as in organizational behaviour and human resource management, and are often termed career management approaches. Career development is then seen as a spectrum, with career planning at one end and career management at the other, as presented in figure 10.1.

▶ The Current Situation on Careers

The actual situation on managerial careers is a matter of some disagreement, especially in Britain. In the USA, the workforce appears to be becoming increasingly 'market-driven', and now needs to be managed through offering 'new deals' based around enhancing employability and marketability rather than job security and career advancement within the company. Belton (1999: 1), drawing on a variety of sources, points out that, despite the apparently booming US economy, employee insecurity persists. Whilst anxiety about job security had lessened since its peak in 1997, it was three times higher than in the 1980–1 recession. Typical employees had changed jobs nine times before the age of 32, and among executives job insecurity had apparently increased in recent years, attributed to increased global competitiveness and technological advances. In some ways, job destruction appears nothing new (around 10–12 per cent of jobs have disappeared annually since 1945), but what appears to be new is its spread among white-collar, professional and managerial employees. More are experiencing job losses, fewer are leaving to take up better jobs, and many seem forced to take lower pay to find other jobs. Anxiety about job losses appears to have changed the employment relationship, with employees feeling less loyal to their companies and more responsible for developing their own skills. In 1995, 40 per cent of adults were participating in adult education classes, up from 32 per cent in 1991, mostly in work- or qualification-related programmes. Much of this demand appears to be driven by a need to enhance marketability, given the absence of job security.

The perceptions of managers in Britain seem to be very similar, as is exemplified by Benbow's (1995: 48) survey conclusions: 'A high proportion of respondents do not feel in control of their future career development. The pace of change over the past decade has shattered career and financial expectations, generating a need for individuals to re-examine many of the inherited wisdoms of the past. The demise of the job for life and the trend towards a wholly flexible employment market are clear examples of the extent to which new agendas are being set.' Arnold (1997) points to such features as increasing workloads for managers, delayering, downsizing, enhanced global competition, the greater use of team-based and project work, the growth of short-term contracts and part-time work, the need for continuous reskilling in the face of new technology, the rise of self-employment and teleworking, increasing pressure on pension schemes, and the greater diversity and age of the workforce as all changing the nature of jobs and careers.

In a summary of economic trends and their effects on the careers and psychological contracts of managers, Herriot and Pemberton (1995: 58) state that many organizations 'have shattered the old psychological relationship and failed to negotiate a new one'. Similarly, Adamson et al. (1998) argue that some UK organizations are now no longer talking in terms of opportunities for advancement or progression, but in terms of opportunities for enhancing marketability and employability. As Martin et al. (1999) point out, this identifies training, including management development, as an important variable in influencing perceptions of trust and contract violation, and consequently employee job satisfaction, commitment, motivation and performance. However, it is unclear to what extent UK companies have moved beyond a rhetoric of employability.

There is also a debate about the facts. Some commentators in the UK have argued, drawing, for example, on apparently 'objective' economic data showing job tenure to be not significantly different in 1995 than in 1975, that the traditional psychological contract built around job security and career is still alive and surprisingly well (Guest and Conway 1997; Guest 1997; Guest and Mackenzie Davey 1996). One of the issues we will examine later in the chapter is how far our survey data support either side in this debate. Before we move to this, however, it is desirable to review the various approaches to career analysis, starting with the individual perspective.

▶ Individual Career Development

Perhaps the most influential theory of managerial career development, based on research into practising managers, is provided by Schein (1978) who developed the concept of *career anchor* to identify a central area of an individual's occupational self-concept. This has three components: self-perceived talents/abilities, motives/needs, and attitudes/values. The career anchor is seen as guiding, constraining, stabilizing, and integrating a person's career, and the identification of a career anchor is seen as vital to effective career development. From a longitudinal study of MBA graduates, Schein identified five career anchors: technical-functional competence, managerial competence, security/stability, creativity, and autonomy/independence. Schein later added pure challenge, service/dedication, and lifestyle integration/balance, perhaps reflecting changes in career orientations in the 1980s and 1990s, especially the increasing participation of women in the workforce, the rise of dual-career families, and the growth of 'downshifting' in response to greater work demands and longer hours of work, particularly in managerial jobs. Knowledge of career anchors is viewed as helpful to organizations in placing, transferring and promoting people. For example, scientists and engineers committed to technical career anchors may not be able to rise very far without going into general management, which may create problems both for them and for the organization. Some organizations have responded to this by creating dual or multiple career ladders.

An alternative approach to individual career development focuses less on apparently stable career orientations and more on *developmental stages* or phases, each linked to age and each with its own specific concerns and issues. The management development implications of such stage theories are that career stage needs to be taken into account by organizations. Another way of looking at individual career development over time is to explore the process of making career or job changes or *transitions*, including cross-functional and international moves as well as changes of company or career field (Nicholson 1990). The frequency of managerial job change in the UK seems to be increasing, with changes of status, employer and function more common. Inkson (1995) has shown that such mobility has not been slowed by recent recessions, and now often involves declining status changes.

A further approach is based on the *boundaryless career* (Arthur 1994). Here people cross boundaries between organizations, departments, levels, functions and skill sets, either voluntarily or through organizational decisions. Boundaries are in any case becoming more fluid. Careers are seen as becoming increasingly independent of security and promotion, and increasingly less constrained by organizations. As Hall and Mirvis (1995: 277) put it, 'careers too are becoming more complex. We would argue that what we are seeing now . . . is a series of many shorter learning cycles over the span of a person's work-life . . . people's careers will become increasingly a succession of "mini-stages" . . . as they move in and out of various product areas, technologies, functions, organisations and other work environments'.

Recent discussions of the apparently rapidly changing context of organizational careers have led researchers to revise traditional models and accounts of individual career development to take account of new economic and organizational contexts. This has brought into popularity the concept of the *psychological contract* (e.g. Herriot and Pemberton 1995, 1996; Rousseau 1995). This term, defined by Robinson and Rousseau (1994: 246) as 'an individual's belief regarding the terms and conditions of a reciprocal exchange agreement between that focal person and another party', has proved useful in exploring individual responses to the changing organizational context of careers, and so may provide a bridge between the career-planning and career management literatures. Herriot and Pemberton (1995) acknowledge that there cannot be a return to the old relational, employment security contract; new deals must be negotiated, monitored and renegotiated in an explicit manner and with mutuality with respect to the existence and terms of the contract. They identify three potentially useful types of contract: the lifestyle contract (e.g. flexible work), the autonomy contract (for those with technical/functional or autonomy career anchors), and the development contract (for core employees prepared to be generalists).

The psychological contract is very often regarded as a helpful way of analysing managers' responses to this changing career context. In some ways, interest in this concept parallels a wider interest in the rise of a *contract culture* in management and HRM more widely. The concept was first developed by Schein (1978) in terms of the mutual perceptions of the individual employee and the organization of the obligations implied in the relationship between them. But Arnold (1997) points out that if a contract is purely perceptual it is not a contract at all, as there is no formal or informal agreement with the other party. It is also unclear as to how an 'organization', composed of competing interest groups and parties, can be a party to a psychological contract.

A common theme in the North American literature in particular has been that the psychological contract is moving from a focus on employment security towards one based on employability security, and that as a consequence individuals need to display and develop *career resilience* (Waterman et al. 1994) or *career self-reliance* (e.g. Bridges 1998). The old managerial contract is often depicted as offering employment security in the context of a paternalistic, dependent relationship. The new transactional contract is seen as emerging, rather than fully fledged, and has often been unilaterally imposed by the company. Changes of function, employer, sector and country have become ever more frequent and necessary, hence the boundaryless career. The changing nature of work and employment in contemporary industrial societies is often seen as advancing this change of contract, as 'job shift' (Bridges 1998) is held to accompany the rise of a 'jobless society'. This is seen in terms of a decline in the importance of job hierarchies, descriptions, and matrices in the face of a growth in project-based work, portfolio careers and new opportunities (such as consultancy, contract work and self-employment) outside the conventional job matrix. Work still needs to be done, but it no longer comes in job-sized chunks, nor is it bundled up into 'jobs'.

An important dimension in this conception of the changing nature of careers and contracts is *flexibility*. Individuals are often considered to need to display ever more personal 'flexibility' in their jobs and careers. 'Resilient' employees will show flexibility in return for challenging work, development opportunities and career-planning support (e.g. Waterman et al. 1994). They will move quickly to keep pace with change, be dedicated to continuous learning and take ownership of their own career management. Such employees will stay connected and well networked, be flexible, and show commitment to life-long learning, not only in their own interests but also in the interests of their organization.

▶ Organizational Career Management Strategies

In this section we turn to an examination of organizational career management practices, using labour market segmentation theory and theories of corporate strategy and HR systems. A useful framework linking career systems and HR strategies is provided by Miles and

Snow (1978), and it is this framework which will be adopted here. Their approach is related to that of Sonnenfeld et al. (1988) which was introduced in chapter 2 and which linked corporate strategies to the way organizations go about recruiting and promoting people (in particular, managers and executives) and to the assessment criteria used to make placement decisions, identifying four basic types: clubs, academies, baseball teams, and fortresses.

Miles and Snow (1978) have demonstrated how human resource systems can support, and even drive, an organization's business strategy. They also identify four basic organizational types, termed prospectors, defenders, analysers, and reactors. Prospectors seek to locate and exploit new opportunities, develop new products and create new markets. Their HR systems must therefore locate, recruit, develop and retain technical experts who are creative and independent. They particularly emphasize innovation and flexibility. They are likely to recruit extensively in the primary external labour market for employees with specialized skills. Defenders tend to have narrow and relatively stable product/market domains, which they seek to protect through efficient production, strong control mechanisms and continuity and reliability. Their human resource systems must therefore seek to recruit, develop and retain long-term, loyal members high in commitment to the organization. They are likely to rely heavily on an internal labour market strategy, seeking to develop employees with flexible but specific skills. Analysers fall between the first two groups, taking fewer risks than prospectors but excelling in the delivery of new products and services. Their HR systems need to recruit and develop people who take moderate risks but who also remain loyal to the organization. They are likely also to rely on an internal labour market strategy, but with some recruitment of external specialists. Reactors are firms which display little ability to adapt to their environment. Their human resource systems often try to dispense with staff through lay-offs, discharges, early retirements and outplacements, whilst at the same time engaging in a limited recruitment of 'turnaround' experts. They may make heavy use of the external labour market for temporary and casual staff, with limited use of the internal labour market. In the Miles and Snow typology, as with Sonnenfeld et al., labour market segmentation is seen as a crucial factor in analysing organizational career practices.

A number of authors have provided analyses of career development practices used by organizations (e.g. Bowen and Hall 1977; London and Stumpf 1982). These practices range across the spectrum depicted in figure 10.1, from career planning to career management. Baruch and Peiperl (1997) developed a list of 17 career management practices, using factor analysis to explore how these various practices cluster together. Five factors emerged, as already briefly noted in chapter 7, as part of performance review. These were labelled 'basic' (e.g. elementary practices such as job posting, formal education, pre-retirement programmes, lateral moves), 'active planning' (forward-looking, proactive practices such as career-orientated appraisals, supervisor career counselling, career counselling, and succession planning), 'active management' (bi-directional, information-gathering practices such as assessment centres, formal mentoring, and career workshops), 'formal' (uni-directional, organizational provision of information through written personal career planning, dual career ladders and books/pamphlets on career issues) and 'multidirectional' (increasing options for feedback and development through peer appraisal and upward appraisal). From their analysis they then proposed a two-dimensional model of career practices, involving level of sophistication of the practice and level of involvement by the organization. They also reported on several case-study companies whose career development practices focus on different clusters. Building generalist managers through using lateral moves, succession planning and hierarchical performance appraisals was most emphasized.

In spite of the wide range of approaches to the nature of careers, there is a general consensus that individuals now need to participate more in the management of their own careers, and that employees need to take greater personal responsibility for their own career development. If this is the case, then we might expect to see organizations hand over more responsibility to employees to manage their own careers; to see widespread and increasing use of 'career-planning' techniques; and correspondingly limited and declining use of 'career management' techniques like succession planning. Alternatively, we might expect to see a growth and development of a middle position, representing a recognition of the need for a mutual focus and for an individual–organizational partnership in career development. We now explore to what extent the evidence from the surveys supports these contentions.

▶ Evidence from the Surveys

In analysing the contributions of the surveys, two of them, the larger company survey and the MBA graduate survey, have interesting evidence about the nature of managerial careers. The evidence can in turn be split into that about processes within organizations, and that to do with managerial career patterns. There were three main questions which were common to both the surveys, and we examine their implications in the three tables following.

Table 10.1 Existence of planned career structure

HRD managers (%) (n = 501)		MBAs (%) (n = 450)	
Yes for all	32	Yes	19
Yes for some	5		
No	63	No	80

Table 10.1 asks whether there is a planned career structure. We did not define precisely what was meant by a planned career structure, but took it to mean one where it is possible for managers to discuss career development with the organization, and where career patterns can be perceived in the management cadre. As can be seen, the outstanding feature is that both groups report a low incidence of planned career structure, with the MBAs considerably lower than the company respondents, even though their average size of company was larger. The difference can perhaps partly be explained by the HRD managers knowing more about the issue, but the pattern of MBAs having a less positive response holds across most questions. There are, however, the same clear associations with a planned structure for both groups: a written statement, high priority and company responsibility for management development, and to some extent larger organizations, but even in the largest category the percentage was only 36 for the HRD managers and 26 for the MBAs. A planned career structure is one of the most likely indicators of an internal labour market for managers, and the fact that it is relatively rare suggests that the internal labour market is somewhat rare as well, although as we shall see below, there are some counter-indications.

The second question asked of both groups was on a career management issue, namely whether there was succession planning whereby existing managers were identified to succeed outgoing/retiring senior managers. The results are shown in table 10.2. The differences between the two groups on this answer are much larger than we have

Table 10.2 Existence of succession planning

	HRD managers (%) (n = 501)	MBAs (%) (n = 450)
Yes	60	26
No	40	60
Don't know/not stated	1	14

seen for any previous question. It should not be too surprising to find succession planning in an organization; indeed it might be considered irresponsible not to have some sort of contingency plan in the event that a key manager disappears for whatever reason at short notice. But part of the explanation must also lie in a follow-up question for the HRD managers, asking whether succession planning was a formal or an informal process: 55 per cent reported that it was an informal process, and it is therefore understandable that managers not involved in this area would not be aware of it. There was an unusually high number of don't know/not stated in the MBAs' answers to this question, which may indicate a degree of general uncertainty. Taking only the formal answers would reduce the HRD managers responses to the 'normal' relationship with the MBAs. Nevertheless, it might have been expected that managers generally would be aware even of informal practice, which the MBAs' answers do not suggest. A related issue asked only of the companies was whether different groups of managers were treated differently. One might argue that a key career management tool is to identify high-potential managers and put them on a 'fast track' for more intensive development: 51 per cent of respondents said they did, whereas 49 per cent did not, with a size effect meaning that it was more common in larger companies.

The third question was about whether managerial appointments were for a career or for the specific job. This also has an implication for the existence of an internal labour market. The answers are given in table 10.3. Both sets of answers indicate an overwhelming intention to appoint only for the specific job, with only one in five companies appointing for a career. Interestingly, among the MBAs the largest grouping reported a lower percentage of career-based appointments. The two sets of respondents might, however, have had different attitudes to the question. While the company respondents were thinking about the company's intentions, the MBAs might also have had their own intentions in mind, seeing the job as all they intended to stay for. This would help to endorse the concept of the boundaryless, resilient career mentioned above, and do so as something desirable rather than being forced into it. The company perspective is interesting, since

Table 10.3 Appointment for job or career

	HRD managers (%) (n = 501)	MBAs (%) (n = 450)
Mainly for a job	76	83
Mainly for a career	20	14
Both	3	2

Table 10.4 Filling vacated managerial positions (HRD managers %, n = 501)

No. of vacancies	Internal promotion	External recruitment	Absorption by others
0–30	20	47	75
31–60	51	40	18
61–100	25	7	1
Not stated	5	5	5

appointment for a career might be thought to be a key indicator of an internal labour market. In both groups, moreover, while there is the usual association whereby appointment for a career is linked with variables such as high priority and company responsibility for management development, the extent of this is not as marked as with some other questions.

This issue of the company labour market is taken up even more directly in two other process questions, both only asked of the company representatives. The first of these asked directly from where the company's management stock was recruited; growing them internally, the external labour market, and new graduate recruits. Perhaps not unexpectedly, the great majority of organizations recruited from both internal (89 per cent) and external (77 per cent) sources, while 34 per cent took new graduate recruits. The response to the second question in this area is shown in table 10.4. The question asked what happened when managerial positions were vacated; three alternatives were offered, and respondents were asked what proportion of vacancies had been filled by each of the three methods over the last two or three years. The results indicate that a higher proportion are internally promoted, but that external recruitment is also widely used, and that while absorption by other managers is the least common, it is by no means uncommon; one of our case studies noted that 60 per cent of its vacated management positions were treated in this way, which must be exceptional.

So far we have been talking about organizational processes, but we also obtained some information about the career mobility of managers. An important indicator from the organizational perspective was how many managers spent most of their careers in the one organization, and this is illustrated in table 10.5. These figures make for interesting reading, and indicate that across the board about a third of companies have kept more than three-fifths of their managers for most of their careers. Moreover, although there is relatively little difference between the size groups, if anything it is the smallest grouping which has kept fewer than the others, with the biggest grouping (which is mainly

Table 10.5 HRD managers spending most of their career in the same organization by organization size (%, n = 501)

% of managers	All	100–299	300–499	500–999	1,000–4,999	5,000+
0–30	36	40	44	33	40	23
31–60	28	33	14	28	26	32
61–100	32	23	39	33	31	30
Not stated	5	3	3	5	4	13

where the debate about downsizing and restructuring has taken place), also keeping a low proportion. Admittedly these must be rough estimates, but they do indicate that there have still been many managers who spend most of their careers in one organization. However, it must also be accepted that this is a view of the existing stock of managers looking to the past, and that the present and future may not be the same. At the very least, the average length of career seems likely to have dropped as more managers have retired before achieving the traditional retirement age of 65.

The potential difference between the past and the future may be highlighted by a further question which asked how long, upon promotion or recruitment, a manager would be expected to stay with the organization. In other words it asked about the flow of managers in the future. Table 10.6 provides the data. The pattern here is rather different to that in table 10.5, and more in keeping with the concept of fragmented, portfolio careers. Here almost half of the respondents expected managers to stay only five years or less, while about a quarter each expected them to stay between six and 10 years and longer than this. If organizations expect managers to stay only a relatively short time, it may be difficult for them to take a long-term, planned view of their career and may make them focus on job-related training. There are few significant differences between the size categories,

Table 10.6 Expectation of staying with organization by organization size (%)

	All	100–299	300–499	500–999	1,000–4,999	5,000+
Less than 3 years	5	6	5	6	3	2
3–5 years	40	41	46	39	37	38
6–10 years	23	24	17	25	28	22
More than 11 years	26	28	25	29	24	23
Not stated	6	2	6	2	7	14

Table 10.7 Number of previous employers by size of current employer (MBAs %, n = 450)

	All	1–99	100–999	1,000–4,999	5,000+
None	4	1	–	5	6
1	17	17	11	20	18
2	21	13	29	22	21
3	20	21	17	20	20
4	16	19	11	12	18
5	10	7	16	10	7
More than 5	13	20	16	11	10

although in this question, as with the previous one, there was quite a high percentage of the largest grouping who did not answer the question. It was also noticeable that in this question, as with several others dealing with career patterns, there are few of the differentiating influences of management development policy variables.

And what about the managers? What did they report about their careers? Table 10.7 indicates how many previous employers the MBA graduates had had. Only 4 per cent had worked with their present employer for the whole of their career; respondents had served on average in 4.2 organizations, including their present employer. A comparison is with Kotter's (1995) Harvard MBA graduates, who had served on average in 3.3 companies between 1974 and 1992, while his 'leaders' amongst the class had served in only 2.6. This seems to indicate a higher level of mobility amongst MBAs in Britain than the US, not what many people would have surmised. Many of the British group had crossed size and sector categories; there is not only mobility between employers but also between sectors and size groups. There was an interesting extent to which the MBAs had experience of different size categories: 7 per cent had been self-employed but were no longer so; 34 per cent had worked for businesses with under 100 employees, and 38 per cent for those in the 100–999 medium-sized category, compared with 16 and 18 per cent currently in those categories. Similarly, 55 per cent had at one time worked in the public sector, even though the vast majority now work in the private sector. The overall picture is not just moving from one large company to another, but more complicated than that. In contrast to other issues, mobility was not linked to policy or size variables.

Another pair of questions in this area asked the MBAs whether they anticipated a change of employer or a change of level within the same

Table 10.8 Anticipated change of employer by priority (MBAs %, n = 450)

	All	High priority (7–10)	Mid-priority (5–6)	Low priority (1–4)
Yes	50	36	54	55
No	49	62	45	44
Not stated	1	1	1	1

Table 10.9 Change of level anticipated by priority (MBAs %, n = 450)

	All	High priority (1–7)	Mid-priority (5–6)	Low priority (1–4)
Anticipated	57	57	58	56
Not anticipated	42	42	41	43

organization, both in the foreseeable future. Tables 10.8 and 10.9 are shown together for comparative purposes. The implications of table 10.8 are interesting in their own right and in relation to table 10.9. Half of the MBAs anticipated a change of employer, but as the relationship with priority shows, the percentage is considerably less where the employer gives a high priority to management development. It may be that high priority is a proxy for other things, such as an internal labour market and an organizationally planned career; alternatively, it may be important in its own right, namely that where there is a high priority managers value management development so much that they do not want to leave. By contrast, table 10.9 is significant for what it does not show. Although about the same proportion felt they were likely to move within the organization, there is no association with any of the normally differentiating variables.

A final question deals with attitude rather than process or career patterns. We asked the companies whether responsibility for career development lay with the organization or the individual, with a 1–10 scale where individual responsibility lay at the low end and company responsibility at the high end. The results are shown in table 10.10. Of all the questions we asked throughout the surveys, this one showed the highest percentage taking the middle ground. Although the companies clearly did not see career development as mainly their responsibility, as perhaps used to be the case when large companies had strongly defined internal labour markets and career structures, nor did they see it as primarily the responsibility of the individual alone. Only 2 per cent in each case suggested that individuals or

Table 10.10 Responsibility for career development by impact of management development

	All (%)	Impact of management development (%)		
		High	Medium	Low
Primarily manager's responsibility (1–4)	26	22	25	43
Balance of responsibility (5–6)	57	56	59	52
Primarily company's responsibility (7–10)	17	19	17	4
Mean	5.04	5.28	5.09	4.23

companies were the prime movers in this area to the extent of giving a score of 1 or 10. There was very little variation by the policy variables in this pattern of results, and organizational size failed to make a difference. However, as the table indicates, there was a difference in the association with the impact of management development. It is also instructive to compare responsibility for career development with that for management development. Again, there was a tendency, if not so marked, to report in the middle ground but the balance of responsibility for management development fell on the company side (mean 5.71), so it appears that individuals are seen as having more responsibility for career development than for management development.

So what conclusions can be drawn from these survey results? There are pointers in two separate directions, towards a fragmented career, and towards a more stable one within the organization. On the one hand, three-quarters of the companies and even more of the MBAs noted that appointments were more for the job than a career; organizations do not expect their managers to stay for anything like a career, with half thinking the period will be five years or less; and half the managers expect to leave in the foreseeable future. On the other hand there are many organizations where managers have spent the majority of their careers; organizations accept at least an equal share of responsibility for career development; a considerable majority of organizations do have succession planning; and the internal labour market generally fills a higher percentage of vacancies than external recruitment. On these data, we would argue that the argument about the end of career is overstated in the sense that companies are still very concerned about their managers, whilst accepting that there is substantial mobility on the part of the managers and also that there are several features which indicate a short-term view on the part of companies.

And what are the conclusions to be drawn from our results in respect of the wider literature about careers as reviewed earlier in the chapter? Our surveys do not suggest that the extreme view that the 'career is dead' can be supported. If this was accurate we might have expected the following to be reported:

1. a decline in the use of career management techniques, alongside a rise in the use of career-planning techniques, as depicted in figure 10.1;
2. a decline in those features characteristic of 'relational' or 'employment security' contracts, such as long-term planning and diffuse obligations;
3. a rise in those features associated with 'transactional' or 'employability' contracts, such as short time horizons and specific obligations;
4. a rise in the behavioural characteristic of 'career resilience';
5. a rise in 'cellular' or 'protean' career behaviours, with the individual, not the organization, taking responsibility for career development. (Allred et al. 1996)

The MBAs clearly seem resilient in their commitment to continuous professional development; clearly networked in their membership of professional associations; and career resilient in their commitment to life-long learning. However, there is also some indication that they have not turned their backs entirely on organizational support in a purely 'cellular' or 'transactional' way. They still see the value of in-company training, albeit having a low opinion of what they have experienced. There is some indication that they see career development as moving towards the middle position in figure 10.1, where responsibility for career development is shared between employee and employer. We might characterize this position as a 'partnership' model, and infer that the psychological contract of the MBA graduate respondents includes the provision of in-company training.

Taking the survey results in relation to the literature, these findings seem to support the contention that careers are changing towards a market-driven focus. There seems to be much evidence of career planning, of career-resilient behaviours, of transactional contracts, of the market-driven nature of career development, of the search for employability, and of 'boundaryless' careers. However, a substantial minority also report being appointed for a career, of staying with their employer, of remaining at the same level, and also report the existence of planned career structures and succession-planning programmes. These features of more 'relational' contracts and of career management by the company seem particularly marked where the company is reported as having a 'strong' management development policy.

▶ A Framework for Understanding Career Development

In figure 2.2, a model of management development was presented, identifying the context (internal and external environmental inputs), management development policy, management development practice (process and outputs) and management development impact (outcomes). Figure 10.2 presents a version of this model, with specific

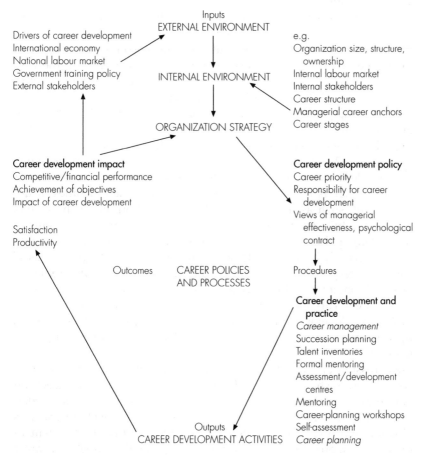

Figure 10.2 A model of managerial career development

reference to career development issues. Career development policy is here seen as influenced by inputs from the internal and external environments. Building on the earlier analyses, this is seen as influenced by corporate strategy (for example, prospect, analyse, defend, react). A major distinction here is between organizations that develop a 'strong' policy and those that develop a 'weak' one. Earlier analyses identified elements of a 'strong' policy: written policy, giving priority to development, taking responsibility for it. Here we can extend this analysis to include career issues, and propose that a 'strong' policy may include the offer of more 'relational' contracts and internal labour market and career management opportunities (probably emphasizing basic, formal, and active planning activities). Such strong policies seem to be associated with defenders and analysers, though analysers may use a hybrid, 'partnership' model with greater use of active management activities.

In contrast, organizations with 'weak' policies may be reactors, but may also be prospectors, making heavy use of the external labour market, offering transactional contracts, and encouraging employees to engage in individual career-planning with less support in the way of career management (except perhaps from 'multidirectional' activities such as 360-degree feedback and peer appraisal).

Figure 10.3 presents a framework for exploring these links between organization type, business strategy, HR strategy, career type, psychological contract, development policy, and career anchors.

Figure 10.2 postulates that career development procedures (such as those depicted in figure 10.1) determine the outputs of career development, such as how much is undertaken, and the outcomes of development, such as its impact on the organization. From the results reported in this chapter, and those reported in appendix 2, it seems as if a 'strong' policy is associated with positive impacts and outcomes.

In terms of the model depicted in figure 10.2, it appears as if company responsibility for career development is highly predictive of development activities having a positive impact on the organization. Career variables also predicted whether the organization gave priority to development, especially the presence of career structures, upward progress, and the existence of fast-track career management systems.

Regression analysis (appendix 2) shows that the policy variables contribute much more strongly than external or internal structural variables or career variables to explaining variance, in that order. Interestingly, company responsibility for career development was also strongly predictive of positive impact and the achievement of development objectives. However, the career variables cluster of career structure, upward progress, and existence of fast-track programmes

Type	Business strategy	HR strategy	Career type	Contract	Anchor	Cluster	Focus	Development policy
Defender	Small no. of stable products	Make: promote and develop from internal labour market	Club	Relational	Security/stability Lifestyle General managerial Service/dedication	Basic, formal Active planning	Career management	Strong
Prospector	First to market	Buy: hire expertise as needed from external labour market	Baseball team	Transactional	Technical/functional Entrepreneurial/creativity Challenge Autonomy/independence	Multidirectional	Career planning	Weak
Analyser	Blend of above	Blend of above	Academy	Both, differentiated	General managerial Technical/functional Challenge	Active management Active planning Multidirectional	Mutual	Strong but differentiated
Reactor	Inconsistent hybrid	Inconsistent hybrid	Fortress	Inconsistent hybrid	Challenge	Formal basic	Unclear	Weak

Figure 10.3 Psychological contract types, organizational strategies, management development policy and career types

Source: adapted from Miles and Snow 1978; Sonnenfeld et al. 1988; Rousseau 1995; Baruch and Peiperl 2000.

did not prove to be significant in most of our regression analyses compared with the policy cluster.

Many UK managers seem to be taking responsibility for their own career development in ways resonant of 'transactional', 'cellular' and 'resilient' managers, as the MBA graduate study shows, especially in their commitment to career-planning and to continuous professional development and networking. This has not, however, meant that organizations have simply abandoned responsibility for career development. Iles (1997) argues in favour of 'sustainable' career development, where fostering career resilience is seen as in the interests of both organization and employee. Here, partnership between the parties involves commitments and entitlements on both sides. These might include individuals offering high performance, life-long learning, flexibility and commitment in return for development, challenge, and enhanced marketability and employability. The organization may therefore need to provide continuing career support in the form of opportunities for self-assessment, benchmarking of skills, and continuous development, as well as lateral and other moves, communication on strategic direction and changes, the training of managers as career coaches and counsellors, and the provision of career and learning resource centres. Rather than seeing a move away from purely 'relational' towards purely 'transactional' contracts, we may see the emergence of a diversity of contracts, mixing transactional elements (such as high pay for high performance, the assessment of goals and the achievement of targets) alongside 'relational' aspects, such as commitment to internal labour markets and long-term development.

This analysis of career strategies suggests that the mix of practices depicted in figure 10.1 will vary with the organizational strategy and management development policy of the organization. Further research will be necessary to test this, as well as what influences policy choice.

▶ The Future Direction of Managerial Careers

There has recently been much interest in knowledge management as the global economy becomes increasingly knowledge-driven (e.g. Leadbeater 1999), but less attention has been given to the implications of this for managerial careers. Whilst there has been recognition of the implications of developing cultures that encourage information-sharing (Scarbrough et al. 1999), less attention has been paid to career issues.

As organizations seek to develop new sources of competitive advantage based around knowledge creation and management, they will seek knowledge outside the company through networks. Management of the knowledge supply chain may become more important than labour supply (Leadbeater 1999), with implications for employment, as the kinds of psychological contracts used to secure knowledge may be very different from those used to secure labour. Self-employment and portfolio careers may become more common, with organizations increasingly becoming cellular coalitions of self-employed knowledge workers. The increasingly self-managed nature of work, the need to consider other forms of reward, such as equity pay, as workers become more entrepreneurial, and recognition of knowledge as a form of personal 'equity' may lead to training being seen as an investment in knowledge creation and knowledge workers being offered a direct stake in the organization (e.g. Scarbrough et al. 1999). Careers may become an HR strategy for integrating and sharing knowledge, as people transfer between jobs, functions and organizations.

It is likely that different organizations will pursue different strategies (figure 10.3). Following from Sonnenfeld et al. (1988), in baseball teams, knowledge management may be seen more as a way of servicing the knowledge needs of star performers, whereas in clubs there may be greater emphasis on group contribution, the development of systems for codifying and disseminating collective knowledge, and emphasis on translating knowledge into collective assets. Managerial careers may come to resemble those of performing artists, where individuals with distinctive contributions come together to work on short-term projects. Parties will share an interest in effective collaboration, the long-term management of reputation, image, and visibility, and the development of distinctive portfolios. Perhaps concepts like trust, teamwork and professional commitment will grow in importance as organizational commitment and loyalty decline, with organizations resembling collections of fluid projects.

Not much empirical work has addressed this issue (e.g. Jackson et al. 1998; Hirsch and Jackson 1996). For performers in particular, a variety of skills are necessary: networking, flexibility, versatility, managing a variety of work roles, working outside the profession, continuous professional development, perseverance, resilience, entrepreneurial skills, the need for good agents, the importance of reputation, and time management skills all seem important determinants of career success.

One of the strongest statements that managerial careers will become increasingly 'boundaryless' and require a similar range of skills to performers is provided by Allred et al. (1996). They argue that organizational form has always driven managerial careers, and that organization structure has dictated core managerial competencies. Different structures require different competencies, now including commercial, self-governing and collaborative as well as technical skills. Functional organizations with primarily technical/specialist managerial careers have given way to divisional structures requiring commercial competencies and career paths. The evolving network form of organization (firms linking to provide the critical expertise needed for specific projects, internal or external partners used at various points of the value chain, and suppliers embraced as full partners) is seen as also requiring collaborative skills, such as referral, partnering, and relationship management skills.

Careers in network organizations require management across flat, multi-company partnerships rather than long climbs up steep corporate hierarchies. Careers in the twenty-first century may no longer involve hierarchies, but cellular organizations more akin to minimalist, professional service organizations. Here, the organization acts not as employer but as facilitator, whilst members take full charge of their own careers. As organizations increasingly adopt or encounter cellular structures, managers and professionals become team cells, responsible for a range of activities, especially the development of leadership and self-governance skills.

Individuals may increasingly control their own careers, with limited assistance from and reliance on organizations. Knowledge-based technical speciality, cross-functional and international experience, collaborative leadership, self-management (including career-planning and time management), continuous learning and personal traits such as flexibility, integrity and trustworthiness will be key attributes of successful managerial careers in cellular organizations. Managerial careers will increasingly be seen as do-it-yourself projects: organizations of the future will be less employers and more tools to advance careers.

However, our surveys show that though there are glimmerings of such career strategies, especially in our MBA graduate sample, many organizations remain committed to career management responsibilities. A diversity of strategies may emerge, in part driven by diverse corporate strategies and differentiated by labour market segmentation. We may not be seeing the end of the career, but the beginning of a multiplicity of career paths and strategies.

Conclusions

Figure 10.2 presented a framework for understanding managerial career development in organizations, adapted from the general framework for understanding management development discussed in figure 2.2. It puts forward a number of testable propositions which can guide further research in this area; not all of these have been tested in the current round of surveys. The framework hypothesizes that organizational strategies (and in particular, as far as this chapter is concerned, career-development policies) are shaped by the external and internal environment of the organization. In particular, external factors like government policy, the national and international economy, and the national and regional labour market will influence career paths and strategies, whereas internal factors such as whether the organization operates an internal labour market or whether it adopts a planned career structure will also drive career policies (as will the kinds of career anchors managers have, and at what career stages they are).

The framework further asserts that career development policy (in particular, what priority is given to career development, what responsibility the organization assumes for it, and what psychological contracts are offered) will in turn influence what career development practices and procedures are employed (an organization with a 'strong' career development policy is likely to take responsibility, give high priority, and express it in written form, as well as offer more 'relational' contracts, succession-planning and planned career structures, and perhaps also attracting, selecting and retaining managers with particular career anchors, as figure 10.3 shows).

In turn, the kind of policy adopted is likely to influence the outputs of career development practice (an organization with a 'strong' policy is likely to carry out more of the activities across the whole spectrum depicted in figure 10.1; one with a 'weak' policy may do much less, or restrict itself to activities on the right-hand side of figure 10.1, merely encouraging individual career-planning). In turn, output is likely to influence satisfaction with career development and positive assessments of its success and impact on the organization.

However, though there is evidence in the regression analyses discussed in appendix 2 that, in general, 'strong' development policies are associated with high levels of development, high levels of satisfaction with it, and positive assessments of impact, the career-specific relationships have yet to be fully tested (though taking responsibility for career development was predictive of positive impacts). Though the 'policy' variables, rather than the internal or external environment variables, seemed most strongly predictive of output and outcome, what determines a 'strong' or 'weak' policy remains to be investigated. Figure 10.3 suggests that the labour market segmentation and strategic type are likely to be associated with 'strong' or 'weak' career policies. Organizations operating a managerial labour market (for example, the clubs in Sonnenfeld et al.'s (1988) typology) are more likely to develop a 'strong' policy; those operating an external labour market (for example baseball teams) a 'weak' one. Both kinds of organization appear to be represented in our sample; but increasingly former 'clubs' are engaging in some recruitment externally (even, for example, the Civil Service), whilst some baseball teams are increasingly operating an internal market, with succession-planning and planned career structures. This suggests the growth of a 'partnership' model, with a mutual focus (the midpoint of figure 10.1), and indeed many organizations in our sample did appear to be operating career-development systems which reflected this mutual focus and joint position of responsibility between individual and organization – perhaps a position closest to the 'academy' position in figure 10.3.

However, the rise in importance of knowledge management may change things yet again, with a greater focus in some organizations on acquiring knowledge from the external knowledge market rather than the labour market (for example, not necessarily employing knowledge workers as direct employees but as suppliers, consultants or partners in networking). Other organizations may attempt to build and retain knowledge in individuals and teams as well as in databases and documents (for example, clubs).

This also raises the issue of career anchors, regarded as an aspect of the internal environment in figure 10.2 and related to organizational type in figure 10.3. It is likely that, in many sectors, employees with technical/functional, autonomy/independence, security/stability or entrepreneurial career anchors felt drawn to pursue general managerial careers in the 1980s, given the increasing disparity between rewards allocated to those pursuing general management as opposed to technical/functional careers. The replacement of a professional/departmental ethos in central and local government and even in the health service by a corporate/managerial ethos, and the increasingly felt insecurity of professional and managerial employment may have also threatened those whose anchor lay in other than general management. The increasing adoption of 'presenteeism' and the practice of working long hours in British managerial cultures (like the US, but unlike continental Europe) now threatens those with 'lifestyle' career anchors, though the use of 'downshifting' to less stressed, but perhaps lower-paid, jobs or moves into self-employment by some groups of managers, suggests a reaction against this. Those with security/stability or 'service' anchors may find their preferred career options under threat, both, for example, in the financial services and utilities sectors and in the public sector as 'managerialism' has grown in importance. This suggests both that those with career anchors other than general management may find that their preferred career anchors are unobtainable, and that there may well be a mismatch between individual and organizational aspirations to career development. However, it may also be that the increasing importance of knowledge management may not only favour those with entrepreneurial/creative career anchors, but also raise the aspirations of those seeking to pursue technical/functional careers, as technical/specialist knowledge, expertise and competence become once again highly valued and marketable within both internal and external knowledge markets. Delayering, the growth of project work, and the rise in portfolio careers may also all impact negatively on those with general managerial anchors, and suit those with challenge, autonomy or lifestyle anchors. Those with 'security/stability' anchors, however, are increasingly likely to feel under threat from the rise of 'transactional' contracts and the stress on employability. Protean or boundaryless careers are likely to appeal more to those with technical/functional, lifestyle, entrepreneurial, challenge and autonomy anchors, and less to those with general managerial or security/stability anchors. So, as well as diversity of career management strategies, we may also be witnessing the emergence of a variety of career anchors, and paths at the individual level as well.

11

Management Development in Small Businesses

INTRODUCTION

Management development literature and practice are very firmly rooted in the culture of large organizations, and indeed, the model we have developed in figure 2.2 to explain the system of management development also appears to share a large-organization perspective. Yet the vast majority of firms in Britain, Europe and elsewhere employ fewer than 50 people. We now need to see whether the model is useful in improving our understanding of management development in small firms. To understand what management development practices and issues discussed in this book mean in the context of small organizations, we need to have very clear ideas on the overall purpose of management development in the sector and, indeed, on the nature of small firms and how they may differ from larger firms.

▶ Models of Small Firm Management Development

Leaving aside for the moment the personal benefits for individual managers of developing their management capabilities, the management development model developed in this book also reflects a perspective that the organizational and economic benefits of effective management development lie in the improved efficiency of organizational performance internally which, in turn, leads to improved competitive positions for organizations externally (and, eventually, for the economy as a whole). At first glance, and certainly from the perspective of the small business development policies pursued by most national governments, the size of an organization may not appear to be an issue. Effective management development can be seen as a 'good' that can be applied with beneficial results to all types and sizes of organization.

This 'official' view of small businesses generally does not admit that the managers of small organizations face special management development issues, although it does concede that these managers suffer a host of managerial weaknesses. Management development in this model is seen as a necessary condition for these 'weak' small firms to begin their trajectories of upward growth into becoming significant large firms (Churchill and Lewis 1983; ACOST 1990; Gray 1993). For policy-makers, growth is seen almost exclusively in terms of increases in the size of the small organization's workforce. Indeed, small business development is frequently justified on its capacity to absorb unemployment. Management development is often reduced to the provision of enterprise training – a mixture of training in the basic concepts and skills of marketing, human resource management, financial management and planning. This view, however, springs from an economic model of small businesses as large firms scaled down, a model which many consider is deeply flawed.

An alternative view espoused by many small business representative bodies holds that small businesses are fundamentally different from larger firms. This model recognizes that small firms suffer real disadvantages as competitors in their own product markets and in crucial factor markets, particularly those for finance and skilled labour (Bolton 1971; Wilson 1979; Silver 1984; NEDO 1986). A strong case is made that small businesses suffer particular size disadvantages with respect to information-gathering and processing and to compliance with various regulations and reporting requirements (Stanworth and Gray 1991). Management development is seen as a subordinate priority to the need to improve the institutional and structural framework within which small firms operate. The point is often made that these size effects are so strong at the smaller end of the small and medium-sized enterprise (SME) sector that it makes little practical sense to lump these very small businesses, numerous though they are, with other small and medium-sized firms. The distinction made between self-employed sole traders who employ no other people and small firms employing at least a couple of workers is well established (Storey 1994; Gray 1998). The smallest firms (which were excluded from our survey) are mainly self-employed individuals or very small social organizations that can provide a position and livelihood for their owner-managers, their behaviour determined as much by personal and cultural motivations as by economic logic. This is reflected in the informal approaches to management and training that pervade this small business end of the sector.

Finally, there is a more commercially determined model which views small businesses as part of the fabric of local and national economies. In this view of the small business, a view often held by larger firms and regional development bodies, small businesses are seen as part of commercial networks, complex supply–production–distribution chains and as important elements in the contracting out of services as larger organizations 'vertically disintegrate' (Drucker 1985; Williamson 1985; Lazerson 1988; Pettigrew and Whipp 1991). These small businesses are part of the minority that are more 'business-minded' and recognize the need to manage relations with other firms (especially with important larger-firm customers). It is these small businesses that need to develop their own management structures and systems to cope with change and growth, including the development of employed managers capable of operating effectively in local environments like the owner-managers described in the second model. Although this is a comparatively under-researched field, the research that does exist indicates that these businesses face formidable and intense problems in developing appropriate management cadres and structures as they grow (Bolton 1971; Barry 1980; Flamholtz 1986; Bates and Wilson 1989; Stanworth and Gray 1991; Storey 1994; Gray 1998). It is mainly these small businesses, which can range in size from half a dozen employees to up to 100, that are the focus of this chapter. However, we also accept it as axiomatic that the quality of management, and therefore its development, is a key issue for any definition of small business.

In order to facilitate comparison with the larger organizations that have tended to feature in this book, it is worthwhile returning to a brief consideration of our own model that we introduced in chapter 1 and extended in figure 2.2. Apart from the very smallest micro-firms and self-employed sole traders which are too small to have a management structure, there is nothing in the model that is inherently inapplicable to small firms. The external environment will, in any case, be much the same for all firms except that small firms generally face more demanding competitive and regulatory pressures. It may be that small businesses are subject to more influence from the external environment than larger firms because they have fewer internal resources. Certainly, there is little doubt that small firms face disproportionately higher compliance costs in dealing with regulations, financial and bureaucratic paperwork and the demand from large customers. They also suffer more from time constraints which inhibit formal discussion and planning. The internal environment is likely to be more intense, with the ownership being more dominated by founder-managers, sometimes wider families and often partnerships, rather than formal company structures. There is a stronger expectation that small firm managers will be multi-functional. Also, management styles within small firms, compared with larger public companies, tend to be either more paternalistic or else more inclusive, depending on size and the social relations that influence the owner. In identifying this background, therefore, we have assumed that the key influences differ in their impact on small and large firms more in degree than in character.

▶ ## Recent Management Development Research in Small Firms

It is worth noting that the small business sector shares a certain theoretical immaturity with the management development field more generally in that very few testable models have been developed to explain the processes and determinants of development. One recent exception has been Wong et al. (1997), who used a model (or 'schema' as they more accurately describe it) developed by Arthur and Hendry (1990) to test the impact of the Business Growth Training scheme (a government initiative that provided a mix of financial support and consultancy to a small number of small businesses). Their conclusions closely support the findings of our small business managers survey reported below in this chapter and, indeed, the more general conclusions of this book as they relate to firms of all sizes.

The role of the state has had the effect that most of the development activities focused on small firms in Britain have fallen under the rubric of 'enterprise training'. This is particularly ironic or misplaced because the small firm sector is one where informality rules and there is little evidence that small business owners are particularly attracted to training either for themselves or for their staff. Indeed, there is compelling evidence that government-supported enterprise training programmes have not reached significant numbers of small firms, have not been cost-effective and have had little impact on the performance of the small firms that have attended these courses (National Audit Office 1988; Stanworth and Gray 1991; Storey 1994; Storey and Westhead 1994; Gray 1998). Informal and more directly personal management development from mentors and consultants seems to dominate the small firm sector (Stanworth et al. 1992; Curran et al. 1996).

Most studies in this field have tended to focus on the general lack of response by small business owners to the wide range of training programmes developed in order to help them survive, manage themselves more professionally, grow successfully, market their products and a whole host of other worthy objectives. Only a handful have looked closely at how small businesses actually do manage their own management development. Curran and Stanworth (1989) point out that there is no real consensus on what management skills should be emphasized in enterprise training, that most enterprise training programmes are of too short a duration to have lasting educational effects and that they are very simplistic when confronted with the complexity involved in successfully managing a small firm. Later, Stanworth et al. (1992), in an in-depth longitudinal study of several individual firms, were able to demonstrate the effectiveness of individual, consultancy-like training relationships in identifying appropriate training and information needs in a small business and in successfully helping an owner-manager and key workers develop the right skills for addressing those needs. Surveys by Curran et al. (1996) reinforced the point that small firms do engage in management development and other activities which may not be regarded as formal training but are nevertheless targeted at achieving certain precise objectives which have relevance for the firm and its current economic circumstances.

One of the few organizations that has tried to track small business management development nationally among its small firm members has been the national employers' organization, the Confederation of British Industry (CBI). A joint sponsor of the original Constable and McCormick Report (1987), the CBI also conducted a parallel survey at that time among its Smaller Firms Council members to gauge management training attitudes and needs. This survey confirmed that little had changed since the Bolton Report (1971), but did highlight interesting differences in perceived management development needs between the small and medium-sized firms (CBI 1986). More recently, the CBI (1994) published another small business membership survey directly on management development and extended its range of enquiry beyond a narrow focus on training.

Table 11.1 Small business staff development in 1998 by size

	Under 5	5–9	10–14	15–24	25–49	50+	Total
No formal training	53	36	31	20	17	8	38
Internal training	10	24	32	33	45	44	22
External training	20	45	46	61	80	72	40
Time off	13	34	22	33	38	48	25
Other	5	5	3	11	10	4	6

Source: Small Business Research Trust, 1998.

Research by the Small Business Research Trust (SBRT), which provided the bulk of the small business sample in our survey, shows clearly that the size effects in relation to planned development increase to a point where the self-employed and the very small microfirms provide very little formal training at all. The surveys in 1995 and 1998 were on staff development practices and in 1999 on management development (SBRT, 11, 4 (1995); 14, 3 (1998); 7, 3 (1999)). The size effects can be clearly seen in table 11.1 which summarizes multiple responses to the 1998 survey. The 1999 management development survey found that by far the biggest barrier to management was insufficient time, and moreover the smallest businesses, with arguably the greatest need, had the least time.

It is clear that firms with fewer than five employees remain significantly less active and less clear about their overall management and staff development objectives than medium-sized firms. With more than half (53 per cent) reporting that they conduct no formal training, their expected aversion to formal training policies is also clear (and more pronounced than in the 1995 survey). There is a direct relation between firm size and the provision of internal and external training courses, as there is in allowing employees time off to pursue their own development. It is likely that these effects relate both to the resource constraints faced by very small businesses and to their aversion to external control. This does not mean, however, that no management development takes place in the smallest firms, but more that it tends to be informal and very task- or crisis-related; Curran and colleagues at Kingston University found that some 80 per cent of small businesses provide informal training to their staff and managers (Curran et al. 1996).

It is interesting that the 15–24-employee band, which includes many fast-growth businesses and has been dubbed the 'growth corridor' (Stanworth and Gray 1991; Stanworth et al. 1992), shows a distinct increase in training and development. It is now recognized that these firms face particular challenges in having to introduce more professional management systems (Bates and Wilson 1989; Gray 1998). A stronger awareness of their needs for management development and a more formal approach might, therefore, be expected from these higher-growth firms. Because their growth depends on their ability to meet demand from consumers or other businesses, they are also more likely to be exposed to fluctuations in their external economic environments. For similar reasons, they are also more likely to have developed stronger links with larger firms and to be influenced by their management development practices. However, these more active small firms also find themselves in competition with larger firms not only for customers but also for resources such as finance or skilled labour. The 1998 SBRT survey identified a sub-set of 190 firms suffering from skills shortages. Some 52 per cent of these small firms paid for external courses while 37 per cent gave their staff time off to pursue their own courses and only 27 per cent admitted to having no formal training policy. This provides clear evidence of external labour market effects on small business management development policies.

The most interesting overall finding, however, was the sharp rise in externally provided training courses between 1995 and 1998. The patterns of management development reported in the 1998 SBRT survey reflect more closely the practice of the larger firms discussed in the earlier chapters of this book. The provision of external courses dominates firms of all sizes as the preferred option, even among the smallest firms. There was also a positive but patchy increase in the numbers of small firms giving their managers and employees time off for study and the provision of internal training courses. Indeed, the vast majority of firms with more than 25 employees report that they use external courses and roughly half provide training organized internally. As many internally designed programmes make use of consultants as training designers, facilitators or deliverers, this finding accords with 1995 CBI survey.

As mentioned earlier, our main tool for examining these issues is our small firm managers' survey which was based on the national database of small businesses held by the Small Business Research Trust together with some of the CBI Small Firms Council and which is described in more detail in appendix 1. The sample consisted of 389 small businesses, of which 30 per cent were micro-firms with fewer than 10 employees, with similar proportions (28 per cent) in both the 10–19-employee and the 20–49-employee bands, while 14 per cent had more than 50. In addition to this main survey, we also use a much smaller survey of 90 managers from firms in the main survey, who provide a perspective as 'clients' of management development. This survey is also described in appendix 1. We now proceed to examine some features of the surveys, starting with the policy frameworks.

Table 11.2 Management development policy frameworks (%, n = 389)

	1–9	10–19	20–49	50+	Growth firms	All
Formality of policy						
Explicit formal policy	5	6	11	11	19	8
Informal policy	33	46	44	39	42	41
None, react to need	50	36	39	46	38	42
No system at all	13	12	6	2	2	9
Extent of priority						
Low priority	27	15	10	15	15	17
Rather low priority	38	43	36	28	31	37
Quite high priority	28	35	43	46	40	37
Very high priority	4	6	9	11	15	7
Assessed for training needs						
Yes	46	59	56	65	67	55
No	40	35	40	35	31	38

▶ **Policy Frameworks and Firm Characteristics**

Our small firms survey was able to explore in more detail the variations between different types of small business in their approach to management development. In particular, we were able to identify the main influences that drive a positive approach towards management development among the small firms that take a more formal approach. In table 11.2, using numbers of employees as the measure of firm size the expected size effects are evident in relation to the degree of planned formality and relative importance of management development. We have used three variables which we also used for the policy cluster in our regression analyses of the survey, namely formality of management development policy, extent of priority given to management development, and whether managers are regularly assessed for training needs. These are of course very similar to the policy variables used for the other surveys, and provide the basis of our strong–weak policy spectrum. However, the categories in the questions are somewhat different, and we did not ask about company versus individual responsibility (on the grounds that most of the companies were too small for this to be meaningful) and replaced it by regular assessment of training needs. Next to the size-band columns in table 11.2 there is a column called 'growth firms' which gives the responses from the 12 per cent of firms that reported an explicit and strong intention to grow and increase their staff (as expected, their responses differ considerably from the rest of the sample and can be monitored against the average responses for the whole sample). We have assumed that these growth businesses are closest to the small firms described in the third model of economically proactive small firms mentioned above.

As expected, the smallest firms were, on balance, generally averse to adopting a formal management development policy, though the differences between the size bands were not large. This reflects a number of external factors – scale effects on resources and time, relative organizational simplicity (also reflected in the effects of number of sites) and a need to be flexible (hence the dominance of 'react to need' among the micro-firms). Further analysis revealed that, generally speaking, the smaller the firm, the less likely it is to exhibit high growth. Nearly 60 per cent of the small firms with formal management development policies were the high-growth firms. Interestingly, firms that operate on more than one site tend to be larger and also tend to have more need for more formal policies (10 per cent compared with just 6 per cent of single-site firms reported having an explicit formal policy). Two-thirds of micro-firms allocated management development a low or rather low priority, whereas a majority of firms with 20 or more employees, and those with more than one site, felt that it should have a quite high or very high priority. The final policy question, assessment of training needs, also follows the same pattern of lower positive responses from the smaller size bands and more positive ones from the bigger firms, with the growth firms category highest of all. It is also to be noted that more than half the total sample answered positively.

These results accord with the findings of Wong and colleagues (1997), who used a matched-sample evaluation of 138 small firms and multivariate analysis to reveal a positive impact of a management development initiative on business performance and found that size-effects and having a formal business plan were linked significantly to business growth. This suggests there is a small but significant minority of small firms with a more structured approach to their management and stronger systems of management development. In interpreting these findings it may be helpful to take into account interesting tendencies towards growth among small firms in general. Psychological resistance to growth is much stronger among the very small micro-firms, mainly because of their focus on survival and fear of loss of independence (Barry 1980; Bates and Wilson 1989; Davidsson 1989; Gray 1998). Researchers using large databases have detected a 'growth barrier' at the 20-employee mark, beyond which as few as 5 per cent of firms pass successfully (Daly et al. 1991; Storey 1994). Our findings indicate that this phenomenon is related to the more positive approach to management development by growth-oriented firms.

Another interesting tendency to emerge is the finding that the formal, planned and even successful nature of management development appears to be linked to the complexity of the business and that these firms stand out as having a more systematic approach to their business. This finding is clearer in relation to the use of budgets to monitor performances (78 per cent of multi-site firms and 83 per cent of 20+-employee firms) and in the use of a written business plan (62 per cent of multi-site and 74 per cent of 50+-employee firms). There were also clear industry differences in the perceived need for a more structured approach to management development, with manufacturers (especially those of industrial rather than consumer products) and business services (the professions and providers of financial services) much more in favour of having a formal management development plan. Small firms in these sectors were also more likely to monitor the actual performance of managers against the plan and against their budgets compared with firms in the distribution sectors and providers of personal services.

What lies behind policy? It is interesting to see what the survey revealed about the motivations identified as the key drivers of management development by the small business managers, as we did for the HRD managers' views of their companies' drivers in chapter 6. Table 11.3 summarizes multiple responses to a number of current influences on the decision to undertake management development across industries and among growth-oriented firms. The 17 influences have been listed in order of number of mentions. The 'others' category was negligible (4 per cent) and has been omitted.

There is an interesting mix of external and internal factors that appear to drive the implementation of management development policies among most small firms. Furthermore, the main drivers of management development among small firms do not share the same priorities as those for larger firms or of the MBA graduates. Given the pressures of competition and recent recession on small businesses, the number 1 slot for a general measure of business health and good performance, 'business efficiency', is not surprising. The relatively low score among services probably reflects the non-commercial 'lifestyle' motivations frequently observed among small-firm owners, especially those in catering and personal services (Stanworth and Gray 1991; Storey 1994; Gray 1998). The much higher priority accorded 'staff motivation' as the second-highest driver, compared with its lowly 25 per cent rating among the larger firms and the 38 per cent rating among MBA graduates discussed in earlier chapters, may reflect the shortages of skilled labour mentioned above. Overall, small firms seem to be less driven by strategic considerations in their approach

Table 11.3 Management development drivers (multiple mentions, %, n = 389)

	Manufacturing	Distribution	Services	Growth firms	Total
Influences – internal					
Business efficiency	64	66	58	65	62
Staff motivation	53	62	55	63	56
Firm's growth strategy	55	56	42	65	50
Retain staff/managers	42	42	35	48	40
Skills shortages	41	26	28	38	32
Structural change to firm	33	32	28	40	31
Cost of management development	25	32	23	33	25
Provide career paths	25	18	20	21	22
Pressure from managers	22	15	16	13	18
Pressure from board	12	3	8	6	8
Influences – external					
Competition from other firms	45	51	41	44	44
Pressure from large customers	38	34	18	38	29
Structural change to industry	14	27	28	19	23
Investors in People	19	18	24	38	21
Cost of recruitment	17	18	21	25	19
Norm among other firms	17	12	18	15	17
Pressure to obtain NVQs	14	14	16	17	15
Not stated/no reply	15	18	20	6	17

to management development. However, it is perhaps not surprising that manufacturers and the active, growth-oriented small firms are more like larger firms in ranking growth strategies as a strong driver for engaging in active management development (and fully 74 per cent of the self-employed MBA consultants ranked strategy as the strongest driver – possibly a reflection of their trade rather than the main small firm preoccupations). The task-focused, short-term nature of many small businesses is revealed in the low ranking given to structural changes to their industry which was the third driver among larger firms.

The really interesting findings to policy-makers are those that reflect the apparent success of various campaigns in favour of concepts and practices associated with human resource development and life-long learning. The need to maintain staff motivation, retain staff (though this also appears to be linked to increasing skills shortages, especially among manufacturers), provide career paths and, most significantly, address the requirements of Investors in People (IiP), are clear manifestations of the impact of HRD ideas on small firm management development practice. It is also interesting to compare the importance accorded IiP in relation to NVQs; this normative approach appears to find less relevance among small firms to the more developmental approach of IiP which holds that development must be made relevant to the needs of the organization and the individual manager.

▶ Amounts, Topics, and Methods of Training

Since the mid-1980s there has been a tremendous amount of public and private sector pressure to upgrade vocational skills at all levels, and educational standards in general. There have been a number of initiatives aimed at forging a partnership between the public and private sectors to provide relevant and effective training, the introduction of standards such as the IiP award and a steady stream of publicity and initiatives, not just in Britain but across the whole European Union (EU), attempting to foster a culture of life-long learning. It is heartening to discover that, on average, our panel of small firms report spending 4.6 days a year on formal training, as shown in table 11.4.

It is particularly impressive that the growth companies average 7.3 days a year. Admittedly the average is strongly influenced by almost one in five doing more than 15 days a year, and admittedly almost the same percentage did none. We should perhaps also note that the substantial proportion of 'not stated' have not been counted in the mean, and if this were counted as none the average would obviously be lower. All this said both the sample as a whole and the growth companies in particular reflect quite well compared to any of the groupings in chapter 8. But even the growth companies are not the highest category.

Table 11.4 Amount of formal training (%, n = 389)

Days per year	1–9	10–19	2–49	50+	Growth firms	All
None	19	13	22	25	17	20
1–2	23	15	12	13	13	16
3–5	17	22	23	23	19	21
6–9	9	5	9	6	4	7
10–14	6	13	16	10	13	11
15+	2	11	5	4	19	6
Not stated	21	22	14	19	15	19
Mean	3.4	6.2	4.9	4.2	7.3	4.6

The average for those companies which reported a quite high or very high priority for management development was 7.9 days, while the relatively small number which had an explicit management development policy had an average of 9.1. A considerable number of the companies in these three categories of growth, priority and explicit policy are of course the same companies, but what the figures indicate is that there is a small proportion of small companies which are very seriously involved with training, and by any of the standards applied in the earlier chapters have a strong policy framework. Although the management development studies of the mid-1980s did not establish benchmarks for the amount of training conducted by small firms then, it is clear that there has been a significant increase in management development in the sector, both formal and informal. This points to strong links between explicit management development policies and small firm development. Clearly, small business owners do recognize their own management development needs, and many are very active in addressing those needs.

Although many managers in small firms will need similar abilities, competencies and skills to their counterparts in medium-sized and large firms, the owner-managers of the small firms are under greater pressure to develop multi-functional competencies. Because so many of them operate within strong resource constraints yet have spans of responsibilities like top executives in large corporations, their management development needs are likely to be both special and more intense. This is an area that has been fairly well researched in terms of basic management skills. Indeed the eight areas identified by Bolton (1971) more than a quarter of a century ago seem to be still valid as small business management development targets today, although their content and relative importance have certainly changed considerably. As an *aide mémoire* Bolton's list is certainly still useful:

1. raising and using finance;
2. costing and control information;
3. organization and delegation;
4. marketing;
5. information use and retrieval;
6. personnel management;
7. technological change;
8. production scheduling and purchase control.

Clearly the importance of information-gathering and knowledge management has increased enormously in all firms and the bureaucratic side of personnel management has given way to the more behavioural ideas of human resource development (which is basically the subject

Table 11.5 Focus areas for development (%, n = 355)

	1–9	10–19	2–49	50+	Growth firms	All
Operations	45	54	57	60	64	53
People	34	24	45	54	49	37
General management	17	19	17	29	32	19
Finance	14	11	16	21	23	15
Planning	14	11	16	21	23	15
Information	13	6	13	13	23	11
Other/specific	3	1	4	0	2	2
Not stated	10	4	3	10	4	6

of this entire book). Also, the need for all organizations and all managers to keep abreast of changes in technology has intensified enormously as the applications of new information and communication technologies have proliferated. Furthermore, as Bolton recognized, management practices, roles, duties and development needs will often vary considerably between different industries. On closer analysis, the main differences revealed in our small business managers survey appear to be between those involved in supply and distribution chain relationships with other businesses (such as providers of business services and manufacturers of components, semi-finished goods, machine tools, etc.) and those that interface directly with consumers.

The survey focused exclusively on the management development practices and the perceptions as reported by the managers themselves. The sample was stratified into manufacturing, retail and distribution, and business services but, apart from the broad differences between consumer and industrial orientation, differences between industries were generally neither significant nor consistent. However, other variables reflect these two underlying business orientations more directly and produced clear and consistent findings. Strong size effects reappear in relation to the functional areas of management that are the focus of management development (the 355 base of table 11.5 is based on multiple responses and excludes those who report having no policy at all).

These replies cast more light on the nature of the specific and internal organizational objectives, with more than half of the sample (53 per cent) identifying a need for management development in their own operations. There was a much stronger emphasis on the development of financial management skills among the larger 50+-employee firms but, generally, the ranking of the areas of functional focus is the same for firms of all sizes. There was also a stronger perceived need among the 10–19-employee firms in the areas of general management

Table 11.6 Development methods (multiple mentions, %, n = 389)

	1–9	10–19	20–49	50+	Growth firms	All
Time off for courses	71	79	77	83	77	77
External courses	67	74	80	80	81	74
On-the-job training	63	71	79	83	77	72
In-house training	53	61	73	65	60	62
Coaching managers	26	40	43	41	42	37
Use consultants	21	29	41	39	48	31
Formal induction	18	35	30	50	56	31
Mentoring	21	29	35	39	35	30
Job rotation	17	13	18	20	19	17

competencies and the skills of information management. Size effects were most pronounced in the area of operations management and seemed to be linked to growth and the need to manage across more than one site. Growth-oriented firms place much stronger emphasis than other small firms on developing strong management in operations, people, finance and, most interestingly, information. Firms with more complex structures (the multi-site firms and the medium-sized firms with more than 50 employees) had a stronger focus on developing management capacity in their operations (58 per cent and 60 per cent respectively). There were also differences between industries, though not in all areas.

By now, it is becoming clear that management training in small firms is influenced by factors that are perceived to be appropriate and relevant to the industry, to the firm and, especially amongst the micro-firms, to the owner-manager. This suggests that management development activities will also reflect a diversity of approaches. Table 11.6 (permitting multiple mentions), confirms the interesting differences revealed in the SBRT surveys (table 11.1) between small businesses of different sizes on the activities they undertake as their management development. In general there is a lower level of all types of activity compared with larger firms but particularly in the provision of in-house training and the use of mentors and consultants. As there are clear size effects, this seems to be related to resource constraints and costs of disruption to work. The main industrial differences of interest appear to reflect a stronger reliance on internal provision of training (courses, on-the-job training, etc.) by firms in the distribution and service sectors.

Overall, providing time off for training is the most commonly used management development activity (this was especially so among the multi-site firms which provided considerably more opportunities across all activities than single-site firms). The larger, multi-site and growth-oriented firms are the most likely to use external courses, which is not surprising as they are likely to have more resources at their disposal and suffer less from disruption to work from the absence of key staff. It is more surprising that these firms are also more likely to offer on-the-job training than the small firms which are usually more associated with this form of informal training. It is particularly interesting to see how growth-oriented firms, the targets of policy-makers, rely much more on external consultants and formal internal employee induction systems than other small businesses. However, it is worth noting that a large proportion of these growth firms are manufacturers which, as we have seen, tend to have more formal systems and tend to have more contact with the systems operated by larger firms.

One last issue on training methods which we need to report concerns the balance between formal and informal development. Here we asked the question on a 5-point scale rather than the 3-point scale for the larger firms reported in chapter 8. Much more or rather more formal development was noted by 12 per cent, about the same by 18 per cent and rather or much more informal development by 58 per cent, with 11 per cent not answering. This reflects a very much stronger balance towards informal development than was the case with the larger firms; this might have been predicted by the differences of size, but as we have seen throughout the book, size is by no means always the dominant influence. There is, however, a strong relationship to the policy variables such that an explicit policy and high priority are associated with formal methods.

▶ Management Development Processes and Responsibilities

Chapter 7 examined how larger firms organized the processes of management development. Some of those issues are taken up in this section. These differences are also reflected in how small business owners manage and monitor management performance and the effects of their management development activities. Table 11.7 is based on multiple responses and shows the differences between the size categories of firm, as well as the high growth and multi-site firms, with respect to monitoring managers' performance and the setting of management development objectives.

There are clear size effects present in the degree to which management performance is monitored and managed. It is also clear that multi-site small firms feel a greater need to monitor performance and

Table 11.7 Management development needs assessment (multiple mentions %, n = 389)

Type of firm	Set individual performance targets	Appoint managers for specific jobs	Assess managers on performance	Managers assessed for training needs
1–9	38	44	51	46
10–19	43	58	62	59
20–49	46	66	70	56
50+	56	76	65	65
Single site	39	56	56	52
Multi-site	53	65	69	59
Growth firms	58	71	81	67
Total	44	58	61	55

development needs. To some extent this reflects the organizational complexity and control aspects of managing multi-site businesses and the narrower scope for smaller firms to have one or more additional levels of management (only 8 per cent of micro-firms had more than two levels of management compared with an average of 21 per cent for the whole sample). It is interesting to note that these size effects are not so clear in the assessment of management performance where there is some evidence that the 20–49-employee firms are more efficient in their working practices. This is reflected in the high level of importance placed on management assessment by firms that anticipate strong growth (as table 11.2 shows, these firms are also more likely to have explicit management development policies). The informality that characterizes the micro-firms is evident in the fact that one-third were unable or unwilling to state their management development objectives and another 20 per cent related their management development to very specific or non-classified objectives. It is interesting that the larger 50+-employee firms were concerned to develop management skills connected with business planning and other internal and specific issues. Firms with explicit management development policies generally had a stronger focus on meeting the development needs of both the organization (47 per cent) and of individual managers (58 per cent).

Another set of processes is derived from the client managers. One question was how development activities were triggered; there were three main triggers reported, all scoring between 40 and 50 per cent, namely informal discussion with boss, own initiative and senior management decision. Appraisal and training needs analysis scored

Table 11.8 Responsibility for initiating policy (%, n = 190)

	1–9	10–19	20–49	50+	Single site	Multi-site	Growth firms	All
CEO/MD	63	70	70	74	66	73	79	69
Board	4	16	13	7	11	12	7	11
Owner/proprietor	13	2	5	4	9	3	3	6
Director/partner	9	9	5	4	8	2	0	7
A specific manager	2	4	5	11	5	7	10	5
Individual staff	7	4	2	4	4	3	0	4
Other/not stated	2	2	4	0	1	5	3	3

considerably lower, in the twenties. A second question was how far development was linked to organizationally defined skills or competencies; only 32 per cent said that there was a high linkage on a 1–10 scale, although this rose to 59 per cent where high priority was also reported. A third question was to what extent development had arisen from a personal development plan; in a similar pattern of answers 35 per cent said it was to a high extent, rising to 48 per cent where priority was high. In general, these answers are similar to those provided by the larger-company client managers reported in chapter 7.

Table 11.8 summarizes how the management development process is managed and implemented inside small businesses, showing the areas of prime responsibility for formulating management development policy for the 190 firms who report having such a policy – explicit or informal. The dominance of chief executives and managing directors in the process of setting the management development policy may be interpreted two ways – either as evidence of commitment from the top (recommended by human resource specialists) or as a reflection of top-down autocratic or paternalist management styles. There is a slight size effect, but quite a strong concentration of this approach among the growth-oriented firms. The relative importance of the owner in the micro-firms and the allocation of a specialist or line manager to this role in the larger 50+-employee firms (and among growth-oriented firms) is to be expected. This fits the findings of Curran et al. (1996) on the importance of the owner-manager as a 'gatekeeper' to all staff-development activities. Although high-level commitment is important, however, the real interest lies in who has responsibility for implementing the policy. This is summarized in table 11.9.

It is interesting, if rather expected, to see the reduced role of chief executives, managing directors and board members in the implementation of management development and (except in the

Table 11.9 Implementation responsibility for development (%, n = 389)

	1–9	10–19	20–49	50+	Growth firms	All
CEO/MD	61	65	55	56	55	69
Board	9	9	7	7	7	11
Owner/proprietor	11	2	3	4	3	6
Director/partner	11	8	6	0	3	7
A specific manager	2	9	18	37	35	5
Individual staff	9	11	8	11	10	4
Other/not stated	0	2	5	0	3	3

micro-firms) a corresponding rise in the role of specialist and line managers in the implementation process. It is also interesting that responsibility for implementing management development seems to be more devolved in multi-site small firms which are more likely to reflect the organizational complexity of larger firms (21 per cent of multi-site small firms gave responsibility for implementation to a specific manager compared with just 12 per cent of single-site firms). Also, as might be expected in keeping with the aims of IiP, the role of individual managers in implementing their own management development increases. A final issue in this section is how small businesses become aware of management development opportunities. The impression that small firm managers are well informed and likely to have considered views on management development was confirmed by a question about their own management education backgrounds. A very high 22 per cent reported that they had received some training and courses from a business school and 20 per cent had received some form of management training from a Training and Enterprise Council or other government source. These are overlapping categories because 19 per cent reported no training or did not reply and more than half (55 per cent) reported they received their own management development 'at work'. Interestingly, the growth-oriented small business managers were less likely to have had formal management training themselves. Nevertheless, all displayed awareness of these sources of training and, as table 11.10 shows, most were aware of the management training opportunities on offer.

One of the most significant findings from the perspective of public policy is the prime position as a source of information enjoyed by the TECs (Training and Enterprise Councils), their Scottish equivalents the LECs (Local Enterprise Companies) and the one-stop-shop advice centres they established, increasingly as joint ventures with chambers of commerce, the Business Links. Another significant finding, from an

Table 11.10 Source of information for courses (%, n = 389)

	Manufacturers	Distribution	Services	Growth	All
TEC/LEC/Business Link	58	51	40	62	50
Business association	42	40	43	45	43
Direct mail	38	32	41	47	38
Trade press	32	32	38	26	34
Specialist newsletters	24	20	31	34	26
Word of mouth	10	8	19	11	13
Local press	7	5	10	4	8
National press	5	2	1	9	3
Not stated	6	5	4	6	5

advertising and marketing perspective, is the high degree of recognition and apparent effectiveness of direct mail, especially among growth-oriented firms. The opposite side of that coin, the relatively poor reach of national and local press, confirms the experience of the Open University Business School in its attempts to market its own self-study packs for small businesses. These mass media contrast weakly with the more targeted trade press and, to a lesser extent, specialist newsletters which, however, appear to be particularly effective with the growth-oriented firms. Interestingly, the much-touted informal method, 'word of mouth', seems to be used mainly by services. Whatever the channel of communication, it seems clear that the management development 'message' is beginning to reach small firms and that they acknowledge its positive impact.

▶ Outcomes of Management Development in Small Firms

In the main outcome-oriented question in the small company survey, the respondents were asked how successful the organization's management development practices had been in achieving their objectives and producing the type of manager required. Almost two-thirds of the whole sample (64 per cent) reported that practices had been rather or very successful; perhaps unsurprisingly now, this figure rose to 90 per cent where there was an explicit development policy, and to 82 per cent where high priority was also reported. There was, however, no clear size effect, but rapid growth was more likely to be associated with reported success. Overall, this was a very positive result.

Another set of outcome measures came from the client managers. They gave a less positive verdict on the achievement of objectives than their firms, with only 33 per cent giving a high rating on a 10-point scale, although their mean score of 5.48 was very considerably higher than the average of 4.84 by the larger-company client managers. Their score on the impact of management development on the organization was similar at 5.51, also higher than their larger-company counterparts. There were also other outcome measures where they reported a higher score than their counterparts: how effectively progress against development needs is reviewed by the organization; how far recognition and reward policies reinforced learning outputs; and how far the business impact of the development had been assessed by the organization. However, in each of these cases they took a negative view of the outcomes, just a less negative one. In another two cases, where they took an overall positive view about the relevance of the development to performance in the job and the important issue of satisfaction with management development since joining the organization, their score was nevertheless less positive than the score of their counterparts, and in a final case, the extent to which they had been able to transfer learning to the job, the scores were exactly the same. The purpose of this set of results is to show that in most instances the small business client managers had a more positive view of management development in their organizations than those in the larger companies. These results may be explained in terms of their having lower expectations of management development, or being 'closer to the action', but the findings are that the small businesses being reported on come out quite well in the view of their customers when compared to their equivalents in the larger companies.

▶ Small Business Development in the Future

Three different models of the role of small business development were mentioned at the beginning of this chapter: (i) small firms as scaled-down large firms; (ii) small firms as a distinct social milieu where informality and lifestyle values are the norm; (iii) small firms as key players in an economic and innovative fabric dominated by larger firms. We then proceeded to examine the issues of small firm management development in relation to our general model of management development. In the light of all serious small business research over the past 30 years, the first model – that small businesses are merely scaled-down versions of large organizations and that their management development needs are not materially different – is clearly not generally tenable. However, in relation to something as conscious and structured as management development this survey has shown that the aims, needs and performance of small firms are not very different from those of larger firms. Small firm owner-managers tend to identify themselves in terms of the industry in which they operate rather than in terms of size. Consequently, the technical skills required for their businesses are likely to overlap considerably with some larger firms even if their working environments differ considerably. They often draw on the same labour markets, albeit at different ends of those markets. This means that some form of informal benchmarking against larger firms is inevitable and this has been clearly reflected in these findings.

However, it is the second model which is most clearly reflected in the overwhelming prevalence of informality and lack of written management development policies. Also, it has to be recognized that the sample is over-represented by older respondents. More than three-quarters of the sample (78 per cent) were aged 45 years or older. They are evidently much more experienced than the average self-employed or small business managing director. Nationally, the largest cohorts of new self-employed are aged under 35 years and a large proportion are women (also under-represented in the small firm survey). There is strong and consistent evidence that many small firms, especially the micro-firms and the self-employed, do hold a range of rather non-commercial attitudes and values, and that economic motivation is by no means dominant (Storey 1994; Gray 1998).

From an economic perspective, the most interesting model is the third one which focuses only on those firms which participate actively in the value-added exchanges with other firms as part of supply and distribution chains. These firms are often specialist providers of business services, machine tools or components to other firms and dominate many aspects of distribution. They are an essential part of the production and distribution process that makes up commercial life and it has long been recognized that they often face strong management development challenges as they grow and prosper (Bolton 1971; Barry 1980; Bannock 1981; Flamholtz 1986; Bates and Wilson 1989; Storey 1994; Gray 1998). In our survey, they have been identified as the growth-oriented firms and they are clearly identifiable as a distinct category. Of particular interest here, these active growth-oriented small firms clearly have a more structured approach to business and a stronger awareness of what they expect from their management development activities. They appear to have turned their backs on the constraining individualism that afflicts the small business sector and they are clearly an important part of the national economic fabric (Drucker 1985; Gray 1998).

Certainly, for this type of small business our model is very useful in understanding the processes and drivers of management development (and provides a useful model for analysing the internal organizational issues confronting more informal small firms as they move through different stages of growth). Their concern for improving their business efficiency through management development is interesting both because it reflects the instrumental and practical nature of many successful small firm owners and because it represents an oblique acknowledgement that the concerns of policy-makers over managerial weaknesses in the small firm sector may not have been completely misplaced. Turning to the future, it is useful to see what the main drivers of management development are likely to be according to small business owners themselves, especially the growth-oriented ones.

Business efficiency and strategy continue to dominate as drivers of future management development, followed by concerns relating to staff. Compared with the current situation small firms seem to feel that shortages of appropriate managerial labour will pose less of a problem in the future and that the costs of management development are likely to fall. However, there also seems to be a stronger awareness that structural changes in industries and within firms will continue to pose management challenges. The growth in the average number of days spent on management development perhaps reflects this. However, regression analysis to determine causal directions in the model found that it was internal structural variables and the management development policy variables as practised in the firm that determined the number of days' training rather than the external structural variables or personal characteristics of the owner-managers (Thomson and Gray 1999). This suggests that a deeper awareness and consistent approach to management development must become embedded in the small firm's culture before extensive management development takes place and has an impact on the firm. The growth-oriented firms confirm the picture of them as resembling larger firms much more than they resemble other small firms. As with the larger firms reported in previous chapters, their growth strategy is very much their top driver, business efficiency second and likely structural changes to the firm third. IiP will continue to be a positive influence on management development, especially among growth-oriented small firms.

At the start of this chapter on the findings of our small firm survey, we mentioned three different concepts of the small firm. It is clear from our findings that a particular category of small firm is very significant – the growth-oriented small business with a more professional and formal approach to management. Interestingly, the sub-sample of self-employed consultants in the MBA graduates survey revealed that gaining their MBA was an import step in their career switch to running their own small consultancy businesses. Although they tended to be older than the main MBA panel, they had a strong need to keep their management skills up to date, mainly through continuing professional development, and a very structured approach to their own management development. This further supports the findings of the small firms survey that these 'structured' small firms appear to be more integrated in their relations with larger firms and capable of adapting their internal structures and human resource development policies to the demands of external competition and change. In this sense, they appear to be an integral part of the national and more global economy. They occupy an analogous role to that of small firms in northern Italy and the *Mittelstand* in Germany, a sector that has been relatively underdeveloped in Britain (Bannock and Albach 1991; Meagher et al. 1992; Gray 1998). Our survey indicates that the equivalent firms in Britain are also keen to develop and face up to the management challenges facing them in the competitive markets of the future.

Conclusions

The findings of most small business research agree that there was a generally poor level of management development among small firms in Britain during the mid-1980s (Stanworth and Gray 1991; Storey 1994). Therefore, the relatively high levels of management development found in this survey and in other recent studies (CBI 1994; Curran et al. 1996) provide heartening evidence that small firms may be beginning to take a more positive approach to the development of management competencies. As already mentioned, the mean amount of training reported in our small business survey was 4.6 days, but 20 per cent of the survey reported no training at all. Nevertheless, given the concern about training in the small firm sector, 4.6 days is not far off the 5 days per year often recommended for all organizations, and must be considered a substantial amount in terms of public policy objectives. It appears that many of the small firms that do have a training policy are every bit as active as the best large firms with their much more substantial resources. The main finding of the small firms survey is that there has been a significant increase in the amount of management development by small firms in Britain over the past ten years. Indeed, it is clear that certain growth-oriented and slightly larger small firms – the more 'structured' small firms – behave more like larger firms in their approach towards management development. Certainly, the same pattern of management development being driven more by internal cultural and organizational issues, with success being associated with a strong lead from top management, is present in the more active small firms as it is among the larger firms. Indeed, these firms in our small firm survey were more likely to engage in formal management development than many of the firms in the large firms survey. Although comparatively few of the small firms in our sample had strong systems of management development, those that did (and across a range of different types of small firm) had very strong systems.

Indeed, the perceived drivers of management development in the future among these structured small firms reveal a powerful strategic approach to management development. Once again, this indicates that a strong approach towards management development is a product of choice on the part of the firms' decision-makers (in this case mainly the owner-managers) rather than just reaction to external circumstances. It also appears from our surveys that systematic management development holds the key to the further development of this important sector of small firms and that our model offers clues to how this necessary management development may be implemented more widely.

chapter 12

Conclusions

INTRODUCTION

There are three main purposes to this final chapter, and a subsidiary one. The first is to examine the extent of change since the mid-1980s and to produce a balance sheet of positive and less positive features. The second is to reflect on wider issues in management development in Britain at the turn of the century, amongst them briefly examining where Britain stands in an international context. The third main purpose is to take up research issues relating to the status of our model of the management development system in the light of our findings, and look to the need for future research in the area. The subsidiary objective is to look briefly at the future of management development.

▶ The Extent of Change Since the Mid-1980s

The main message of this book is one of considerable change since the surveys and reports of the mid-1980s, even though the most important secondary message is one of substantial differences between otherwise similar organizations. The essential message of the seminal reports of the mid-1980s on management development was pessimistic, strongly arguing that Britain was ineffective in developing its managers and well behind its main competitors. Chapter 3 chronicled the historical lack of coherence and commitment to management development which led up to the reports.

Our message, built on the basis of the most extensive set of surveys carried out in the 1990s, is considerably more upbeat, and the first task of these conclusions is to review the main dimensions of change (or lack of it), creating a balance sheet for the mid- to late 1990s compared to that of a decade earlier. There are many positive things to report:

The increased coverage of training. Almost no larger companies and only a limited minority of small companies in the surveys do not report some management training. There are few differences by sector or other breakdowns. Training takes place even where there is no explicit policy statement or budget, nor any other of the formal accoutrements of development. In addition, training is no longer reserved for the high-fliers, but is extended in the vast majority of medium-sized and large companies to managers of average potential, while in over two-thirds of cases some provision is made for low-potential managers as well. Moreover, training covers all levels and competency role areas.

The amount of formal training *has increased substantially*, measured against what was reported a decade previously and against the estimates which the company respondents gave of training at that time. The average amount of training meets the frequently recommended target of some 5 days per manager per year in the larger organizations and falls only a little short in the smaller ones. This was also the figure used in the Handy Report (1987) to describe practice in the main competitor countries. Even so, company respondents are only moderately satisfied with the amount of training being done and look to do more in the future. Individual managers, both MBAs and in the panel companies, reported very much the same level of training as the company respondents. It is particularly heartening to be able to report the extent of training in the small company panel. While the survey did not cover the micro-organizations with five or fewer employees, and we cannot be absolutely sure about the representativeness of the respondents, the strong relationship between amount of training and growth in this group was also noteworthy.

There is a strongly positive view of the present in relation to the past, and of the future in relation to the present, as far as amount of training is concerned. The view of the future, and a commitment to Continuing Professional Development, is especially strong in the MBA panel. It is also worth noting that the 1986 survey anticipated considerable growth in training, and this prediction has been borne out. The priority given to management development is likewise positively viewed from the past to the present to the future. Indeed the change from past to future is truly remarkable; from a situation where almost two-thirds perceived their organization as having a low priority for development 10 years ago there is one where almost three-quarters envisage their organization as having a high one in the foreseeable future.

Organizations feel that they take the balance of responsibility for management development. This view is not shared to the same extent by managers, either MBAs or members of panel companies, but they too recognize that the organization does have an important role to play in this area. There is strong organizational commitment to supplying resources for development as opposed to expecting the individual to share these, and to a lesser extent the same is true for management qualifications. This does not mean that individuals may not make additional commitments on their own, as indeed many do. As far as career development is concerned there is a finer balance, but still one in which companies see themselves as accepting an equal share. These positions are some way removed from the assumptions associated with the end of career arguments. Certainly there were few signs that companies felt that management development could safely be left to the individual; if this had been true in the late 1980s, there seems to have been what Hirsch and Jackson (1996) call 'a shift back from the over-to-you attitude'. Moreover, succession planning at senior levels was an important issue for many organizations.

The objectives of training have been greatly aided by a substantial move forward in the language and definition of managerial competencies, something that was badly missing a decade ago, when Mangham and Silver (1986) pointed to a picture of conceptual poverty as to what sort of training was needed. The national management standards may not be an important driver of development, but they have certainly provided a framework for the competency movement. Almost all of our face-to-face interviewees referred to a competency framework of some kind. The growth of appraisal and its link to management development has also been important in this area, at least amongst the larger companies. This makes it much more likely that the training provided is relevant to the individual manager's needs. Moreover, in terms of what makes a good manager, in-company training and post-experience education are seen as relatively more important than a decade ago, even if inherent ability and job experience are still seen as the most important.

Most respondents believe that their management development activities are meeting organizational objectives to a satisfactory extent and are having a substantial impact on the organization. While these outcome measures are limited compared to the desirability of measuring bottom-line achievements, they are nevertheless useful measures. Individual managers do not share these optimistic views to the same extent, but are far from being entirely negative. The MBAs, not surprisingly, were generally less satisfied with their employer's development system than the client managers.

There has been a very considerable surge in demand for management development. Although this factor does not show up strongly on our statistical analysis, we feel that it has an underlying significance in what organizations have done. In addition, manager interest in management development went beyond the organization. Irrespective of their views and experiences about management development in the organization, the MBA respondents for the most part participated in some form of management development outside the organization, and we feel confident in extending this to many other managers. Moreover, from the point of view of the individual, there has been a recognizable payback from development; this is of course what has largely been responsible for the surge in demand. Some measure of the financial extent of this can be found in the Association of MBAs salary reviews, but at another level it must also be seen in less easily measurable terms of an insurance policy against redundancy.

There has been a shift in attitude amongst senior managers. Another aspect of change, which although not measurable we derived from the attitudes and comments of respondents, is that management development has jumped the generation gap which existed even 10 years ago, whereby most senior managers had not themselves been educated, trained or developed by any other means than experientially. Consequently, while paying lip-service they were not fully convinced that anything other than experiential development was necessary. Now the majority of senior managers have themselves been through a more coherent development process and are therefore much more prepared to believe in it both for themselves and their subordinates.

So what about the other side of the balance sheet, those areas which counsel caution about too much complacency? There is a list of these as well:

There are many missing dimensions in moving towards a stronger system of management development. A majority of organizations do not have a policy statement on management development, even in the larger-company panel. Nor did a majority even of the company representatives report a high priority for management development, or company responsibility for management development, the other two components of the policy cluster of which we have made a good deal throughout this book as constituting the basis of a strong policy. Just to remind ourselves, only 214 out of 501 reported a written policy statement, only 224 said their company had a high priority and only 81 said that the company took primary responsibility for management development. From these figures, we certainly cannot say that a majority of organizations have a strong policy framework. And these figures were provided by the very people who have a vested interest in talking up the importance of management development; as we have seen, the customer groups reported a lower incidence of the desirable features than the HRD managers. The same is true of other features associated with a positive attitude to management development. A majority do not have a budget for management development. Most organizations do not have a planned career structure for managers; managers are mainly appointed for a job rather than a career. When to these is added an expectation that most managers will move on, the assumption must be that most training is short-term and job-oriented. Even the link of development to appraisal, desirable though it is, carries the potential for focusing on immediate training needs. Thus while the general thrust of our conclusions is that a lot has changed for the better in the last decade or so, this must be set against the range of findings that there is still a long way to go until it has become established as a serious strategic priority in most British companies.

There is little sense of effective evaluation of management development being carried out, or of it being an integrated part of wider strategy. In spite of expressed satisfaction with its achievements and impact, there is still a considerable element of an act of faith involved. The demand for incontrovertible proof is arguably unreasonable – the best is enemy of the good. Yet there are still enough questions to engage the sceptics. *Management Development to the Millennium* (Institute of Management 1994) voiced a paradox which may be a key to the future of management development. While the top executive interviewees argued that people were their most important asset, they had only limited familiarity with their organization's HRD policy or the provider industry other than the major business schools. And while we were not directly concerned with the current debates over integrated business and human resource strategies, we did not come across situations where the respondents noted that their management development was part of an integrated high-commitment or high-performance HR policy, and the two individual manager surveys indicated doubts about links to business strategy. And although the surveys consistently saw business strategy as the main driver of management development, we never saw a clear articulation of how this works in practice.

There is also a lack of vision or deep thinking about the future of management development. Respondents found it hard to look ahead for a specific period, hence the use of 'the foreseeable future'. In the same area, there was a low expectation of possible new training methods in the future; few respondents envisaged a role for new technology, for instance. Moreover, although many aspects of management development were more sophisticated than 10 years earlier, there was not a great deal of evidence of thinking about topics such as learning processes or how to link management development to organizational strategies. Indeed from our case studies we got the feeling that management development is lagging behind and derived from change rather than helping to shape it. While management development is certainly recognized, other, usually short-term and bottom-line, pressures are often greater. As a result there is no stable organizational state for management development to plan from. In many cases this means a basic lack of continuity; in one sense, and while recognizing that change is desirable, it was disturbing that over 70 per cent of organizations foresaw different methods of development in the future implying that they lack the courage of their convictions about their present system.

British management development still does not have any real self-confidence about its provenance or abilities, and hence continuity in operating policies, including management development, has been very limited. Many management policies are determined by short-term fads imported from the United States and based on the sayings of the latest guru rather than any depth of research. Not all of these have to do with management development, but they have an impact upon it, and indeed it is arguable that one of the worst features of management development is that it has relatively little continuity, being derived from structural or policy changes rather than helping to shape these. Thus Storey et al. note:

> it is fair to say that some of the senior figures in our British companies did not believe that there could be a programme of corporate reorganisation without a change from top to bottom in training and development – and since they were repeatedly reorganising, this often meant that individual managers were sometimes phases behind in their knowledge of the current development arrangements. Regardless of the merits of the individual schemes themselves, too much change can disrupt expectations. (1997: 227)

We found in our discussions with the 1986 survey companies that trying to make comparisons with a decade earlier was of limited usefulness because our respondents' frames of reference did not extend that far back.

On a slightly different tack, we detected some reservations about the move of responsibility for development to line management. There may have been an element of self-interest in such reservations, but they also sounded reasonable. Line managers are on the whole not trained for their development role; it is not high on their list of priorities and there are few incentives or rewards for them in this area. As a result some central training people felt that they needed to be more proactive, possibly another pendulum which is swinging back. Although companies with a 'strong' policy had successful perceived outcomes, this was associated with centralized leadership in implementation. Yet the current HRM theory is that such activities should be decentralized down to line management. This may be good theory, but we are far from sure that it provides good practice unless the responsibility is recognized and provided with a system of evaluation and personal reward for the manager. As far as we could ascertain, this was not often the case. Without it, the natural concentration of the managers is on those things for which they will be rewarded, that is, those with a closer relevance to financial, production, or sales targets. We think this is a weakness in management development.

▶ Where Does Management Development Stand Now?

So what is the balance between these differing perspectives on where management development stands? As we noted at the beginning of these considerations, our report is upbeat compared with the major reports of 10 years ago. The balance of points above undoubtedly comes down on the positive side, although there is quite sufficient on the other side to conclude that there is no room for complacency. Britain has moved a step or two up the ladder of sophistication, but it is some way from the top yet. Demand is no longer a real problem; the weaknesses are on the supply side in terms of a need for more focus on quality and less on quantity, and for a more integrated system. Nevertheless, the overall situation has improved considerably, and we do not think it solely a matter of coincidence that the recent improvement in Britain's economic standing in the world has coincided with the new framework of management development.

So far in these conclusions, we have primarily used our own findings to evaluate the extent of positive change and remaining weaknesses. But of course our work has only covered part of the total system of management development, that at the organizational level, and we would like to reflect on three related wider issues.

The first relates to the nature of the managerial career. We have argued that organizations do not subscribe to the *end of career* perspective. However, this is by no means the same as saying that managers do not feel insecure; they manifestly do (Benbow 1995), and a considerable part of the enthusiasm for development amongst managers arguably has as much to do with this as the desire for higher skills for their own sake. There has been a good deal of pessimism about the changing nature of managerial careers, perhaps most evocatively portrayed by Herriott et al. (1998) as being cast adrift on a stormy ocean. Storey et al. are also dubious about the British system as it relates to individuals: 'To the extent that there was a generic British approach, it lay in a "sink or swim" attitude to early career development, a reliance on specific performance targets, and a stress on the "ownership" of the career by the individual who then has to find a way through the internal and external labour market, drawing where relevant on an organization's resources' (1997: 228). The 'sink or swim' approach had meant 'an individualistic switching around between firms and jobs' (1997: 226). We would not be as pessimistic as this; we have found that companies do have a perception of responsibility for careers, and indeed need some continuity of personnel to maintain the corporate culture and memory. We would, however, agree that the psychological climate has changed, that managers are losing the sense of their companies being the career anchors to which they attach expectations of ongoing support, and that there is a general move towards a more external labour market. There is something of a paradox here, since the existence of an external labour market would normally mean a lower level of interest in management development. Clearly the drive towards better-developed managers has overcome the move towards an external labour market. There may be another dimension of this issue: where very few managers are developed, employers fear they will leave or be poached, but if most managers are being developed, this fear diminishes because there will be other trained managers available on the external labour market to replace them.

A second issue is the various strands of management development that chapter 3 identified, namely industrial, educational, and professional, and the state of knowledge regarding them. In reviewing the main strands we should also again acknowledge the role of consultants, whose work continues to have significance. This book has mainly dealt with the industrial dimension of management development, and has indicated a very considerable shift in attitudes and level of activity even in the last two decades. The level of further and higher educational provision has also increased enormously, to the point where it now takes up over a fifth of total provision. Even so, a minority of all managers have a degree, although the majority of those moving into management now do. Development of the professional strand has also been significant, with considerable growth in the various institutes which cater for managers. Even so, and allowing for many members of other institutes in engineering, accounting, and other professions having a managerial role, a relatively small minority of all managers are members of any institute. Nevertheless, the institutes are probably now at their strongest position yet in relation to the whole occupation of management, and there may be an increase in membership as managers lose their expectation of corporate commitment to their longer-term career, and search for an alternative career anchor. If the institutes find a coherent operational way of providing a system of continuing professional development, such an increase could be even greater in the future. But taking the three strands together there is still relatively little complementarity between them; rather they run on separate but parallel tracks, although one interesting recent development bringing two of them together has been the emergence of the corporate university. The final question, originally raised in chapter 3, was about whether there is now a body of knowledge which can inform and be instilled in managers. At one level the amount of education, training and development would suggest that there is, but further reflection suggests that if so, it is still a weak framework. It also tends to be concerned with fads, which implies a lack of self-confidence about its core activities and beliefs. A closely related issue is about the nature of managerial knowledge. Although some formal developmental processes are now regarded as universally necessary, there is still a very reputable school of thought which argues that much of the knowledge which makes management successful is tacit knowledge, which is derived from experience, not capable of being defined or learned formally, and therefore cannot be part of programmes of management development. This means that management is closer to an art than a science, in spite of some 'scientific' dimension derived from accumulated research. We will pick up again on this issue in the final section.

In a third dimension, the long-running question of whether management is a profession in any wider sense is still unanswered. Management is still an art, in that according to our survey question on the making of a good manager the main requirements are still personality and experiential development, but the role of systematic training is now firmly established. It may still not be a profession in the strict sense of having standards of entry, but it has moved away from the cult of amateurism that bedevilled its past. Amateurism may still exist in pockets, but it is on the defensive. And the social status of industry has risen, at the expense of sectors like public service, although not to the level of the City of London. However, it would be far from the reality to argue that British managers have developed any strong core of professional identity, either institutionally or by unity of definition or purpose. Managers are still a very loose grouping, and indeed more and more people are carrying out at least some managerial tasks. A related issue is concerned with the nature of management itself. Downsizing and delayering along with new technology have been seen by many as signalling major threats to the managerial occupations and to middle managers in particular (Kanter 1986; Goffee and Scase 1986), although it has been disputed by others (Dopson and Stewart 1990), who see in middle managers a willingness to rise to the new challenges. Using a third approach which focuses on the 'institutionalisation of meaning', Scarbrough (1998) argues that it is the change in meaning systems which is crucial and suggests that managerial groups have been subject to polarization and intensification while managerial work practices have been diffused throughout work practices across all levels of organization.

Our final issue regarding the current situation is how Britain has met the hopes and recommendations of the 1980s. A brief answer must be – substantially but far from completely. Every manager does not have his or her own development plan. There is little evidence that learning material is based on best practice, or even little recognition of what comprises best practice. And there is no measuring rod of what progress is being made. The Management Indicators Framework has some promise, but is too recent and too complex to be sure of such progress. But although few of the explicit recommendations of the 1980s reports and agendas have been completely fulfilled, there has been substantial progress which their authors would surely acknowledge, especially when, in the context of their time, such progress did not look likely. Nevertheless, according to the hopes and recommendations of the mid-1980s, we would give an assessment of 7 out of 10 for progress at the onset of the millennium.

An obviously important test of progress is the question, where does Britain now stand internationally? All countries must face the spread of globalization and the ubiquity of change as factors in management development. Thus one issue is whether there is any trend towards international convergence in management development away from the highly differentiated systems identified by Handy (1987). We believe that there is such a trend, led by the MBA and the effect of globalization, which has resulted in the need to create 'international' managers by the multinationals. How far such people have a common set of competencies, values, or roles, and how far their development has an impact on national systems of development is a subject which requires researching. Certainly it is some way from becoming dominant. Beyond this, however, any comparison between British progress and the situation in other countries necessitates a brief review of what direction the other countries are moving in.

In Japan, there seems to be a move away from lifetime employment and a collective framework of living and working towards a greater amount of individualism and self-reliance. The implication is that management development will move to being owned by the individual and become more market-oriented. In the United States, there is a tendency for the personnel/human resource function to be seen as useful only in terms of its proven contribution to the bottom line. There is a good deal of work going on to try to link the two, but most commentators seem to be pessimistic about a concern for longer-term people-related issues within the organization. Business schools, for their part, are trying to recognize that management is at least as much of an art as a science. In Germany there is a move towards a more academic framework for putative managers, although the apprenticeship tradition is by no means dead. The academic framework itself looks likely to have to move in a more internationally focused direction, and towards the MBA as something that many young managers will see as valuable for their careers. In France the fundamental elitism of the *grandes écoles* seems likely to continue, although the business-related ones seem likely to gain at the expense of those in engineering. The MBA is infiltrating France, too and, what is more, it is increasingly frequently taught in English as an option.

Each country retains a great deal of its distinctiveness in spite of the slight move to convergence noted above. But where does Britain stand in relation to these other countries, and how competitive is British management now? Neither question is at all easy to answer. Certainly the issue of management development has been a greater focus of concern than in the other countries. But without being able to give a precise answer we would argue that Britain has closed a very considerable part of the gap in management development which was apparent in the Handy Report (1987) and indeed for a long time before it. Even so, a survey which has been carried out by some members of the present team in Ireland, with many of the same questions, suggests that Irish small companies have developed a greater orientation towards training their managers than their British counterparts (Graham et al. 2000). Nevertheless Britain has moved a considerable way towards creating a coherent system of its own, one leaning towards the American system rather than any of the others.

Inevitably, many of the arguments about British progress are relative as well as absolute. Much of the fashionable pessimism of the 1980s was based on Britain's demonstrated inadequacy vis-à-vis its main competitors; if we have moved in the last decade, it may be that they have done so even more, leaving the relative position as bad or worse. Certainly headlines about Britain's educational and training deficiencies are still all too common. The Price Waterhouse Cranfield survey (Brewster and Hegewisch 1994) suggests that when compared by indicators such as number of days spent on management training and changes in the amount of expenditure on it, Britain is very much in line at least with the rest of Europe, but in the same survey Britain comes near the bottom of European rankings in percentages of companies with training and development as the main objective of human resource policy and in companies spending more than 2 per cent of the total wage and salary bill on training for all the workforce. Britain may have improved relatively in management development, but this is not necessarily the case for other occupations, and the Skills Audit suggests that there is a relative weakness particularly at the intermediate and technician levels. As noted in chapter 4, the most recent White Paper on training, *Learning to Succeed* (DfEE 1999b), suggests that Britain still has a 20 per cent productivity gap vis-à-vis its main European competitors France and Germany, and almost 40 per cent behind the United States. Thus while training is by no means the only component of productivity, and while management may have improved, it requires skills at all levels to be a successful company or country, and overall Britain still has some catching up to do. As for management itself, the most recent pronouncement on the existing situation is from the Skills Audit of 1996: 'As the Competitiveness White Papers have shown, the best UK companies are as good as the best in the world. . . . However, surveys have shown that UK managers often think their performance is better than it is. Moreover we have a longer tail of poorly performing companies than our competitors' (DfEE 1996: 43).

▶ Towards a Model of Management Development?

The 'working' model which we propounded in chapter 2 argued that there is a feedback loop between four dimensions of management development, namely the contextual aspects or inputs, the management development policy framework, the activities and outputs, and the outcomes or impacts. It also noted that a similar framework could also apply to the individual and the state in respect of their management development activities and perspectives. Where does it stand after the exposition of our findings and, equally important, what does our analysis of the model add to the general framework of conclusions that we have been sketching so far in this last chapter?

It would be far too much to claim that we have captured anything like the range of potential causal relationships in figure 2.2, in either our statistical or descriptive analysis. There is a massive number of these and many of them are very difficult to measure. There is also a very considerable loss of causality as one proceeds around the 'clock'; thus the policy framework, however sophisticated (and the vast majority are not), will not explain all the processes and activities actually occurring, nor will these latter explain all the outcomes, nor will the outcomes explain changes in organizational policy.

What we think we have been able to do is to take a first step towards examining some of these relationships, along the lines of the Chinese proverb which notes that a journey of a thousand miles must start with a single step. We have used a number of different methods to utilize a rich range of data consisting of several surveys derived from different perspectives. Some of our reporting is based on single items of data, but much more, especially in the tables, uses cross-tabulations to illustrate relationships between two sets of data. We also use comparisons between the different surveys to indicate differences or similarities between the findings of the various surveys. Such triangulations are especially important in creating reassurance that the results of any one survey are not isolated and therefore potentially unreliable. We have then additionally carried out a number of multivariate regression analyses on three of the survey databases, using similar independent and dependent variables to seek comparable results in the various equations. The cumulative outcome of all these approaches does, we feel, provide a reasonable level of confidence in the results, since the level of compatibility of the findings from the different surveys is high, or where there are differences, these are explicable in commonsense terms.

In the two previous sections we have provided a broad sweep of descriptive analysis of the extent of change in management development and the current state of play, but we also need to reiterate the key findings as they relate to the model, and to the aspects of causality mentioned in the previous paragraph. We have reported consistent associations between the 'desirable' outputs and outcomes of management development (such as greater amounts of development, higher levels of achievement of development objectives, and impact on the organization) and three key policy dimensions, namely whether there is a written statement, the priority given to management development, and the extent to which the organization assumes responsibility for it. These lead to the central proposition at the heart of the book that there are strong and weak policies which are a matter of choice rather than circumstance. This is derived from both very clear findings of cross-tabular association and regression results, which are particularly striking in our organizational sample of HRD managers. We also reported a cluster of practices concerning the management of the development cycle, which could likewise be termed 'strong' management development practices (including such features as competency frameworks, personal development plans, opportunities for learning transfer and so on) which also led to favourable outcomes. Thus it is important to recognize that the cluster of policy practices, which first led us to the concept of a strong–weak spectrum, only reflects one part of a much wider set of practices which need to be taken together to appreciate the real meaning of a strong system of management development. Finally, there were statistically significant associations between the context and the outputs/outcomes, but at a considerably lower level. Thus a clear causal link between the second and third stages of the cycle was apparent, together with a pattern of policies and processes influencing the perceived outcomes of management development. Moreover the organizational perspectives of the HRD managers were supported by those of the MBAs and client managers on this pattern of relationships, even though they held discrepant views on other issues.

Putting this another way, over the decade or so between the 1986 Constable–McCormick survey and the surveys which we have carried out there has been a very considerable move towards a stronger policy framework, and towards the desirable follow-on implications of improvements in management development practice with which this is associated. We do not want to use the term 'improvements' in a definitive or pejorative way; there are undoubtedly organizations, including some of the very large ones, which have decided quite logically to move towards a weaker policy framework. But this seems to have been associated with those organizations which have already operated a strong framework; the great majority were nowhere near this in 1986. From a national perspective, given the historical background of under-investment in management development, this is surely a good thing.

There is an element of commonsense expectation in these results, although it is always pleasant to have these confirmed by more rigorous analysis. But there are several issues which remain:

- What are the determinants of policy? It is one thing to say that policy is a matter of choice, but economists would argue that choice is not generally random, and depends on other considerations not included in the analysis to date. This might be achieved by disaggregating the results we have reported into the strong and weak policy frameworks, and following up in more detail on each category. There are almost certainly contingent factors, such as the nature of labour markets and career patterns, which influence the general/specific natures of required competencies and set the balance between external and internal recruitment and promotion policies. But the issue of choice is also a very real one, and, we would argue, certainly plays a part. We are experimenting with statistical pathways through various groups of factors, but this is at too early a stage to be reported.
- How robust is this set of associations over time? So far we have only examined them in the relative weakness of cross-sectional surveys. Our data from 1986, while valuable for intermittent cross-referencing, were not sufficiently structured to permit statistical tests. One of the key needs in this as in other areas is to obtain good longitudinal data.
- The better linking of management development with financial and competitive performance, following up work begun in the US.
- The external context might well yield other groupings of variables which would produce interesting results. In particular, the arguments of Sonnenfeld, Peiperl and Kotter (1988) that different industries have different labour market dynamics might provide a contingent basis for inter-industrial differences in management development.
- Similarly, there is no lack of different internal structural variables which would repay closer investigation, among them the extent to which policies at the level of the business, the HR system, and management development are complementary, and also some measure of structural change.
- Better investigation into different facets of informal management development, and a search, which will admittedly be problematic, for a method of treating it on an equal footing with formal methods.

- We have argued that the difference between 'strong' and 'weak' management development policies is a matter of choice rather than circumstance. It is now desirable to step back and examine the nature of choice in more detail. It is not likely that choice is a random factor, so what controls it is a matter of considerable interest.
- Is it feasible to use the working model to pursue a stakeholder-focused analysis?
- The above possibilities are focused at the level of the organization. There may also be valuable work in the area of the relationship between individual career patterns and management development, especially where there are differing perceptions of responsibility for both career and management development. In addition, where there is a weak policy, what drives the development process? It would be interesting to analyse this from differing individual perceptions of career management.

All these possibilities require either different, or better, measurement of both dependent and independent variables. None seriously challenges the working model as we have presented it, and all should help to reinforce it. Indeed it might be reasonable to extend the strong and weak policies in the organizational model to the individual and state models also put forward in chapter 2. We would hope to pursue many of these objectives in further research.

Conclusion: Towards the Future

All the indicators of the future in our survey suggest that more training will be done and that the priority will be greater. Expectations of this sort in the 1980s surveys were largely borne out and it would be surprising if the trends shown up by our respondents since then did not continue. And meanwhile, the rate of change will continue to accelerate and provide a rationale for organizations to see development as a necessary and not just an optional response. Change will have a number of different dimensions. Thus technology and globalization will continue to change industrial and job structures and organizations, labour markets, and careers. All of these will have an impact on the nature of management and therefore management development. But there is a slightly different factor as well. We have mentioned the term 'cultural glue' several times in this book, and it is clear that management development provides a focus for organizational identity and coherence. In the light of continuing radical change, organizations will need such focal points.

It would also be surprising if the present trends on the demand side did not continue. Life-long learning and continuing professional development are ideas and intentions more than a structured reality at present, but seem likely to take off and give a more coherent and formal structure to the ongoing development process. How far there will be a policy framework at the national level or how far a laissez-faire system is a moot point. But it is still a somewhat shadowy concept in terms of a coherent policy structure, especially in providing a means of reconciling the various different modes of learning, and in providing a means of recognizing all learning on an equal basis. Individual managers will certainly seek recognition for their learning activities. If the Council for Excellence in Management and Learning can help to provide such a framework it will have been successful.

But there is an even more persuasive reason for thinking that management development will become more important in the future, and it is to do with the role of knowledge. Organizations are increasingly driven by the demands of the financial markets, and these measures, rather than stakeholder-based measures, have become central to policy-making. Financial markets are also exerting an influence on the competition for capital between industries, as well as within industries. The role of knowledge is also central to this and nothing demonstrates changing views of relative value more than the rise of communications and information technology (CIT) shares on stock markets compared with those of more traditional industries such as retailing.

The role of the manager will become more influential in a knowledge-based economy. For managers, in an economy where skill is based on knowledge, and where all aspects of the situation are likely to change rapidly, job security will be dependent on the ability to learn the new aspects. This will be the real driver of continuing professional development, and as we saw from our MBA survey, many managers have already appreciated the need for this. Indeed the MBA and other qualifications may be more important for the ability to learn that it inculcates than for the actual learning *per se*.

For organizations the key resource for competitive advantage and success will largely be in the heads of the managers. But even then, most managers will possess tacit knowledge which they apply without codifying it, making it difficult for such knowledge to be transferred, but at the same time raising their market value. Indeed all knowledge has a tacit dimension in the sense that codified knowledge can only be utilized where some element of tacit knowledge, that is, the best application of codified knowledge, is brought to bear. How to develop and exploit this knowledge will be the task of the organization. Management development will have much to do with ensuring that managers create, absorb, transfer, and apply knowledge.

Appendix 1

This appendix is intended to provide a basic framework of the surveys; further information is provided in the publications dealing with some of the separate surveys (Thomson et al. 1997; Thomson et al. 1998). The questionnaire for each of the surveys can be obtained from the lead author at the Open University Business School; we regret that we do not have the space in this book to provide them in full.

The Surveys

Panel A (1996)

This comprised 18 large organizations which had also participated in the 1986 Thomson Working Party Survey. It was not intended that they should be a representative cross-section of the economy; nevertheless they do provide reasonably broad coverage. Nor was it intended that they should form a database; rather we were looking for anecdotal evidence, particularly of change since the mid-1980s. The main reason for approaching this particular group was in fact that we had a copy of the organization's written management development policy from the 1980s and invited respondents to draw comparisons. The organizations were:

Government
   Cabinet Office
   Borough of Bromley
Utilities
   United Utilities

Manufacturing
  GKN
  Ciba-Geigy
  Vickers
  Unilever
  Whitbread
  British Steel
  3M
Retail
  Dixons Stores
  John Menzies
Financial Services
  Woolwich Building Society
  Alliance and Leicester Building Society
Transport
  Transport Development Group
Trading
  Inchcape

Panel B (1996) (referred to as the HRD managers survey)

This comprised 501 organizations with more than 100 employees each. The individual with responsibility for management development was interviewed by telephone according to a questionnaire which had been sent in advance; each interview took approximately 40 minutes. A copy of the full questionnaire is provided in Thomson et al. (1997). It is important for the discussion in this book to note that the median size of organization in the sample is around 650. In conventional ways of viewing size groupings, it is therefore much more representative of medium-sized organizations than it is of large organizations.

Overall, however, we are satisfied that the sample is a reasonably representative one. The creation of the initial population of some 23,000 was based on Dun and Bradstreet company information together with the *Civil Service Year Book* and the *Municipal Year Book*. In drawing up the sample the intention was to provide a reasonable coverage of organizations within the population; a breakdown by employment would of course have produced a very different outcome. Even so, although only 61 organizations with more than 5,000 employees were interviewed, this category was nevertheless greatly over-represented to the extent of some three times more than the next three size categories, which in turn were three times more heavily represented than the smallest size category. This skewing was accepted in the target sample structure, and the quotas were achieved. In all, an initial attempt was made to contact 1,693 organizations; 765 were actually contacted; the difference between these two figures is because the person responsible for management development was not initially available and was not re-contacted owing to quotas having already been filled. Of the 765 contacted, 578 agreed to an interview and 187 refused; in the event 501 interviews were carried out, with some appointments being cancelled because the quotas were full. However the refusal rate of 24.44 per cent is lower than in many other surveys of a similar kind, and given also the care taken in structuring the sample, the overall conclusion must be that Panel B is a representative sample of its population. The main characteristics of the organizations were:

Number of employees (%)

100–299	24
300–499	19
500–999	22
1,000–4,999	19
5,000+	17

Turnover

£5 million or under	7
£6–20 million	25
£21–50 million	21
£51–100 million	15
£101–400 million	13
More than £400 million	18

Sector

Manufacturing	26
Distribution	20
Services	29
Holding companies	10
Government	14

Nationality of ownership

British	83
Other	17

UK company growth over last three years

Increasing	67
Decreasing	9
Stable	21

Panel C (1996) (referred to as the small business survey)

This panel comprised returns to a postal questionnaire sent to the owner/ manager or chief executive of small companies. The questionnaire was based on that used for Panel B above, but with some modifications and shortening to make it more suitable for small businesses. Most of the 1,275 questionnaires were sent to those members of the panel of the Small Business Research Trust which had previously reported six or more employees; however, 50 members of the CBI Small Firms Council were also included in the mailing. Of the 1,275 questionnaires sent out with prepaid return envelopes, 24 were returned as not being at the address, and 403 responses were received, of which 389 were usable. This gives a usable response rate of 31.1 per cent, which compares well with most small business questionnaire return rates. It is accepted that there is no fully representative small business perspective because of the problems of contact and obtaining a response. Nevertheless the SBRT panel surveys are generally accepted as being the most continuous and accurate monitoring of small business opinions and intentions, and there is no reason to think that the panel's views on management development are any less reliable. Even so, we recognize that the panel does not include many new or young firms and that the members of the panel are perhaps unusual in being willing to answer both this and other questionnaires. Thus we do not claim a fully representative sample, even of those with more than five employees, and it is likely that our results need caution in interpretation in the light of the frequently observed lack of response of many small businesses to training opportunities.

The characteristics of the organizations in the sample are as follows:

Number of employees (%)
1–9	30
10–19	28
20–29	15
30–49	13
50+	14

Turnover
£250 thousand or under	20
£251–500 thousand	22
£501 thousand – £1 million	19
Over £1 million	36

Sector
Manufacturing	40
Distribution	19
Services	41

Number of sites
1	64
2	16
3	6
4–5	3
6–9	3
10+	1

Number of managers
1	20
2	26
3	18
4	15
5	6
6–9	9
10+	5

Anticipated staffing in one year's time
Increase	49
Stay the same	45
Decrease	5

MBA graduate panel (1997)

This survey was based on postal questionnaires sent to the membership of the Association of MBAs. The questionnaire was also based on that used in Panel B above, modified to relate to being answered by individuals rather than on behalf of organizations, and also to take account of intended future personal development. Some 8,000 questionnaires were sent out and 1,398 returned. A series of quotas was set up to provide a structured sample of the membership; these quotas were primarily based on date an individual joined the Association, level of manager, and industrial sector. 450 questionnaires were selected to meet these quotas, and this is the main grouping from which information has been drawn. It is not possible to say how far this sampling procedure reflects the total membership of the Association, since records are not kept in a way that reflects these particular categorizations. A stronger rationale was to provide suitable categories which could be susceptible to statistical analysis. In addition, a further sample of 50 was set up to reflect those members of the Association who are self-employed, usually as consultants.

The response rate of 17.4 per cent is acceptable for a postal questionnaire but not so high as to dispel questions about how far it reflects Association membership. Those responding were likely to have a higher level of interest in management development than those who did not. Moreover, those institutions whose graduates are eligible for membership of the Association are by no means representative of the total spectrum of MBA-providing institutions. A third caveat is that MBA graduates cannot be said to be representative of managers as a whole. These three factors should be borne in mind when interpreting the results. Nevertheless MBAs almost by definition have a commitment to management development and may be expected to hold informed views about it, and this makes the group of very considerable interest in a review of the subject.

The main characteristics of the individuals in the main sample of the survey are:

Age (%)
Under 35	20
35–44	49
45 or over	31

Gender
Male	72
Female	17
Not stated	10

Current management level
Junior/middle	30
Senior	35
Director	33

Function/discipline
Marketing	18
Finance	20

Production/operations	3
Personnel	3
General	35
Other	11

Length of time a manager

Less than 3 years	6
3–5 years	16
6–10 years	30
11–20 years	35
More than 20 years	12
Not stated	2

Size of current employer by employees

1–9	4
10–99	12
100–499	12
500–999	6
1,000–4,999	18
5,000+	47

'Client' manager panels (1997)

This survey related to managers in organizations which had already participated in either Panel B or Panel C as described above. References in the text are to the Panel B group of managers, unless otherwise stated. In the questionnaires to these companies, we asked if they would be prepared to engage in follow-up research. Those which did so were sent up to twelve questionnaires (depending on the number of managers in the organization) to be distributed to their managers who were 'consumers' of management development. The questionnaires were also based on the original Panel B questionnaire, and were designed both to have some point of comparison with the organizational viewpoint expressed through Panels B and C, and also to elicit information on how the managers perceived the process of management development. As a result of this procedure 215 completed questionnaires were received from managers, 125 from Panel B organizations and 90 from Panel C. We have, however, mainly used the 125 from Panel B, who came from 35 separate organizations, as the source of comparative information.

Given that the organizations were only a small proportion of the original sample, that we had no control over the selection of managers to whom the questionnaires were distributed, and that there was only a limited numerical response, it would be wrong to claim any true representativeness of the sample actually achieved. Nevertheless, the respondents do reflect a grouping whose perspective is valuable as a broad cross-check against the answers of the organizations, and also as a very different group of managers to those represented by the MBA panel.

The main characteristics of the managers in the Panel B and C groups are shown in the table below.

	Panel B (%)	Panel C (%)
Age		
Under 35	42	28
35–44	34	34
45 or over	23	38
Current level of management		
Junior	17	10
Middle	42	38
Senior	31	24
Director	10	27
Length of current employment		
Up to 3 years	21	23
4–5 years	9	13
6 years and more	70	62

We have tried in the above to indicate the degree of representativeness of each of the surveys. We accept that there is considerable variability in this. However, the credibility of all the surveys is enhanced by the extent to which they produce compatible results, and, as will have been seen, this was generally the case.

Appendix 2: Statistical Analysis

The purpose of this second appendix is to explain the nature of the statistical analysis carried out on the surveys, and to provide some examples of the results. Fuller articles have been produced describing the methodology and results: Thomson, Mabey and Storey (1998) for Panel B, Thomson and Gray (1999) for Panel C and Mabey and Thomson (2000) for the MBA graduate panel.

The questionnaires deliberately contained the same or very similar questions, enabling comparisons to be drawn between the results of one survey and another. This also enabled the regression analysis to be composed of the same or very similar variables, and for essentially the same methodology to be used in each case. A number of independent variables were regressed against dependent variables such as the amount of training reported to be carried out, and the results from these independent variables were then aggregated into clusters, giving a composite level of causality from several variables. The clusters then became the key focus of analysis and discussion.

The main clusters were as follows (the example is taken from the MBA graduate survey, but the others are almost identical):

'External' variables (size of organization by number of employees) + (industrial sector) + (ownership by nationality of parent organization)

'Internal' variables (growth of organization over last three years) + (centralization of management development) + (responsibility for implementation of management development)

'Policy' variables (existence of a written policy statement on management development) + (extent of perceived priority given to management development) + (perceived responsibility for management development)

'**Career'** **variables** (existence of planned career structure) + (managers appointed for a specific job or a career) + (existence of succession planning programme in organization). In the case of the small company survey, because of the very low number of managers in the companies, it was thought better to substitute a cluster which picked up the personal facets of the key figure. Thus the new cluster became '**Personal'** **variables** (age band of key manager) + (membership of work-related organizations) + (educational level)

A range of dependent variables was utilized. Some related to outputs as defined in the explanation of our theoretical model in chapter 2, while others related to 'outcomes' as similarly defined, and yet others were components of the policy cluster. Perhaps the most important in the first group was the amount of days of training reported per annum, while in the second group the achievement of management development objectives and the impact of management development on the organization were utilized. In the third group we took the existence of a written statement and the priority given to management development as examples.

The objectives of the regression analysis in each case were to examine causality in the determinants of management development outputs and outcomes, again using the model defined in chapter 2. Table A1 gives examples of the results, in each case using the reported amount of training as the dependent variable. These results are commented on in the separate papers. Here it is only necessary to note the generally high level of significance of the results, and in particular, the uniformly highest level of significance of the policy cluster. It is these results which have led to the strength of our conviction about the importance of the strong versus weak policy framework for the operation of management development. Even where several clusters achieve a high level of significance, the policy cluster has much higher Beta scores; thus in the MBA survey regression the Beta score for the policy cluster was .272, while for the external cluster it was .078 and for the internal cluster .061. In addition, we would note that although there is not sufficient space to provide all the results, there is a consistency between the results within each survey (thus using an outcome variable such as the achievement of management

Table A1   Determinants of management development by clusters of variables

	Larger companies survey	Small companies survey	MBA survey
R square	.201	.203	.247
Regressor-set	SigB	SigB	SigB
External cluster	.001 ***	.041 *	.000 ***
Internal cluster	.017*	.001 ***	.001 ***
Policy cluster	.000 ***	.000 ***	.000 ***
Career cluster	.312		.003 **
Personal cluster		.080	

* $p < 0.05$; ** $p < 0.01$; *** $p < 0.001$

Table A2 Priority in relation to external, internal and career clusters

R square	0.155
Listing of variables	Beta
External cluster	0.190***
Internal cluster	0.146***
Career cluster	0.255***

*** $p < 0.001$

development objectives also shows the policy cluster to have the highest significance) as well as between the surveys. It is obviously very important for our overall argument that the results from these different surveys reinforce each other both internally and comparatively.

Table AR takes up a rather different issue. It was clear that the policy cluster was the key cluster so we thought it important to explore what lay behind the components of the cluster. Table A2, which is based on the reporting of priority by the HRD managers, provides an attempt to relate the level of priority to the three clusters of variables other than the policy cluster itself, while part of table A3 does the same with the existence of a written statement. What table A2 indicates is that although all three clusters are highly significant, the career cluster on this occasion emerges as the most important; indeed taken separately, all three of its component variables as defined above are strongly significant. The career cluster in turn is related to the nature of the managerial labour market within the organization, and the implications are that high priority is associated with an internally focused labour market.

A third use of regression analysis was to examine another approach to causality, namely by asking respondents to score a range of prospective influences on management development in the organization. No clusters were used for these equations, partly because there was some potential overlap between the issues. These 'drivers' were then regressed against two different sorts of dependent variable, with the results as shown in table A3. One dependent variable was an output of the system, namely the amount of training reported, as a parallel to the dependent variable in table A1, while the other is concerned, like table A2, with explaining a component of the policy cluster. The variables are listed in the order of the mean scores on a 1–10 scale as ranked by the HRD managers, and this mean ranking is also provided below.

The two equations involved in table A3 (and so presented in order to save space) are carrying out different tasks, so are not directly comparable. The results from the amount of training equation are interesting because none of the variables that are highly ranked by the respondents emerge as significant, while three near the bottom of the scale do so, if only weakly. The explanation for this would seem to lie in whether the respondents were identifying general or specific drivers. Thus although NVQs are identified as an important driver by very few respondents, those that do so are likely to report high amounts of training. By contrast, the existence of a written statement is more

Table A3 Amount of training and written statement related to perceived drivers

R square	0.168	0.158	
Perceived driver	Beta (amount)	Mean on 1–10 scale	Beta (statement)
Business efficiency	0.070	7.23	0.089
Company strategy	0.097	7.21	−0.201 ***
Support of board	−0.088	6.84	−0.163 **
Ability to do job	0.063	6.60	−0.013
Company culture	−0.017	6.38	−0.057
Customers/clients	−0.030	6.36	−0.048
Potential to progress	−0.038	6.36	0.059
Structural change	0.063	6.25	0.049
Staff motivation	0.000	6.02	0.020
Career development	0.119	5.98	−0.126
Demand from managers	0.113 *	5.89	−0.030
Retention of personnel	0.038	5.58	0.134 *
Competitive activity	0.129 *	5.40	0.004
Cost of management development	−0.087	5.07	−0.009
Investors in People	0.010	4.54	−0.192 ***
NVQs	0.130 *	3.49	−0.017

* $p < 0.05$; ** $p < 0.01$; *** $p < 0.001$

strongly associated with several factors, including the high-level issues of company strategy and support of the board, although also Investors in People, which almost by definition is associated with written documentation.

References

Aaronson, S. (1996). Dinosaurs in the global economy? American graduate business schools in the 1980s and 1990s. In R. P. Amdam (ed.), *Management, Education and Competitiveness*. London: Routledge.

ACOST (Advisory Council on Science and Technology), Cabinet Office (1990). *The Enterprise Challenge: Overcoming Barriers to Growth in Small Firms*. London: HMSO.

Adamson, S. J., Doherty, N. and Viney, C. (1998). The meaning of career revisited: Implications for theory and practice. *British Journal of Management*, 9(4), 251–60.

Alexander, G. P. (1987). Establishing shared values through management training. *Training and Development Journal*, 41(2).

Alimo-Metcalfe, B. (1998). 360-degree feedback and leadership development. *International Journal of Selection and Assessment*, 6(1), 35–44.

Allred, B., Snow, C. and Miles, R. (1996). Characteristics of managerial careers in the 21st century. *Academy of Management Executive*, 10(4), 17–27.

AMBA (1992). *The MBA Experience*. London: Association of MBAs.

AMBA (1997). *MBA Salary and Career Survey*. London: Association of MBAs.

Amdam, R. P. (ed.) (1996). *Management, Education and Competitiveness*. London: Routledge.

Arnold, J. (1997). *Managing Careers into the 21st Century*. London: Paul Chapman Publishing.

Arthur, M. and Hendry, C. (1990). Human resource management and the emergent strategy of small and medium sized business units. *Journal of Human Resource Management*, 1(3), 233–50.

Arthur, M. B. (1994). The boundaryless career: A new perspective for organizational inquiry. *Journal of Organizational Behaviour*, 15(4), 295–306.

Ascher, K. (1984). *Masters of Business: The MBA and British Industry.* London: Harbridge House.

Ashton, D. and Felstead, A. (1995). Training and development. In J. Storey (ed.), *Human Resource Management: A Critical Text.* London: Routledge.

Bannock, G. (1981). *The Economics of Small Firms.* Oxford: Basil Blackwell.

Bannock, G. and Albach, H. (1991). *Small Business Policy in Europe.* London: Anglo-German Foundation.

Barnett, C. (1972). *The Collapse of British Power.* London: Eyre Methuen.

Barnett, C. (1987). *The Audit of War.* London: Macmillan.

Barry, B. (1980). Human and organizational problems affecting growth in the smaller enterprise. *Management Review,* 5(4), 14–16.

Baruch, Y. and Peiperl, M. A. (1997). High flyers: Glorious past, gloomy present, any future? *Career Development International,* 2(7), 354–8.

Baruch, Y. and Peiperl, M. (1999). The impact of an MBA: A comparative study. ny of Management Conference, Manchester. urning points in business growth: Implent in small businesses. 12th UK Small Firms London.

Beaumont, P. (1993). *Human Resource Management.* London: Sage.

Becker, G. (1964). *Human Capital.* Chicago: University of Chicago Press.

Belton, B. (1999). Despite humming economy, workers job insecurity. *USA Today.*

Benbow, N. (1995). *Survival of the Fittest.* London: Institute of Management.

Berry, J. (1990). Linking management development to business strategy. *Training and Development Journal,* 44(8), 22.

Black, J. (2000). The development of professional management in the public sector in the UK 1855–1925. Ph.D. thesis, Open University.

Bolton, J. (1971). *Small Firms.* Report of the Committee of Inquiry on Small Firms, Cmnd. 4811. London: HMSO.

Bowen, D. and Hall, D. T. (1997). Career planning for employee development: A primer for managers. *California Management Review,* 20(2), 33–5.

Boyatzis, R. (1982). *The Competent Manager.* New York: Wiley.

Bramley, P. (1991). *Evaluating Training Effectiveness: Translating Theory into Practice.* Maidenhead: McGraw Hill.

Brech, E. (1997). *The Concept and Gestation of Britain's Central Institute of Management 1902–1976.* London: Institute of Management.

Brewster, C. and Hegewisch, A. (eds) (1994). *Policy and Practice in European Human Resource Management.* London: Routledge.

Bridges, W. (1998). *Creating You and Co.* London: Brealey Publishing.

Buller, P. F. (1988). For successful strategic change: Blend OD practice with strategic management. *Organization Dynamics,* 16, 42–55.

Burgoyne, J. (1977). Management learning developments. *BACIE Journal,* 31(9), 158–60.

Burgoyne, J. (1988). Management development for the individual and the organization. *Personnel Management* (June), 20–4.

Burgoyne, J. and Jackson, B. (1997). The arena thesis: Management development as a pluralistic meeting point. In J. Burgoyne and M. Reynolds (eds), *Management Learning.* London: Sage.

Burgoyne, J. and Stuart, R. (1976). The nature, use and acquisition of managerial skills and other attributes. *Personnel Review*, 15(4).

Cannon, F. (1995). The role of education and training in organizational climate change: A case study. *Journal of Professional HRM*, 1 (October), 10–18.

Carter, J. (1996). Degrees of support: Employer commitment to staff development on postgraduate courses. In I. Woodward (ed.), *Continuing Professional Development*. London: Cassell.

Caves, R. (1968). *Britain's Economic Prospects*. London: George Allen & Unwin.

CBI (1986). *Management Training for Small Businesses*. London: Confederation of British Industry.

CBI (1994). *Management Development: Survey of Small and Medium Sized Business*, November 1994. London: Confederation of British Industry.

Chandler, A. D. (1962). *Strategy and Structure*. Cambridge, Mass.: MIT Press.

Chandler, A. D. (1976). The development of modern management structure in the US and the UK. In L. Hannah (ed.), *Management Strategy and Business Development*. London: Macmillan.

Chandler, A. D. (1977). *The Visible Hand: The Managerial Revolution in American Business*. Cambridge, Mass.: Harvard University Press.

Chandler, A. D. (1990). *Scale and Scope: The Dynamics of Industrial Capitalism*. Cambridge, Mass.: Harvard University Press.

Channon, D. F. (1973). *The Strategy and Structure of British Enterprise*, London: Macmillan.

Chapman, P. (1993). *The Economics of Training*. London: Wheatsheaf.

Child, J. (1969). *British Management Thought*. London: George Allen & Unwin.

Churchill, N. and Lewis, V. (1983). The five stages of small business growth. *Harvard Business Review*, 61, 30–51.

Clark, T. and Salaman, G. (1996). The management guru as organisational witchdoctor. *Organization*, 31(1), 85–107.

Clarke, M. (1999). Management development as a game of meaningless outcomes. *Human Resource Management Journal*, 9(2), 38–49.

Constable, J. and McCormick, R. (1987). *The Making of British Managers*. London: British Institute of Management/CBI.

Coopers Lybrand Associates (1985). *A Challenge to Complacency: Changing Attitudes to Training*. London: NEDO.

Coulson-Thomas, C. and Coe, T. (1991). *The Flat Organization: Philosophy and Practice*. London: British Institute of Management.

Crockett, G. and Elias, P. (1984). British managers: A study of their education, training, mobility, and earnings. *British Journal of Industrial Relations*, 1, 34–46.

Cunningham, I. and Dawes, G. (1997). Problematic premises, presumptions, presuppositions and practices in management education and training. In J. Burgoyne and M. Reynolds (eds), *Management Learning*. London: Sage.

Curran, J., Blackburn, R., Kitching, J. and North, J. (1996). *Establishing Small Firms' Training Practices, Needs, Difficulties and Use of Industry Training Organizations*, DfEE Research Studies. London: HMSO.

Curran, J. and Stanworth, J. (1989). Education and training for enterprise: Some problems of classification, policy, evaluation and research. *International Small Business Journal*, 7(2).

Daly, M., Campbell, M., Robson, M. and Gallagher, C. (1991). Job creation 1987–89: The contributions of small and large firms. *Employment Gazette* (November).

Davidsson, P. (1989). *Continued Entrepreneurship and Small Firm Growth*. Stockholm: Economic Research Institute.

Davies, J. and Easterby-Smith, M. C. (1984). Learning and developing from managerial work experiences. *Journal of Management Studies*, 21(2), 169–84.

Dawes, G., Bennett, B., Cunningham, C. and Cunningham, I. (1996). *Learning and Development in Organizations*. St Albans: Strategic Developments.

De Geus, A. (1988). Planning as learning. *Harvard Business Review* (March–April), 70–4.

Deloitte, Haskins & Sells (1989). *Management Challenge for the 1990s: Current Education, Training and Development Debate*. Sheffield: Training Agency.

DfEE (1996). *The National Development Agenda 1996*. London.

DfEE (1998a). *Research Report No 6*. London.

DfEE (1998b). *The Learning Age*. London.

DfEE (1999a). *Education and Training Statistics for the United Kingdom 1998*. London.

DfEE (1999b). *Learning to Succeed: A New Framework for Post-16 Learning*. London.

DfEE and Cabinet Office (1996). *The Skills Audit: A Report from an Interdepartmental Group*. London.

Dibella, A., Nevis, E., Gould, J. and Moingeon, B. (1996). Organizational learning as a core capability. In A. Edmondson (ed.), *Organizational Learning and Competitive Advantages*. London: Sage.

Doeringer, P. and Piore, M. (1971). *Internal Labor Markets and Manpower Analysis*. Boston and Lexington: D. C. Heath.

Dopson, D. and Stewart, R. (1990). What is happening to middle management? *British Journal of Management*, 1(1), 3–16.

Dore, R. (1989). *Japan at Work: Markets, Management and Flexibility*. Paris: OECD.

Doyle, M. (1996). Organizational transformation and renewal: A case for reframing management development. *Personnel Review*, 24(6), 6–18.

Drucker, P. (1985). *Innovation and Entrepreneurship: Practice and Principles*. New York: Harper & Row.

DTI (1998). *Our Competitive Future: Building the Knowledge Driven Economy*, Cm 4176. London: HMSO.

du Gay, P. (1996). *Consumption and Identity at Work*. London: Sage.

Dyer, L. and Reeves, T. (1995). Human resource strategies and firm performance: What do we know and where do we need to go? *International Journal of Human Resources Management*, 6(3), 656–70.

Easterby-Smith, M. (1986). *Evaluation of Management Education, Training and Development*. Aldershot: Gower.

Easterby-Smith, M. and Thorpe, R. (1997). Research traditions in management learning. In J. Burgoyne and M. Reynolds (eds), *Management Learning*. London: Sage.

Elbourne, E. T. (1914). *Factory Administration and Accounts*. London: Library Press.

Evans, P., Lank, E. and Farquhar, A. (1989). Managing human resources in the international firm. In P. Evans, Y. Doz and A. Laurent (eds), *Human Resource*

Management in International Firms: Change, Globalisation and Innovation. London: Macmillan.

Everard, B. (1991). The costs and benefits of training. *Training and Development* (December), 26–8.

Ferguson, M. (1999). The origin, gestation and evolution of management consultancy within Britain 1869–1965. Ph.D. thesis, Open University.

Flamholtz, E. G. (1986). *How to Make the Transition from Entrepreneurship to a Professionally Managed Firm*. London: Jossey-Bass.

Fonda, N. (1988). Management development: The missing link in sustained business performance. *Personnel Management* (December), 50–3.

Fonda, N. (1989). *Strategies and People: The Prospect Centre Perspective*. Kingston upon Thames: The Prospect Centre.

Forrester, P. (1985). Postgraduate management education in UK universities. Unpublished.

Fox, S. (1989). The politics of evaluating management development. *Management Education and Development*, 20(3), 191–207.

Fox, S. (1997). From management education and development to the study of management learning. In J. Burgoyne and M. Reynolds (eds), *Management Learning*. London: Sage.

Fox, S. and McLeay, S. (1991). An approach to researching managerial labour markets: HRM, corporate strategy and financial performance in UK manufacturing. British Academy of Management Annual Conference, Bath University.

Franks, Lord (1963). *British Business Schools*. London: British Institute of Management.

Furnham, A. and Stringfield, P. (1998). Congruence in job-performance ratings: A study of 360-degree feedback examining self, managers, peers and consultant ratings. *Human Relations*, 51(4), 517–30.

Gallie, D. and White, M. (1993). *Employee Commitment and the Skills Revolution*. London: Policy Studies Institute.

Garavan, T. (1991). Strategic human resource development. *Journal of European Industrial Training*, 15(1), 17–30.

Garavan, T., Costine, P. and Heraty, N. (1995). *Training and Development in Ireland: Context, Policy and Practice*. Dublin: Oak Tree Press.

Garavan, T., Heraty, N. and Morley, M. (1998). Actors in the HRD process: An exploration study. *International Studies of Management and Organization*, 28(1), 114–35.

Garratt, B. (1994). *The Learning Organization*. London: HarperCollins.

Goffee, F. and Scase, R. (1986). Are the rewards worth the effort? Changing managerial values in the 1980s. *Personnel Review*, 15.

Goold, M. and Campbell, A. (1987). *Strategies and Styles: The Role of the Centre in Managing Diversified Companies*. Oxford: Blackwell.

Graham, R., Donoghue, K., Gray, C. and Mabey, C. (2000). *Management Development in the Republic of Ireland: Pattern and Trends*. Milton Keynes: Open University Business School.

Granick, D. (1971). *Managerial Comparisons of Four Developed Countries: France, Britain, United States and Russia*. Cambridge, Mass.: MIT Press.

Grant, R. M. (1995). *Contemporary Strategic Analysis*. Oxford: Blackwell.

Gratton, L. (1996). Implementing a strategic vision: Key factors for success. *Long-Range Planning*, 29(3), 290–303.

Gray, C. (1993). Stages of growth and entrepreneurial career motivation. In F. Chittenden, M. Robertson and D. Watkins (eds), *Small Firms: Recession and Recovery*. London: ISBA/Paul Chapman.

Gray, C. (1998). *Enterprise and Culture*. London: Routledge.

Guest, D. (1992). Employee commitment and control. In J. Hartley and G. Stephenson (eds), *Employee Relations*. Oxford: Blackwell.

Guest, D. (1997). Human resource management and performance: A review and research agenda. *International Journal of Human Resource Management*, 8(3), 263–76.

Guest, D. E. and Conway, N. (1997). Employee motivation and the psychological contract. *Issues in People Management*, 21.

Guest, D. and Mackenzie Davey, K. (1996). Don't write off the traditional career. *People Management*, 2(4).

Guest, D. and Peccei, R. (1994). The nature and causes of effective human resource management. *British Journal of Industrial Relations*, 32(2), 219–62.

Hall, D. (1984). Human resource development and organizational effectiveness. In C. Fornbrun, N. Ticky and M. Devanna (eds), *Strategic Human Resource Management*. New York: Wiley.

Hall, P. J. and Mirvis, P. H. (1995). Careers as lifelong learning. In A. Howard (ed.), *The Changing Nature of Work*. San Francisco: Jossey-Bass.

Hamel, G. and Prahalad, C. K. (1994). *Competing for the Future*. Boston, Mass.: Harvard Business School Press.

Handy, C. (1987). *The Making of Managers*. London: NEDO.

Handy, C., Gordon, C., Gow, I. and Randlesome, C. (1988). *Making Managers*. London: Pitman.

Harrison, R. (1997). *Employee Development*. London: Institute of Personnel and Development.

Harvey, C. and Press, J. (1989). Overseas investment and the professional advance of British mining engineers, 1851–1914. *Economic History Review*, 42(1), 64–89.

Hendy, C. and Pettigrew, A. (1990). Human resource management: An agenda for the 1990s. *International Journal of Human Resource Management*, 1(1), 17–43.

Herriot, P., Hirsch, W. and Reilly, P. (1998). *Trust and Transition: Managing the Employment Relationship*. Chichester: John Wiley.

Herriot, P. and Pemberton, C. (1995). *New Deals*. Chichester: John Wiley.

Herriot, P. and Pemberton, C. (1996). Contracting careers. *Human Relations*, 49(6), 757–90.

Hillage, J. and Moralee, J. (1996). *The Return on Investors*. Brighton: Institute of Employment Studies.

Hirsch, W. and Jackson, C. (1996). *Strategies for Career Development: Promise, Practice and Pretence*. Brighton: Institute of Employment Studies.

Holden, L. (1992). Does strategic training policy exist? Some evidence from ten European countries. *Personnel Review*, 21(1), 12–23.

Holden, L. (1994). NEC: International HRM with vision. *International Human Resource Management*, 2(2), 113–31.

Holland, G. (1986). Management education policy. Presented at the British Institute of Management Conference on Management Education and Training (February), London.

Holmes, L. (1996). HRM and the irresistible rise of the discourse of competence. *Personnel Review*, 24(4), 34–49.

Huselid, M. (1995). The impact of human resource management practices on turnover, productivity and corporate financial performance. *Academy of Management Journal*, 38(3), 635–72.

IFF (1996). *Employer-Provided Training in the UK 1993*. London: IFF Research Ltd.

Iles, P. A. (1997). Sustainable career development: A resource-based view. *Career Development International*, 2(7), 347–53.

Inkson, K. C. (1995). Effects of changing economic conditions on managerial job changes and careers. *British Journal of Management*, 6, 183–94.

Institute of Management (1994). *Management Development to the Millennium*. London.

Institute of Personnel and Development (1998). *Impact of People Management Practices on Business Performance*, London.

Institute of Personnel and Development (1999). *Organizational Development: Whose Responsibility?* London.

Jackson, C., Arnold, J., Nicholson, N. and Watts, A. G. (1998). *Managing Careers in 2000 and Beyond*. Brighton: Institute of Employment Studies.

Jones, G. and Barnes, M. (1967). *Britain on Borrowed Time*. London: Penguin.

Kamoche, K. (1996). Human resources as a strategic asset: An evolutionary resource-based theory. *Journal of Management Studies*, 33(6), 757–85.

Kanter, R. M. (1986). The reshaping of middle management. *Management Review* (January).

Kanter, R. M. (1989). *When Giants Learn to Dance*. New York: Simon & Schuster.

Katz, L. (1955). The skills of an effective administrator. *Harvard Business Review* (January–February).

Kearns, P. and Miller, T. (1993). The financial return from training and investment: Hard facts of act or faith? *Transition*, 9 (October), 22–3.

Keeble, S. (1982). *The Ability to Manage*. Manchester: Manchester University Press.

Kempner, T. (1984). Education for management in five countries: Myth and reality. *Journal of General Management* (Winter).

Kirkpatrick, D. (1958). Techniques for evaluating training programmes. *Journal for American Society of Training Directors*, 13 (November).

Knowles, M. S. (1984). *The Adult Learner: A Neglected Species*, 3rd edn. Houston: Gulf.

Kolb, D. (1984). *Experimental Learning*. Englewood Cliffs, NJ: Prentice-Hall.

Kotter, J. (1995). *The New Rules: How to Succeed in Today's Post-Corporate World*. New York: The Free Press.

Larsen, H. H. (1996). In search of management development in Europe: From self-fulfilling prophecies to organizational competence. *The International Journal of Human Resource Management*, 7(3), 657–76.

Lazerson, M. (1988). Organizational growth of small firms: An outcome of markets and hierarchies? *American Sociological Review*, 53 (June), 330–42.

Leadbeater, C. (1999). The knowledge-driven economy. Association for Management Education and Development Conference, (August), Cranfield.

Lee, G., Coaley, K. and Beard, D. (1993). Management training: Cost or investment? *Financial Services Training Journal*, 1(3), 29–37.

Lee, J. (1921). *Management: A Study of Industrial Organization*. London: Pitman.

Leggatt, T. (1972). *The Training of British Managers: A Study of Need and Demand*. London: NEDO.

Legge, K. (1984). *The Evaluation of Planned Organizational Change*. London: Academic Press.

Lewis, J. S. (1896). *The Commercial Organization of Factories*. London: Spon.

Lindley, R. (1991). Individuals, human resources, and markets. In J. Stevens and R. Mackay (eds), *Training and Competitiveness*. London: Kogan Page.

Lippitt, G. (1982). Management development as the key to organizational renewal. *Journal of Management Development*, 1(2).

Locke, R. (1984). *The End of the Practical Man: Entrepreneurship and Higher Education in Germany, France, and Great Britain 1880–1940*. Greenwich, Conn.: JAI Press.

London, M. and Stumpf, S. A. (1982). *Managing Careers*. Reading, Mass.: Addison-Wesley.

McCauley, C., Ruderman, M., Ohlott, P. and Morrow, J. (1994). Assessing the developmental components of managerial jobs. *Journal of Applied Psychology*, 79(4), 544–60.

McGovern, P., Stiles, P. and Hope, V. (1995). Career management in an era of insecurity. In *Proceedings of the Employment Research Unit Annual Conference*, Cardiff: Cardiff Business School.

McLagan, P. (1989). Models for HRD practice. *Training and Development Journal* (September), 49–59.

Mabey, C. and Iles, P. A. (1993). The strategic integration of assessment and development practices: Succession planning and new manager development. *Human Resource Management Journal*, 3(4), 16–34.

Mabey, C., Kaye, R. and Topham, P. (1998). Computer-based courseware: A comparative review of the learner's experience. *Accounting Education*, 7(1), 51–64.

Mabey, C. and Mallory, G. (1994). Structure and culture change in two UK organizations: A comparison of assumptions, approaches, and outcomes. *Human Resource Management Journal*, 4(2), 1–18.

Mabey, C., Skinner, D. and Clark, T. (1998). *Experiencing Human Resource Management*. London: Sage.

Mabey, C. and Thomson, A. (2000). The determinants of management development: The views of MBA graduates. *British Journal of Management*, 11 (Special Issue), 53–517.

Management Charter Initiative (1999). *Management Indicators Framework*. London: Management Charter Initiative.

Mangham, I. and Silver, M. (1986). *Management Training: Context and Practice*. London: Economic and Social Research Council.

Mansfield, R. and Poole, M. (1991). *British Management in the Thatcher Years*. London: British Institute of Management.

Mansfield, R., Poole, M., Blyton, P. and Frost, P. (1981). *The British Manager in Profile*. London: British Institute of Management.

Margerison, C. (1990). *Making Management Development Work*. London: McGraw-Hill.

Marginson, P., Edwards, P., Martin, R., Purcell, J. and Sisson, K. (1988). *Beyond the Workplace: Managing Industrial Relations in Multi-Establishment Enterprises*. Oxford: Blackwell.

Martin, G., Pate, J. and McGoldrick, J. (1999). HRD and psychological contracts: A case study of life-long learning. *Academy of HRD Conference Proceedings*, 2, 689–96.

Martin, S. (1995). A futures' market for competencies. *People Management* (March), 20–4.

Matthews, D. (1998). The business doctors: Accountants in British management from the nineteenth century to the present day. *Business History*, 40(3), 72–103.

Maurer, T. and Tarulli, B. (1996). Acceptance of peer/upward appraisal systems: Role of work context factors and beliefs about managers' development capability. *Human Resource Management*, 35(2), 217–41.

Meagher, N., Kaiser, M. and Dietrich, H. (1992). *Self-Employment in the United Kingdom and Germany*. London: Anglo-German Foundation.

Miles, M. and Huberman, A. (1994). *Qualitative Data Analysis*, 2nd edn. Thousand Oaks, Calif.: Sage.

Miles, R. E. and Snow, C. C. (1978). *Organizational Strategy, Structure, and Process*. New York: McGraw-Hill.

Mincer, J. (1970). The distribution of labour incomes: A survey with special reference to the human capital approach. *Journal of Economic Literature*, 8(1), 1–26.

Mole, G. (1996). The management training industry in the UK: An HRD director's critique. *Human Resource Management Journal*, 6(1), 19–26.

Mueller, F. (1996). Human resources as strategic assets: An evolutionary resource-based view. *Journal of Management Studies*, 33(6), 757–85.

Mumford, A. (1993). *Management Development: Strategies for Action*, 2nd edn. London: Institute of Personnel and Development.

Mumford, A. (1997). *Management Development: Strategies for Action*, 3rd edn. London: Institute of Personnel and Development.

Mumford, A., Robinson, G. and Stradling, D. (1987). *Developing Directors: The Learning Processes*. London: Manpower Services Commission.

Nagler, B. (1987). Cummings' efforts to cut costs. *Managing Automation*, 2(7).

National Audit Office (1988). *Assistance to Small Firms*, Cmnd. 655. London: HMSO.

NEDO (1984). *Competence and Competition: Training and Education in the Federal Republic of Germany, the United States and Japan*. London.

NEDO (1986). *External Capital for Small Firms: A Review of Recent Developments*. London.

Newton, T. and Findlay, P. (1998). Playing God? The performance of appraisal. In C. Mabey, G. Salaman and J. Storey (eds), *Strategic Human Resource Management*. London: Sage.

Nicholson, N. (1990). The transition cycle: Causes, outcomes, processes and forms. In S. Fisher and C. L. Cooper (eds), *On the Move: The Psychology of Change and Transition*. Chichester: John Wiley.

Nioche, J. (1992). The war of degrees in European management education. *EFMD Forum*, 1, 21–4.

Nishizawa, T. (1996). Business studies and management education in Japan's economic development: An institutional perspective. In R. Amdam (ed.), *Management, Education and Competitiveness*. London: Routledge.

Nonaka, I. and Takeuchi, H. (1995). *The Knowledge Creating Company*. Oxford: Oxford University Press.

Nordhaug, O. and Grunhaug, K. (1994). Competences as resources in firms. *International Journal of Human Resource Management*, 5(1), 89–106.

Osbaldeston, M. (1987). *The Supply of Management Education*. London: British Institute of Management.

Osbaldeston, M. and Barham, K. (1992). Using management development for competitive advantage. *Long-Range Planning*, 25(6), 18–24.

Parkinson, S. (1990). Management development's strategic role. *Journal of General Management*, 16(2), 63–75.

Patterson, M., West, M., Lawthorn, R. and Nickell, S. (1998). *Impact of People Management Practices on Business Performance*. London: Institute of Personnel and Development.

Pedler, M., Boydell, T. and Burgoyne, J. (1991). *The Learning Company*. Maidenhead: McGraw-Hill.

Personnel Managers' Factbook (1997). London: Professional Publishing.

Pettigrew, A. and Whipp, R. (1991). *Managing for Competitive Success*. Oxford: Basil Blackwell.

Pettigrew, A., Hendry, C. and Sparrow, P. (1988). *The Role of Vocational Education and Training in Employer's Skill Supply Strategies*. Sheffield: Training Agency.

Political and Economic Planning (1966). *Attitudes in British Management*. Harmondsworth: Penguin.

Pollard, S. (1968). *The Genesis of Modern Management*. Harmondsworth: Penguin.

Porter, L. and McKibbin, L. (1988). *Management Education and Development: Drift or Thrust into the 21st Century*. New York: McGraw-Hill.

Preston, D. (1993). Learning the organization: Confusions and contradictions for new managers. *Human Resource Management Journal*, 4(1), 24–33.

Purcell, J. (1996). *Human Resource Bundles of Best Practice: A Utopian Cul-de-Sac?* ESRC/BUIRA Seminar Series.

Raper, P., Ashton, D., Felstead, A. and Storey, J. (1997). Toward the learning organization? Explaining current trends in training practice in the UK. *International Journal of Training and Development*, 1(1), 9–21.

Reed, M. and Anthony, P. (1992). Professionalising management and managing professionalisation: British management in the 1980s. *Journal of Management Studies*, 5 (September), 591–613.

Revans, R. (1980). *Action Learning: New Techniques for Management*. London: Blond & Briggs.

Rigg, M. (1989). *Training in Britain: A Study of Funding, Activity and Attitudes*. Sheffield: Training Agency.

Rix, A., Parkinson, R. and Gaunt, R. (1993). *Investors in People: A Qualitative Study of Employers*. CRG People at Work.

Robbins, Lord (1963). *Report of the Committee on Higher Education*, Cmnd. 2154. London: HMSO.

Robinson, D. and Robinson, J. (1989). *Training for Impact: How to Link Training to Business Needs and Measure the Results*. Oxford: Jossey-Bass.

Robinson, D. and Rousseau, D. (1994).Violating the psychological contract: Not the exception but the norm. *Journal of Organizational Behaviour*, 15, 245–59.

Rogers, A. (1986). *Teaching Adults*. Milton Keynes: Open University Press.

Rousseau, D. M. (1995). *Psychological Contracts in Organizations*. Thousand Oaks, Calif.: Sage.

Rubinstein, W. (1994). *Capitalism, Culture and Decline in Britain 1750–1990*. London: Routledge.

Sadler, P. and Barham, K. (1988). From Franks to the future: 25 years of management training prescriptions. *Personnel Management* (May), 48–51.

SBRT (1985–98). *The NatWest/SBRT Quarterly Survey of Small Business in Britain*, vols 1–14. London: Small Business Research Trust.

Scarbrough, H. (1998).The unmaking of management? Change and continuity in British management in the 1990s. *Human Relations*, 51(6), 691–715.

Scarbrough, H., Swan, J. and Preston, J. (1999). *Knowledge Management: A Literature Review*. Wimbledon: Institute for Personnel and Development.

Schein, E. H. (1978). *Career Dynamics: Matching Individual and Organizational Needs*. Reading, Mass.: Addison-Wesley.

Schein, E. H. (1985). *Organizational Culture and Leadership*. San Francisco: Jossey-Bass.

Schon, D. A. (1983). *The Reflective Practitioner: How Professionals Think in Action*. London: Maurice Temple Smith.

Schuler, R. and Jackson, S. (1987). Linking competitive strategies with human resource management. *Academy of Management Executive*, 1(3).

Seibert, K. W., Hall, D. T. et al. (1995). Strengthening the weak link in strategic executive development: Integrating individual development and global business strategy. *Human Resource Management*, 34(4), 549–67.

Senge, P. (1991). *The Fifth Discipline*. New York: Doubleday.

Shackleton, J. R. (1992). *Training Too Much? A Sceptical Look at the Economics of Skill Provision in the UK*, Hobart Paper 118. London: Institute of Economic Affairs.

Shackleton, V. (1992). Using a competency approach in a business change setting. In R. Boam and P. Sparrow (eds), *Designing and Achieving Competency: A Competency-Based Approach to Managing People and Organisations*. London: McGraw-Hill.

Sheldon, O. (1923). *The Philosophy of Management*. London: Pitman.

Silver, M. (1984). *Enterprise and the Scope of the Firm*. Oxford: Martin Robinson.

Simpson, E. L. (1980). Adult learning theory: A state of the art. In H. Lasker, J. Moore and E. L. Simpson (eds), *Adult Development and Approaches to Learning*. Washington, DC: National Institute of Education.

Sitkin, S., Sutcliffe, S. and Schroeder, R. (1994). Distinguishing control from learning in total quality management: A contingency perspective. *Academy of Management Review*, 19(3), 537–64.

Skoulding, G. and Peppercorn, G. (1987). *Profile of British Industry: The Manager's View.* London: British Institute of Management.

Smith, E. (1996). *Employer-Provided Training in the UK since 1998.* London: IFF Research Ltd.

Smith, M. (1992). *Utility and Human Resource Management,* Supplementary Readings 2, B884 Human Resource Strategies. Milton Keynes: Open University.

Sonnenfeld, J., Peiperl, M. and Kotter, J. (1988). Strategic determinants of managerial labour markets: A career systems view. *Human Resource Management,* 27(4), 369–88.

Sparrow, P. and Bognanno, M. (1993). Competency requirement forecasting: Issues for selection and assessment. *International Journal of Selection and Assessment,* 1(1), 50–8.

Sparrow, P. and Hiltrop, J. (1994). *European Human Resource Management in Transition.* Hemel Hempstead: Prentice Hall.

Spender, J.-C. (1999). Underlying antinomies and perpetuated problems: An historical view of the challenges confronting business schools today. Unpublished manuscript.

Spilsbury, M. and Moralee, J. (1995). *Evaluation of Investors in People in England and Wales.* Brighton: Institute of Employment Studies.

Stanworth, J. and Gray, C. (eds) (1991). *Bolton 20 Years On: The Small Firms in the 1990s.* London: Paul Chapman.

Stanworth, J., Purdy, D. and Kirby, D. (1992). *The Management of Success in Growth Corridor Small Firms.* Milton Keynes: Small Business Research Trust.

Stiles, P., Gratton, L., Truss, C., Hope-Hailey, V. and McGovern, P. (1997). Performance management and the psychological contract. *Human Resource Management Journal,* 7(1), 57–66.

Stoddart, J. (1987). *Demand as Perceived by those who have Passed Through a Course of Management Education.* London: British Institute of Management.

Storey, D. (1994). *Understanding the Small Business Sector.* London: Routledge.

Storey, D. and Westhead, P. (1994). *Management Training and Small Firm Performance,* Working Paper 18. Coventry: SME Centre, Warwick University.

Storey, J., Edwards, P. and Sisson, K. (1997). *Managers in the Making: Careers, Development and Control in Corporate Britain and Japan.* London: Sage.

Storey, J. and Sisson, K. (1993). *Managing Human Relations and Industrial Relations.* Buckingham: Open University Press.

Tamkin, P. and Hillage, J. (1998). *Management Development in the UK: A Framework of Indicators.* Brighton: Institute for Employment Studies.

Tate, W. (1995). *Developing Corporate Competence: A High Performance Agenda for Managing Organizations.* Aldershot: Gower.

Thomson, A. (1987). *Perspectives on Management Training and Education: The Results of a Survey of Employers.* London: British Institute of Management.

Thomson, A. and Gray, C. (1999). Determinants of management development in small businesses. *Journal of Small Business and Enterprise Development,* 6(2), 113–27.

Thomson, R. and Mabey, C. (1995). *Developing Human Resources.* London: Butterworth-Heinemann.

Thomson, A., Mabey, C. and Storey, J. (1998). The determinants of management development: Choice or circumstance? *International Studies in Management and Organisations*, 28(1), 91–113.

Thomson, A., Storey J., Mabey, C., Gray, C., Farmer, E. and Thomson, R. (1997). *A Portrait of Management Development*. London: Institute of Management.

Thomson, A., Storey, J., Mabey, C., Gray, C. and Thomson, R. (1998). *Management Development: The Views of the Association of MBAs*. London: Association of MBAs.

Townley, B. (1993). Performance appraisals and the emergence of management. *Journal of Management Studies*, 30(2), 222–38.

Ulrich, D. (1997). Measuring human resources: An overview of practice and prescription for results. *Human Resource Management*, 36(3), 303–20.

Ulrich, D., Losey, M. and Lake, G. (1997). *Tomorrow's HR Managers*. New York: Wiley.

Urwick, L. (1954). *Is Management a Profession?* London: Urwick, Orr & Partners.

Urwick, L. and Brech, E. (1948). *The Making of Scientific Management*. London: Management Publications.

Van der Krogt, F. and Warmerdam, J. (1997). Training in different types of organisations: Differences and dynamics in the organisation of learning and work. *International Journal of Human Resource Management*, 8(1), 87–105.

Vickerstaff, S. A. (1991). The management of training in the smaller firm. British Academy of Management Annual Conference (September), London.

Wagel, W. H. (1987). Leadership training for a new way of managing. *Personnel*, 64(12).

Warr, P. (1993). *Training for Managers*. London: Institute of Managers.

Waterman, R. H., Waterman, J. A. and Collard, B. A. (1994). Towards a career-resilient workforce. *Harvard Business Review*, 72(4), 87–95.

Watkins, K. and Marsick, V. (1992). Towards a theory of informal and incidental learning in organisations. *International Journal of Lifelong Learning*, 11(4), 287–300.

Whitley, R., Thomas, A. and Marceau, J. (1981). *Masters of Business? Business Schools and Graduates in France and Britain*. London: Tavistock.

Wiener, M. (1981). *English Culture and the Decline of the Industrial Spirit 1850–1980*. London: Penguin.

Wille, E. (1990). *People Development and Improved Business Performance*. Berkhamstead: Ashridge Management Research Group, Ashridge Management College.

Williamson, O. (1985). *The Economic Institutions of Capitalism*. New York: Free Press.

Wilson, J. (1995). *British Business History, 1720–1994*. Manchester: Manchester University Press.

Wilson Report (1979). *The Financing of Small Firms*. London: HMSO.

Winterton, J. and Winterton, R. (1997). Does management development matter? *British Journal of Management*, 8 (June), S65–S76.

Wong, C., Marshall, J., Alderman, N. and Thwaites, A. (1997). Management training in small and medium-sized enterprises: Methodological and conceptual issues. *International Journal of Human Resource Management*, 8(1), 44–65.

Woodall, J. and Winstanley, J. (1998). *Management Development: Strategy and Practice.* Oxford: Blackwell.

Worrall, L. and Cooper, C. (1997). *The Quality of Working Life: 1997 Survey of Managers' Changing Experiences.* London: Institute of Management.

Wren, D. (1994). *The Evolution of Management Thought.* New York: Wiley.

Index

G